AMERICAN
CULTURE
IN EUROPE

AMERICAN CULTURE IN EUROPE

Interdisciplinary Perspectives

Edited by
Mike-Frank G. Epitropoulos
and Victor Roudometof

Westport, Connecticut
London

Library of Congress Cataloging-in-Publication Data

American culture in Europe : interdisciplinary perspectives / edited
    by Mike-Frank G. Epitropoulos and Victor Roudometof.
        p.   cm.
    Includes bibliographical references and index.
    ISBN 0–275–95051–4 (alk. paper)
        1. Europe—Civilization—American influences. 2. Americanization.
    I. Epitropoulos, Mike-Frank G., 1967–   II. Roudometof, Victor, 1964–
    CB205.A44   1998
    940—dc21   98–11131

British Library Cataloguing in Publication Data is available.

Library of Congress Catalog Card Number: 98–11131
ISBN: 0–275–95051–4

First published in 1998

Praeger Publishers, 88 Post Road West, Westport, CT 06881
An imprint of Greenwood Publishing Group, Inc.

Printed in the United States of America

The paper used in this book complies with the
Permanent Paper Standard issued by the National
Information Standards Organization (Z39.48–1984).

10 9 8 7 6 5 4 3 2 1

Copyright Acknowledgment

The editors and publisher gratefully acknowledge permission to reprint the following article:

David Lempert, "Pepsi-Stroika: American Cultural Influence on the Russian
Political and Legal System," *Legal Studies Forum*, 20(3) (Fall 1996).

Contents

Photo essays follow chapters 4 and 6

Preface

Our involvement with this project began in the summer of 1993, when we replied to an announcement by Thomas Cushman from the Sociology Department of Wellesley College, who had issued a call for papers on the topic of American culture in Europe. Over the next three years, this project was plagued by various delays, leading to general disillusionment concerning its future. Cushman was unable to complete the process because of his work load. Therefore, he agreed to pass the responsibility for the volume to us. When, in the summer of 1996, we assumed the editorial responsibility for the volume, we had to ask for a new contract by Greenwood, and we had to initiate contact with the original contributors. In the course of the 1996–97 academic year, it became apparent that many of the original contributors were unable to conclude their chapters in a timely fashion. Nevertheless, we felt compelled to proceed with the process. We invited Thomas Schott (Department of Sociology, University of Pittsburgh) to take the place of some of the original contributors, and we scaled down the original, grandiose design of the volume. Consequently, the chapters collected in this volume represent the outcome of a project that took more than three years to complete.

We feel that, despite the difficulties this project has encountered over the past three years, it represents an important contribution to the general discussion on Americanization. The interdisciplinary character of this compilation aims at recasting the discussion of American culture in

Europe in terms of the substantive categories of culture rather than purely in terms of discussions of particular geographical areas. This allows
readers to see the general processes that occur across time and space in
Europe. It is also an important and novel first step in working toward a
general sociological theory of American cultural influence in Europe.

We thank James Sabin of the Greenwood Publishing Group for his trust
and patience — we had to plead with him more than once for extensions
of the original deadline. We also thank Thomas Schott and his collaborators for undertaking the research project of science in Europe and com-
pleting it in a timely fashion. Finally, we thank Roland Robertson
(Department of Sociology, University of Pittsburgh) for his role as intellectual advisor and commentator for the volume's final chapter.

Victor Roudometof's research and writing for this project during the
1996–97 academic year was generously supported by the Mary Seeger
O'Boyle Post-Doctoral Fellowship of the Program in Hellenic Studies at
Princeton University.

Introduction:
America and Europe,
Fragile Objects of Discourse

Mike-Frank G. Epitropoulos
and Victor Roudometof

The diffusion of American culture across national boundaries is a hall-mark of the twentieth century. The process of this diffusion and the effects of American culture on European societies is a topic of central concern to historians, anthropologists, and sociologists working in individual European countries. This volume is part of a recent wave of studies concentrating on the effect of American culture in European countries (Rollin 1989; Lacorne, Rupnik, & Toinet 1990; Lunden & Asard 1992; Kuisel 1993; Wagnleitner 1994; Melling & Roper 1996; Dean & Gabilliet 1996). Although many scholars work on the "Americanization" of individual European cultures, most works on this subject focus on the presence and effects of American culture in particular European societies. In contrast, this volume represents an attempt to unite the efforts of a diverse group of scholars working on the diffusion of American cultural influence to bring about a more general understanding of the processes, effects, and influences of American culture in Europe. The terms "American culture" and "Europe" are contested and are utilized in this volume as shorthand expressions to convey the broad *problematique* of the collected chapters. The notion of American culture is usually employed as a synonym for commercial mass-produced culture (which, in turn, is American-owned and English-speaking). In fact, the entire discussion on Americanization is not confined to Europe alone (see, for example, Haines 1989; Martin 1993; and some of the essays in Nordenstreng & Schiller 1993).

THE QUESTION OF DEFINITION

America is often identified with modernity per se, with the experience of becoming part of a "brave new world" of sensibilities and action. As such, the attraction of being "modern" is frequently cast in terms of being or becoming American in cultural outlook. Of course, perception is not reality, and the global perception of American culture is far from being an accurate representation of American life. In this regard, Arjun Appadurai's (1996) personal reflections on his encounter with modernity while still in India are worth quoting:

In my own early life in Bombay, the experience of modernity was notably synaesthetic and largely pretheoretical. I saw and smelled modernity reading Life and American college catalogs at the United States Information Service library, seeing B-grade films (and some A-grade ones) from Hollywood at the Eros Theatre, five hundred yards from my apartment building. I begged my brother at Stanford (in the early 1960s) to bring me back blue jeans and smelled America in his Right Guard when he returned. I gradually lost the England that I had earlier imbibed in my Victorian schoolbooks, in rumors of Rhodes scholars from my college, and in Billy Bunter and Biggles books devoured indiscriminately with books by Richmal Crompton and Enid Blyton. Fanny and Zooey, Holden Caulfield, and Rabbit Angstrom slowly eroded that part of me that had been, until then, forever England. Such are the little defeats that explain how England lost the Empire in postcolonial Bombay.

I did not know then that I was drifting from one sort of postcolonial subjectivity (Anglophone diction, fantasies of debates in the Oxford Union, borrowed peeks at Encounter, a patrician interest in the humanities) to another: the harsher, sexier, more addictive New World of Humphrey Bogart reruns, Harold Robbins, Time, and social science, American style. (pp. 1–2)

The last paragraph of the quotation illustrates the peculiar position of postcolonial cultures, cultures in which Europeanization was replaced by Americanization. Nevertheless, within the broader global context, critics have raised the issue of the so-called American "cultural imperialism" thesis. That is, American domination of the culture industries and consumer culture (from McDonalds to CNN) raises the spectrum of the globe becoming increasingly homogenized — thereby threatening human cultural variety as well as local distinct lifestyles (Ritzer 1993; 1997; see also Barber [1995] for a similar, yet more nuanced, viewpoint). Considerable difficulties surround this concept of American cultural imperialism (for critical overviews, see Tomlinson 1991; Ferguson 1992; see also Featherstone 1990). Most important, the claim that local (national, cultural, ethnic, or religious) differences are under siege by the American cultural industries rests on a particular view of the past in European societies (especially con tinental). Namely, the notion of the historical past as part of the national cultural repertoire is deeply embedded in everyday life and continuously reproduced in newspapers, art, museums, and other cultural activities (Horne 1984, Billig 1995). Concomitant with it is the belief in the neces- sity of reproducing national difference. In this regard, Europeans differ from Americans in their strongly held worldview that cultural products are not simply commercial products but bear a special relationship to the collective identity (Schlesinger 1997: 375–77).

Hence, the domination of American commercial culture circumscribes the ability of local cultural entrepreneurs to successfully reproduce their own cultural products. France is perhaps the paradigmatic case of such a clash between commercial modernity and revered tradition. As Denis Lacorne and Jacques Rupnik (1990) describe it,

The problem for a country like France is that its economic ambitions clash with its cultural identity. The French seek economic power in order to maintain their position in the world. This in turn requires the integration of the French economy into world markets and a truly competitive spirit. It implies becoming business- minded, willingness to spend lengthy periods abroad, a decent command of Eng- lish, and so on. But at the same time the French want to preserve a cultural heritage which is intrinsically archaic, those *vielles valeurs* which are the very foundation of *la France eternelle* such as *l'academisme*, distrust of pragmatism, a passion for philosophical abstractions, and a taste for refined fashions and high- brow culture. The upshot is that the country's real or imagined economic power conflicts with the national identity of a people with uninhibited delusions of "grandeur" and a desire to set themselves as a model for the rest of the world. (pp. 1–2)

Not surprisingly, twentieth-century French anti-Americanism has been most intensely felt at times of increased French dependence on the Unit- ed States (Harrison 1990:169). Generally speaking, then, the question of American cultural presence in Europe occupies a space strongly colored by the perception of European decline after World War II and the emer- gence of the United States as the hegemonic power in the modern world- system. Consequently, the substitution of European cultural dominance by American commercial culture makes the issue of American cultural dom- ination deeply important for Western and Central European countries.

Nevertheless, Europe has peculiarities that warrant a differentiation of the problem of American influence in Europe from the general question of cultural imperialism as it pertains to peripheral societies. Europe has been the original homeland of American immigrants, and, hence, there has been considerable cross-cultural interaction between the two shores of the Atlantic (Roper 1996: 1–28; Kroes 1996). Europe and the United States have constructed mirror images of each other, stereotypes that have helped define not only the other but also themselves. In the nineteenth century, Alexis de Tocqueville — the original inventor of the term "individualism" — was responsible for promoting both the image of Americans as individualists and that of Europeans as communitarians. Broadly speaking, Europeans have used bipolar oppositions as metaphors for defining themselves in relation to the Americans: the list includes such pairs as "shallow versus sophisticated," "young or new versus old," and "materialistic versus idealistic" (Kroes 1996: 13–15). Underneath these classifications lie the European intellectuals' admiration for high culture and disdain for low commercial popular culture. In critiques of mass culture, such as *The Dialectic of Enlightenment* (1938), the advent of commercial culture is viewed negatively. We all know that commercial culture is English-speaking and frequently portrayed as exclusively American.

More recently, such authors as Umberto Eco (1986) and Jean Baudrillard (1988) have sought to develop a new image of America. America is viewed as the fulfillment of those promises that European culture has failed to deliver. It is the utopian land where European intellectual obsessions become irrelevant. It stands for the realization of the European project of modernity, a realization that makes obsolete the very act of dreaming about it. For Baudrillard "it is we [that is, the Europeans] who think that everything culminates in its transcendence and that nothing exists without first having been thought through as concept. Not only they [that is, the Americans] hardly care for that at all; they rather see the relationship in reverse. They are interested not in conceptualizing reality, but in realizing the concept and implementing the ideas" (1988: 167).

This point was accurately made when, in reaction to the French protests against Euro-Disney, Michael Eisner, Disney's director, expressed his amazement to the protesters' thesis that Euro-Disney would bring cultural devaluation. "Culture?" Eisner asked: "Sleeping Beauty is culture, and that's French; Peter Pan is English, Pinocchio Italian, Snow White German" (quoted in Kroes 1996: 35). American culture is largely based on commercialization of or adaptation from European cultural items. This peculiar interdependence of American and European culture reinforces the necessity of taking into account the complex processes of transmission and reception across the shores of the Atlantic. Not only is the European culture being reinterpreted by Americans and used as raw material for the construction of American culture but also American culture is being transmitted into Europe and undergoing similar processes of readaption and selective appropriation.

Such processes take place within specific European countries, a factor that also points to the need to examine these processes within the particular cultural configuration in which they occur. Despite the attempts to institute the European Union (EU) as a would-be federation, national sentiment remains a strong component of the European national societies. In the face of increasing migration into the European countries as well as the growing accountability of the state on the basis of international human rights law, exclusionary strategies frequently take the form of claims to protect local culture and authenticity from outsiders (Balibar 1991; Sassen 1996).

The sheer mention of the EU raises the other important question, namely the extent to which Europe represents a cultural configuration with solid boundaries. In 1738, Lord Henry Saint-John Bolingbroke, English statesman and political author, observed in a letter:

The emperor [of Austria, Leopold, 1658–1705] was like the others too but with this difference relative to the political system of the West: Austrian ambitions and religious fanaticism were exercised in *far-off countries, whose affairs were not considered part of the same system.* Otherwise there would have been as much reason to assist the people of Hungary and of Transylvania against the emperor as there had been formerly to assist the people of the seven United Provinces against Spain, or as had been to assist them against France. However, the ambitions and religious fanaticism of Louis XIC were exercised in the Low Countries, on the Rhine, in Italy, and in Spain, in the very center of this system, and I would say, with such success as would fail with the time to subvert the system itself. (Struminski 1995: 98–99, emphasis added)

The strong belief that "Asia begins in the outskirts of Vienna" was not completely consolidated at the time. During the eighteenth century, the notion of Eastern Europe as an essentially backward region was reinforced, in many respects as part of the ideology of the Enlightenment (Wolff 1994; cf. Stoianovich 1994). With the single exception of Greece — which served as the precursor of the Western European Enlightenment — the countries of Eastern Europe were depicted in a negative light. This division of Europe has had long lasting consequences, because, in the aftermath of the 1989 revolutions, it provides a major terrain of ideological conflict. The prizes of this battle concern entrance and acceptance by Western Europe (in the form of the European Union) of membership in a common club of modernity as well as the lucrative material benefits in the form of EU economic assistance to its member states. During the late

1980s and 1990s, Central European intellectuals rather successfully attempted to reconceptualize Europe as exclusively Protestant and Catholic. In doing so, their goal has been to integrate their societies (Poland, the Czech Republic, and Hungary) into the EU and to exclude Russia from the New Europe. Their arguments justify their inclusion in the EU on the basis of their Protestant or Catholic religious affiliation. In turn, this line of thinking frequently involves unwarranted assumptions about Eastern Orthodox countries (Schopflin & Wood 1989; cf. Prodromou 1995). The most recent reincarnation of this divide between the Catholic and Protestant West and the Orthodox East can be found in Huntington's (1993) division of Europe along religious lines separating the Orthodox from the Catholic and Protestant countries.

The ongoing debate concerning the boundaries of Europe represents, in an acute manner, the present inability of the EU to incorporate the countries of Eastern and southeastern Europe. This inability raises reasonable skepticism about the ultimate fate of the European project itself (see Judt 1996).

In order to avoid becoming entangled in this highly ideological political and cultural debate, we have chosen to employ a rather broad conception of Europe for the purposes of this volume. Chapters examine aspects of American culture in France, Germany, Greece, the former Soviet Union, and Eastern Europe. Departing from Cold War classifications, we treat Eastern and Central Europe together with Western Europe. Although this choice may be contested in the context of the debate concerning the boundaries of Europe, it allows us to increase the scope of our inquiry and, thus, the viability of whatever generalizations can be advanced as a result of this research project.

OUTLINE OF THE VOLUME

The concept of culture for the purposes of this volume is a broad one. The chapters range from discussions of science to history of ideas to sociological and anthropological studies of European societies. Certainly, the notion of culture is a problematic one and has a long history within the social sciences (McGrane 1989; Robertson 1988). In studies of film, music, and broadcasting the question of Americanization is raised in direct relation to the proliferation of commercial capitalism around the globe. As Tomlinson (1991) argues, however, the two issues are conceptually distinct — the spread of capitalism is only identical with Americanization if one assumes that the two are inseparable. Discussion in this volume focuses on the topic of Americanization rather than the broader question of the relationship between mass media and global capitalism (Mattelart 1994).

The first two chapters employ network analyses to study the relative power and dynamics of scientific centers from a world-system perspective. They represent a good example of studying science from within a global frame of reference but with specific attention to the uneven power of European states. In the first chapter, Thomas Schott, Jun Kanamitsu, and James F. Luther focus on the themes of deference and influence among the central cluster of nations in world science. They identify the current central cluster as the United States, Western Europe, and Japan and discuss the nature of the relationships among and between the countries in this science triad. The key questions revolve around cooperation, competition, and emulation in scientific endeavors. Within this triad, the U.S.–Japanese rivalry emerges in the form of a "free rider" problem, wherein Japan innovates in private technological goods on the basis of public good (that is, scientific knowledge).

In their discussion of the relationships among the scientific core countries, the authors analyze collaboration, conference participation, and citations as indicators of the level and nature of interaction among scientists. Their findings indicate a high degree of emulation among centers and affirm the communal nature of scientific knowledge in spite of the protectionism that accompanies their competition. The authors note that, although Western Europe has surpassed the United States in achievement within the scientific network, the United States remains central in terms of deference, collaboration, influence, emulation, desired recognition, and professional travel.

This interesting contradiction was revealed in the French popular press when the upscale weekly *Le nouvel observateur* attempted to evaluate the global force of French culture. With data from the American Citation Index, it found that French authors were widely quoted: in 1994 Foucault alone surpassed any other author with 1,085 citations (Cochran 1996: 119). Nevertheless, these authors (Foucault, Bourdieu, Lévi-Strauss, Derrida, Ricoeur, Barthes, Lyotard, Sartre, Braudel) are read, cited, and known almost exclusively in English. Ironically, French intellectual prowess still looks to an English-speaking audience for recognition, a reflection of strong deference to the United States.

Having established the methodology and conceptual framework in Chapter 1, Schott shifts his focus to the periphery in Chapter 2, "Peripheries in World Science: Latin America and Eastern Europe," where he is joined by Samuel A. Kugel, Ruben Berrios, and Keri L. Rodriguez. From the perspective of the scientific periphery, "smallness" emerges as the key theme. That is, among the range of possible alternatives, what option will scientifically "small" countries pursue? The extremes of the range are inward self-reliance, on the one hand, and outward attachment to the center, on the other hand. Schott and colleagues find that in most small countries scientific attachment to the central cluster (identified in Chapter 1) receives high priority as official policy and within the national scientific community. Furthermore, such attachment is endorsed and promoted by international organizations such as the United Nations Educational, Scientific and Cultural Organization, the Organisation for Economic Cooperation and Development, and the World Bank. Empirically, scientific deference to centers often has geopolitically-determined considerations. Western Europe is found to be more central than the United States in collaboration and influence in the world scientific periphery. However, as far as scientific deference is concerned, the United States remains the main center.

Schott's two chapters clearly illustrate the necessity of separating perception from reality in the debate on Americanization. First, they clearly illustrate that Europe is not a coherent unit in the scientific field because different countries occupy markedly different positions in the hierarchy of science. Second, they document that, although Western Europe constitutes one of the core regions of world science, Europeans still display considerable deference to the United States. The symbolic dominance of the United States, then, leads us into a discussion of the manner in which Europeans view the United States, an issue conceptually distinct from the actual power relations between the EU and the United States.

In such a reconceptualization, Americanization constitutes a discourse of misunderstanding, a field where local European power politics interact with the broader global political environment. Political and cultural anti-Americanism has a long history in Europe. From nineteenth-century French intellectuals to the political anti-Americanism of the Greek socialists in the late 1970s, the United States has provided the terrain for the expression of various European political and cultural currents. During the 1990s, for example, the specter of Americanization has been employed by the EU in order to argue in favor of the Europeanization of the mass media market is necessary (Schlesinger 1997: 373).

In the volume's third chapter, Peter Bergmann offers a rich historical analysis of one such example, namely the case history of Americanization in Germany. He traces the dynamic meaning of Americanization in three distinct historical periods. In the nineteenth century, Bergmann notes, Americanization was viewed as an avenue for the future, carrying the promise of democracy and progress. It meant the triumph of capitalism and the negation of anti-Semitism. Following World War I, and with the rise of nazism, America once again became the villain. In Hitler's mind, America was the real enemy. Although the German population preferred losing the war to the Western powers, Hitler's last offensive was against America. In the post-1945 period, Americanization provided a positive model for the development of democracy. From the 1960s forward, U.S. involvement in Vietnam, U.S. foreign policy, and consumer culture tarnished America's shiny image and drove German supporters into active opposition against it. Specifically, Bergmann chronicles the salient role of the Frankfurt School in the Americanization dynamic and the way in which Pax Americana was viewed increasingly as pax atomica.

In Chapter 4, David Lempert provides an anthropologist's view of urban Russia in its recent period of sociopolitical upheaval during the late 1980s and early 1990s. Lempert concentrates on the transfer of U.S. economic, political, and legal systems to Russia. The political economy of this transfer, Lempert notes, centered almost exclusively on property rights, not on social accountability, labor, or human rights. The specifics of legislation were tailored to benefit a coalition of Western capitalist interests and Russian managerial elites. Keeping in line with the comparative historical approach of the volume, Lempert discusses the evolution of the Soviet Union's embrace of Western forms, which typically had been selective, with strong centralization and control by the state.

In the 1980s, Mikhail Gorbachev's perestroika represented an opening for young reformers within the politico-economic system. They sought to oust the older leadership in pursuit of higher standards of living that the young reformers felt could be gained through joint ventures with the West. In this light, it is not surprising that the goal to create the necessary legal and political infrastructure would guarantee managers controlling interest in their companies, albeit without any accountability. The same process included bilateral exchanges of corporate executives, public interest groups, legal scholars, and graduate students all aiming to establish an investor friendly Russian free market. Although Ralph Nader warned Russians not to imitate American culture, his words fell on deaf ears. Ultimately, Lempert portrays how Americanization was used as a shorthand expression for a process of selective appropriation of specific legal and political U.S. practices. This process was marked by huge inequities in terms of wealth, justice, and access to the reform process, inequities justified and rationalized by the new post-Soviet ideology.

In Chapter 5, Mike-Frank G. Epitropoulos and Victor Roudometof examine the generational changes in lifestyle and American-driven consumer culture that have taken place in post–World War II Greece. These changes were the consequence of ever-increasing contact with outsiders through tourism, migration, and mass media. The authors focus on the emergence of Greek youth culture revolving around Western — often American — cultural artifacts and social spaces. During the post-1960 period, a variety of Western establishments (pubs, discos, and cafes) became extremely popular, attracting the overwhelming majority of their audience from the youth. In terms of rituals and modes of communication, the authors reveal both change and continuity with past leisure practices. Contrary to simplistic notions of cultural imperialism, they suggest a model of cultural syncretism wherein local and imported practices are fused with each other, thereby yielding new forms and meanings.

Noting other examples of cultural syncretism, Steve Fox follows the case of blacks in German advertising in the late 1980s through the early 1990s. His chapter studies the impact of two profound period changes in Germany, namely, the xenophobic backlash and the German unification. Fox discusses the various, divergent meanings of blackness and how they are utilized in German advertising, particularly in youth magazines, billboards, and theaters. Consistent with the volume's commitment to a broad concept of Europe, Fox sheds light on the German people's struggle for cultural identity wherein preferences for German television programs are greater than other European ones while American television programs eclipse other European productions in popularity. In this context, Americanness is acceptable and popular while Europeanness is not. In the process, Fox spells out advertising's commodification of racial difference.

In his "Choosing Exile: Richard Wright, the Existentialists, and Cultural Exchange" (Chapter 7), Greg Robinson chronicles the experience of African-American expatriates in France. Militant intellectual Richard Wright was centrally concerned with freedom. As a black intellectual in the 1940s Wright found the French tolerance very appealing, moved to France, and subsequently declared that France had more freedom in one square block than did the entire United States. However, he still retained his U.S. citizenship and exile status, which endeared him to elite, French existential circles. His experience provides an interesting case worth juxtaposing to the well known tradition of French anti-Americanism (cf. Lacorne, Rupnik, & Toinet 1990). In his struggle for a "Third Way" during the Cold War era, Wright argued against both the United States and the Soviet Union. The interpersonal dynamics revealed among the French existentialists, the various political configurations, and Wright himself (among other African-American expatriates) demonstrate the exchange and interplay of ideas and reveal some measures of power and influence across cultures. Robinson makes the case that the French existentialists held ideas in higher regard than people, and that, in syncretic fashion, the French absorbed ideas from Wright selectively.

The volume's final chapter is an attempt to address the problematique of American cultural presence in Europe from a theoretical point of view. If, as Hannerz (1992: 10) suggests, the debate on Americanization is a small part of the wider tendency toward globalization, an increasing inter-connectedness of the world, then it is important to examine the function of Americanization within the general context of the ongoing process of globalization (Robertson 1992). In their contribution, Roudometof and Robertson begin with a discussion of the effects of time-space compression upon social life (Harvey 1989). They argue that economic, political, and cultural globalization bring about a destabilization of our understanding of time and space. Within the intellectual field, this restructuring entails a clash of perspectives between the proponents of time and space. As the contemporary experience of simultaneity restructures our understanding of space, it also questions the very foundations of time-based narratives. The current restructuring of time and space is not the first one in human history. During the nineteenth century, European modernity entailed the celebration of national symbolism and the cultural specificity of the European nations. It represented a particular understanding of time-space relations because it considered the nation-state the central actor in social life. The post-1945 global reality has posed serious challenges to this image of social organization. European integration, the end of colonialism, and the increasing intrusion of global mass media have questioned the solidity of the European nation-state. Commercial culture becomes the hallmark of these processes — the visible manifestation of broader changes in society and culture. For cultural purists, it offers an attractive and highly visible target of protest. Roudometof and Robertson argue that reality is more complex. As a number of chapters show, American cultural items are appropriated selectively and often reinterpreted or fused with local cultural practices or traditions. Hence, although cultural diffusion proceeds, the end result is not a loss of cultural diversity but rather the recreation of new hybrid cultural forms (see Pieterse 1995). These forms illustrate that cultural consumers are not passive agents but active participants who integrate, appropriate, and manipulate cultural objects to represent the social relations of their own communities.

REFERENCES

Appadurai, Arjun. 1996. *Modernity at Large: Cultural Dimensions of Globalization.* Minneapolis: University of Minnesota Press.

Balibar, Etienne. 1991. "Es Gibt Keinen Staat in Europa: Racism and Politics in
Europe Today." *New Left Review* 186 (March/April): 5–19.

Barber, Benjamin R. 1995. *Jihad vs. McWorld: How Globalism and Tribalism
Are Reshaping the World.* New York: Ballantine Books.

Baudrillard, Jean. 1988. *America.* London: Verso.

Billig, Michael. 1995. *Banal Nationalism.* London: Sage.

Cochran, Terry. 1996. "The Emergence of Global Contemporaneity." *Diaspora* 5
(1): 119–140.

Dean, John and Jean-Paul Gabilliet (eds.). 1996. *European Readings of American
Popular Culture* (Contributions to the Study of Popular Culture No. 50).
Westport, Conn.: Greenwood.

Eco, Umberto. 1986. *Travels in Hyperreality.* San Diego, Calif.: Harcourt Brace
Jovanovich.

Featherstone, Mike (ed.). 1990. *Global Culture: Nationalism, Globalization, and
Modernity.* London: Sage.

Ferguson, Marjorie. 1992. "The Mythology about Globalization." *European
Journal of Communication* 7: 69–93.

Haines, Gerald K. 1989. *The Americanization of Brazil.* Wilmington, Del.: Scholarly Resources Imprint.

Hannerz, Ulf. 1992. "Networks of Americanization." In *Networks of Americanization. Aspects of the American Influence in Sweden,* edited by Rolf Lunden and Erik Asard, pp. 9–19. Uppsala: Almqvist and Wiksell
International.

Harrison, Michael M. 1990. "French Anti-Americanism under the Fourth Repub-
lic and the Gaullist Solution." In *The Rise and Fall of Anti-Americanism:
A Century of French Perception,* edited by Denis Lacorne, Jacques
Rupnik, and Marie-Francois Toinet, pp. 169–78. London: Macmillan.

Harvey, David. 1989. *The Condition of Postmodernity.* Oxford: Blackell.

Horkheimer, Max and T. W. Adorno. 1938. *Dialectic of Enlightenment.* London:
Allen Lane.

Horne, Donald. 1984. *The Great Museum: The Re-presentation of History.* London: Pluto.

Huntington, Samuel. 1993. "The Clash of Civilizations?" *Foreign Affairs* 72(3):
22–49.

Judt, Tony. 1996. *A Grand Illusion? An Essay on Europe.* New York: Hill and
Wang.

Kroes, Rob. 1996. *If You've Seen One, You've Seen the Mall: Europeans and
American Mass Culture.* Urbana: University of Illinois Press.

Kuisel, Richard F. 1993. *Seducing the French: The Dilemma of Americanization.*
Berkeley: University of California Press.

Lacorne, Denis and Jacques Rupnik. 1990. "Introduction: France Bewitched by America." In *The Rise and Fall of Anti Americanism: A Century of French Perception*, edited by Denis Lacorne, Jacques Rupnik, and Marie-Francois Toinet, pp. 1–31. London: Macmillan.

Lacorne, Denis, Jacques Rupnik, and Marie-Francois Toinet (eds.). 1990. *The Rise and Fall of Anti-Americanism. A Century of French Perception*. London: Macmillan.

Lunden, Rolf and Erik Asard (eds.). 1992. *Networks of Americanization: Aspects of the American Influence in Sweden*. Uppsala: Almqvist and Wiksell International.

Martin, Lawrence. 1993. *Pledge of Allegiance: The Americanization of Canada in the Mulroney Years*. Toronto: MacClelland and Stewart.

Mattelart, Armand. 1994. *Mapping World Communication: War, Progress, Culture*. Minneapolis: University of Minnesota Press.

McGrane, Bernard. 1989. *Beyond Anthropology: Society and the Other*. New York: Columbia University Press.

Melling, Phil and Jon Roper (eds.). 1996. *Americanization and the Transformation of World Cultures: Melting Pot or Chernobyl?* Lewiston, N.Y.: Edwin Mellen.

Nordenstreng, Kaarle and Herber I. Schiller (eds.). 1993. *Beyond National Sovereignty: International Communication in the 1990s*. Norwood, N.J.: Ablex Publishing Corporation.

Pieterse, Jan N. 1995. "Globalization as Hybridization." In *Global Modernities*, edited by M. Featherstone, S. Lash, and R. Robertson, pp. 45–68. London: Sage.

Prodromou, Elizabeth H. 1995. "Paradigms, Power, and Identity: Rediscovering Orthodoxy and Regionalizing Europe." *European Journal of Political Research* 30: 125–54.

Ritzer, George. 1993. *The McDonaldization of Society: An Investigation into the Changing Character of Contemporary Social Life*. Newbury Park, Calif.: Pine Forge Press.

Ritzer, George. 1997. *The McDonalidization Thesis, Explorations and Extensions*. London: Sage.

Robertson, Roland. 1988. "The Sociological Significance of Culture: Some General Considerations." *Theory, Culture, and Society* 5 (1): 3–23.

Robertson, Roland. 1992. *Globalization: Social Theory and Global Culture*. London: Sage.

Rollin, Roger (ed.). 1989. *The Americanization of the Global Village: Essays in Comparative Popular Culture*. Bowling Green, Ohio: Bowling Green State University Press.

Roper, Jon. 1996. "Encountering America: Altered States." In *Americanization and the Transformation of World Cultures: Melting Pot or Cultural Chenobyl?* edited by Phil Melling and Jon Roper, pp. 1–28. Lewiston, N.Y.: Edwin Mellen.

Sassen, Saskia. 1996. *Losing Control? Sovereignty in An Age of Globalization*. New York: Columbia University Press.

Schlesinger, Philip. 1997. "From Cultural Defence to Political Culture: Media, Politics, and Collective Identity in the European Union." *Media, Culture, and Society* 19 (3): 369–92.

Schopflin, George and Nancy Wood (eds.). 1989. *In Search of Central Europe*. Cambridge: Polity.

Stoianovich, Traian. 1994. *The Balkan Worlds: The First and Last Europe*. New York: M. E. Sharpe.

Struminski, Bohdan. 1995. "Does the 'Bolingbroke-Stempowoski Law' Exist?" *To Be* (2B) 3(7–8): 98–101.

Tomlinson, John. 1991. *Cultural Imperialism: A Critical Introduction*. Baltimore, Md.: Johns Hopkins University Press.

Wagnleitner, Reinhold. 1994. *Coca-colonization and the Cold War: The Cultural Mission of the United States in Austria after the Second World War*. Chapel Hill: University of North Carolina Press.

Wolff, Larry. 1994. *Inventing Eastern Europe: The Map of Civilization on the Mind of the Enlightenment*. Stanford, Calif.: Stanford University Press.

1

The U.S. Center of World Science and Emulating Centers: Japan and Western Europe

Thomas Schott, Jun Kanamitsu, and James F. Luther

WORLD SCIENCE AND ITS CENTERS

Science is a tradition that is widely shared. Scientific knowledge is widely available as a public good, especially through scientific literature with its wide subscriptions that globalize knowledge for collective human ownership. Moreover, the cultivation of the scientific tradition is highly communal. It is cultivated through cooperation and communication that transcend boundaries and span societies. The knowledge created around the world is assimilated as a basis for the creation of new knowledge that is disseminated around the world as a contribution to the tradition. The communal cultivation binds the cultivators around the world into a community, the scientific community. This communal cultivation of the scientific tradition around the world is appropriately called world science (Schott 1993).

World science, however, is not even in its participation around the world. The scientific tradition is cultivated intensely in some societies and hardly in others. Some contributions attract much deference and become exemplars that set standards and influence cultivation around the world. The networks of deference and influence, then, are not a uniform grid but form a hierarchy.

World science has always had its center, but the center has shifted. Up to the seventeenth century the center was in Italy, then it shifted to England, then to France, then to Germany, and in the 1930s the center moved to the United States (Ben-David 1984). The center, though, has not monopolized creativity and has not been a hegemon attracting all deference and exerting all influence. There have been other seats of creativity attracting some deference and exerting some influence. The center is thus not unitary but a cluster of centers. Centrality is continuous, ranging from conceivable hegemony at one extreme, through lesser centrality, toward peripherality and even obscure isolation at another possible extreme. Centrality is high not only in the United States but also in Western Europe, and Japan is also becoming central. The center is less concentrated, it is dispersing.

This chapter examines the dynamics among the centers, addressing the following questions, What are the institutional foundations for cooperation and competition among centers? Is the dynamic among the centers a combination of cooperation or competition or something else? Is the center still located in the United States? Are other participants, such as Japan and Western Europe, emulating the U.S. center? Are they catching up with the U.S. center? Are the centers self-reliant or are they attached to one another? This focus on centers is complemented by the focus on peripheries in the next chapter (Schott et al. 1998).

INSTITUTIONAL FOUNDATIONS FOR COOPERATION AND COMPETITION AMONG CENTERS

The first institutionalization of science occurred in England in the seventeenth century, notably when the cultivation of the tradition was granted legitimacy, autonomy, and organization with the founding of the Royal Society of London. In the charter the King proclaimed,

We have long and fully resolved with Ourself to extend not only the boundaries of the Empire, but also the very arts and sciences. . . . In order, therefore, that such studies, which have not hitherto been sufficiently brilliant in any part of the world, may shine conspicuously amongst our people, and that at length the whole world of letters may always recognize us . . . as the universal lover and patron of

every kind of truth . . . we . . . have . . . established . . . the Royal Society of
London for Promoting Natural Knowledge. (Royal Society 1940: 250)

As the charter indicates, England aimed at institutionalizing science to
promote great scientific achievement in England, compared to the continent, thereby gaining esteem among nations. The charter also granted
autonomy to correspond with foreign peers, to print reports of discover-
ies, and to circulate the publications widely, even abroad.

The intense cultivation of science in England earned deference from
continental Europe, which attributed the English achievement to its institutionalization. To catch up with the English, the continental Europeans
copied the English institutions. The competition for esteem thus led to
imitation of institutions around the European civilization of modernity.
Science was institutionalized as a highly anational endeavor and its cultivators formed a transnational community. When Europeans settled around
the world, they carried with them this scientific tradition and institutionalized it when they established modern societies, such as those in North
America.

When people in other civilizations embarked on modernization they
adopted the scientific tradition and imitated the institutions of science in
Europe and North America. This involved adopting in the invariance of
nature, in both space and time, and a belief in the invariance of the truthfulness of knowledge. This belief was promulgated in Japan by
Fukuzawa when it modernized after 1868,

Since the beginning of the world up to this day, anywhere in the whole world, the
laws governing physical matter have been the same with not a single change ever.
In the ancient period of the gods, water boiled when it reached 212 degrees
Fahrenheit, and in this Meiji era too, water boils at the same temperature. Steam
in the Western world has the same power of expansion as steam in the Orient.
Men in America die taking an excessive dose of morphine, and Japanese also die
taking the same dosage. This is what we call physical law. The learning that studies these laws in order to apply them to human advantage is called physical science. (Fukuzawa [1882] 1985: 123)

Science was, however, nationalized in Japan when it came to be treated as
a national resource. Science was nationalized in the United States when it
became mobilized for World War II. Science was nationalized in Western
Europe mainly in the 1960s when it came to be treated as a means for

economic growth. The faith in social progress, especially in the form of economic growth, has been augmented by a doctrine that progress can be accelerated by the rationalization of science. Thus, rationalization of social activity has been expanded to incorporate science as a means for social progress.

In the latest half-century the United States has been admired as the most successful society, especially when its economy was the most productive in the world. Economic growth has been considered the manifestation of social progress and the United States was the most progressive society, and, as such, posed a challenge to other societies, as expressed in the European best-seller *Le Défi Américain* (Servan-Schreiber 1967). American social progress was attributed to its scientific achievements, which, in turn, were attributed to its institutions. American institutions, therefore, have been considered most efficient and, hence, worthwhile copying in societies around the world (Ben-David 1984). U.S. scientific achievement and institutions have been taken as a frame of reference for comparison and self-assessment in other nations. The United States has been the exemplar for imitation around the world and its policy and institutional arrangements have become doctrine for rationalized progress. During the Cold War the United States allied itself with Western Europe and Japan and let its allies attach themselves to its scientific endeavor. The United States was the great contributor to the public good in world science, was very open to sojourning students and scientists from allied countries, and was not concerned with whether it was contributing especially much, or whether its allies were benefiting more than they were contributing.

Comparisons and assessments of scientific achievement and its institutional conditions are undertaken not only by each nation-state but also by world organizations. World organizations, especially the United Nations Educational, Scientific and Cultural Organization, the Organisation for Economic Co-operation and Development (OECD), and the World Bank, support an epistemic community of counselors on policies for science. They monitor and evaluate the institutions and achievements of science in the various societies, formulate theories about science and its proper management, and recommend policy to nation-states for science. The organizations and the epistemic community promote an international regime for guiding and managing world science (Finnemore 1993).

They currently advocate a policy against intellectual protectionism and for internationalization of scientific endeavors.

The policy is formulated around research and development (R&D) as a category combining science with technology. R&D in a society is performed in an institutional setting conceptualized as a system of innovation within the society, indicating that innovation is the desired goal of this system in the society. Science in a society is treated as an investment in innovation, and support for R&D is measured in terms of expenditure on R&D relative to the economy, as a percentage of the gross national product or gross domestic product (GDP). When the OECD was elaborating its investment doctrine in the 1960s, the percentage was highest in the United States, at 3 percent of GDP. Because the United States was considered the greatest achiever in science as well as the most successful nation in capturing economic benefits, its 3 percent R&D investment became established as a goal for other nations to reach. The United States was an exemplar to imitate; its policy, abstracting from the country itself, became formulated as a model and a recipe for progress.

In the 1970s, Japan's Council for Science and Technology recommended "We should set the goal of 2.5% of GDP spending on R&D in the short run, considering the necessity of future investment and the current actions taken by Western nations, and the 3% in the long run" (Council for Science and Technology 1977). Around 1990, Japan reached its 3 percent goal. Japan, though, specializes in technological innovation rather than in science, much more than either the United States or Western Europe, which has engendered some conflict as examined below.

European nations have also adopted the goal of 3 percent and are trying to catch up, but hardly any have reached the goal. The Commission of the European Community (now Union) provides a self-assessment: "Europe's research and industrial base suffers from a series of weaknesses. . . . The first of these weaknesses is financial. The Community invests proportionately less than its competitors in research and technological development. . . . 2% of GDP in the Community, 2.8% in the USA and 3% in Japan"; the Commission also prescribes solutions: "With regard to overall research funding, the objective of a gradual increase to 3% of GDP should be borne in mind" (European Commission 1994: 101–3).

In the United States, meanwhile, the R&D expenditure has dropped below its previous 3 percent. However, an expenditure of 3 percent has been adopted as a goal also in the United States, as expressed in the major science policy statement by President Clinton:

U.S. investment in fundamental research must be commensurate with our national goals. The Gross Domestic Product (GDP) provides the benchmark for total economic activity and thus the most meaningful measure of the R&D investment. Total U.S. support of non-defense R&D is about 1.9 percent of GDP, below that of Germany (2.5 percent) and Japan (3.0 percent). Including all defense R&D . . . the U.S. total becomes 2.6 percent . . . a reasonable long term goal for the total national R&D investment (both civilian and defense) might be about 3 percent of GDP. (Clinton & Gore 1994: 13–15)

Thus, the U.S. expenditure of 3 percent in the 1960s was a practice that was imitated, but over the decades it has actually become abstracted from its origin and become institutionalized around the world as a goal for nations to attain.

The expenditure on science and technology is not considered cultural consumption but is considered a means to innovation. This is illustrated by the recent *Green Paper of Innovation* from the European Union, in which the summary declares "Innovation is vital . . . countries need to transform new ideas rapidly into new products and commercial successes if they are to maintain growth, competitiveness and jobs. In this regard, Europe seems less well placed than its main rivals. The paradox is that it has an excellent scientific base but it is less successful than others in converting its competence into new products and market shares" (European Commission 1996: 1). Science and innovation are thus considered means to growth, competitiveness, and jobs. In addition to being a source of esteem for a society, scientific achievement has become a means to social progress.

The construed rivals are the United States and Japan. Japan has been especially successful in technological innovation despite its smaller scientific activity. Indeed, Japan has been criticized around the world for being a "free rider" by benefiting from its innovation of privately-owned goods on the basis of a public good — world science — without contributing equitably to this public good (Ancarani 1995). The criticism was apparently accepted in Japan: "In light of 'Japan coexisting with the nations of the world,' Japan is expected to play an important role in the world community and to contribute accordingly. From the viewpoint of international contribution to science . . . Japan has not contributed enough in the way of intellectual resources. The United States and European countries feel that Japan is getting a 'free ride.' Thus, . . . [the Japanese Council on Science and Technology] stated that Japan should take a more international approach by sharing basic research results with other nations" (Science and Technology Agency 1991: 19–20). The rivalry to capture private innovation from public science constrains the publicness of science. Intellectual protectionism occurs in a country by restricting foreigners' access to research facilities in the country, especially to research supported by the government.

The issues are not merely discussed in diplomacy among nation-states but are increasingly formulated into rules governing scientific activities among nations. The creation of rules is orchestrated by world organizations. The OECD promotes the creation of such "rules of the game," as illustrated by a recent meeting of Ministers from OECD countries:

Ministers acknowledge that government support to corporate research . . . may create friction at the international level and may affect international access to science and technology. In this regard, Ministers call on the OECD to deepen its analysis of government support to private sector R&D. . . . Ministers also request the OECD to analyse further the issue of equal access for domestic and foreign-controlled firms to publicly funded research. . . . Ministers ask the OECD, where appropriate, to explore the need for improving existing multilateral instruments and whether there is a need to develop additional "rules of the game". . . . Ministers call on the OECD to examine whether and how international mutually-beneficial co-operation in major research areas could be further improved among governments and research communities on the basis of adequately shared responsibilities. (OECD 1991: 10–11)

These calls indicate the existence and increasing salience in the world of an ideology of justice and fairness according to which a nation should contribute a portion toward the world public good, which is similar to its portion of national private goods derived from the world public good.

Nations compete not only by increasing support for science and technology but also by pursuing policies for adding value through collaborative networking in the local system of research (OECD 1992). Japan has formed its *keiretsu* networks for collaborative scientific research and technological innovation. The *keiretsu* networks are considered loci of innovation and are being imitated by the United States. Similarly, in Western Europe, the European Science Foundation and the European Union have for decades been promoting networking among European researchers (European Commission 1994, 1996). Their policies have increased collaboration among West European nations in scientific research (Moed & de Bruin 1990; National Science Board 1996: 222–23) and in technological invention (Schott 1994a). The West European integration has entailed a cohesion among scientists in Western Europe. Western Europe has emerged as a society that is often compared to Japan and the United States; together they form a triad dominating the global system.

World science is organized around this triad. The societies in the triad are considered actors and each pursues social progress by means of scientific achievement. Science, then, has become nationalized and rationalized as a means for social progress in each society. Social progress of a society is usually measured by economic growth, but the frame of reference is other societies. Science is treated as a means to social ends and is therefore measured partly by investment (both by comparison with the other societies in the triad and by increases toward the common goal of investing 3 percent of GDP in R&D) and partly by outcomes (both by scientific achievement and esteem and by technological innovation based on science). Each actor has a desire or ambition to equal or surpass the others in the triad. Their emulation turns into competition insofar as it becomes a contest among them for the same object, notably technological innovation that is privately appropriated, a contest for innovation as an indivisible object following rules that are agreed upon, such as patenting. Often, if not typically, the competition turns into rivalry insofar as it becomes a struggle among them, a struggle that does not follow rules, because rules are breached or absent. Indeed, the interaction in the triad is conceived to be a combination of competition and cooperation (Group of Lisbon 1995; Ohmae 1985; Ostry & Nelson 1995).

The so-called actors of the triad are thus enacting a script for social progress by means of science. The script prescribes them to play roles as equitable cooperators and competitors for scientific achievement and thereby social progress (McNeely 1995). Science is institutionalized as the communal creation of a public good, a global commons, but this cooperation is accompanied by competition for capturing national private goods from the world public good. This institutionalized cooperation and competition among the triad is an institutional framework for the cultivation of the scientific tradition.

ACHIEVEMENT IN CENTERS AND
ITS ATTRACTION OF DEFERENCE

The questions here are, how intense is the cultivation of science around the world and to what extent does achievement in a society attract deference from around the world? Scientific achievement in a society can be indicated, albeit crudely, by its scientists' publications, as listed in Table 1.1 (science here comprises the natural, technological, and medical sciences). A few decades ago, as indicated by Table 1.1, scientific achievement was higher in the United States than anywhere else. By the mid-1990s, however, Western Europe had not only caught up but forged ahead of the United States. Performance has also been surging in Japan but has not yet caught up with science in the West.

TABLE 1.1
Scientific Publications Authored around the World
(in percent)

Authors' Locations	Scientific Publications	
	1975–79	1995
United States	40.9	33.8
Japan	5.0	7.9
Western Europe	33.0	37.4
France	6.4	7.1
Denmark	0.9	0.9
Greece	0.2	0.4
Other countries	21.1	20.9
Total	100.0	100.0

Notes: Western Europe includes Austria, Belgium, Cyprus, Denmark, Finland, France, Germany (both East and West), Greece, Iceland, Ireland, Italy, Luxembourg, Netherlands, Norway, Portugal, Spain, Sweden, Switzerland, and the United Kingdom.

Publications in a society are indicated as a percentage of the world total.

The percentages in a column total 100 percent (except for rounding) in this and Tables 1.2–1.9.

Source: *Science Citation Index, 1975–79, 1995.* Philadelphia, PA: Institute for Scientific Information.

Deference toward achievement and other relations was tapped in the early and mid-1990s in a survey of a sample of 487 scientists (211 in the United States, 94 in Japan, and 182 in Europe, namely 80 in France, 50 in Denmark and 52 in Greece). The scientists were sampled rather randomly in each site, covering the natural, technological, and medical sciences, and interviewed with a questionnaire that has been validated in earlier studies (Schott 1994b, 1997).

Deference toward scientific achievement was indicated in the survey by asking, "Quite apart from any influence upon your own research, who are the five people in the world who have performed the best scientific research in your area of specialization since 1990?" The American, Japanese, and European scientists' deference toward contributors around the world is listed in Table 1.2. Evidently, scientists defer partly to local achievement and partly to achievement around the world. Specifically, scientists in France, Denmark, and Greece defer much to achievement around Western Europe. Achievements in the United States and Western Europe attract by far the most deference. Juxtaposing Tables 1.1 and 1.2, we see that achievement attracts deference in commensurate amount, except that the Japanese surge in achievement still attracts disproportionately little deference. Contrarily, deference seems to remain especially high toward the declining achievement in the United States.

PEOPLE MOVING AMONG CENTERS

Scientific achievement attracts not only deference but also people. Achievement attracts students who want to become apprentices of the creators of the achievements. Moreover, among people outside the main center, a sojourn for training at the main center is considered part of a well-rounded training for a young scientist. Likewise, a visit to the main center carries some prestige; it is considered part of the role of a scientist. Educational origins of the scientists in the survey were tapped by asking where they received their highest degree. The educational origins are summarized in Table 1.3. Scientists in the United States, obviously, have largely been home bred, although some are immigrants. (None of those born in the United States went abroad to study.) The Japanese scientists have also been trained at home. The scientists in Europe have mostly been trained in their own country (especially those in France) but a significant fraction of scientists (especially in smaller countries such as Denmark and

TABLE 1.2
Scientists' Deference to Contributors around the World
(in percent)

Contributors' Locations	United States	Japan	Western Europe	France	Denmark	Greece
United States	75	50	38	35	35	40
Japan	1	17	1	1	1	1
Western Europe	18	27	53			
Scientist's country				32	20	7
Other Western Europe				25	37	34
Other countries	6	7	8	7	8	9
Total	100	101	100	100	101	100
N contributors	676	125	689	335	199	155

TABLE 1.3

Scientists' Education in Own Country and Abroad

(in percent)

Places of Education	United States	Japan	Western Europe	France	Denmark	Greece
United States	92	0	3	0	6	6
Japan	0	97	0	0	0	0
Western Europe	4	3	95			
Scientist's country				100	80	79
Other Western Europe				0	12	12
Other countries	4	0	2	0	2	4
Total	100	100	100	100	100	101
N scientists	210	89	182	80	50	52

Greece) have studied in another West European country or in the United States. (The scientists in Denmark also include some immigrants, mostly from other West European countries.)

Scientists travel to interact with colleagues at other institutions and at conferences. Travels were tapped in the survey by asking, "Which institutions have you visited in the last 12 months for purposes of your research?" and "To which scientific conferences abroad have you gone in the years 1990 to 1994?" Travels are listed in Table 1.4. Travels are mostly to institutions and conferences in the United States and Western Europe. French, Danish, and Greek scientists, in particular, travel extensively around Western Europe, often with support from European agencies that specifically aim to promote such cohesion among researchers around Europe. The centers of travel are obviously Western Europe and the United States (Martin-Rovet 1995; Martin-Rovet & Carlson 1995). Juxtaposing educational origins and travels (Tables 1.3 and 1.4) with achievement in scientific research (Table 1.1), we see that achievement attracts people, but the surging Japanese achievement is not yet attracting much travel from the American and West European centers.

IDEAS MOVING AMONG CENTERS

An achievement attracts deference and thereby becomes an exemplar that influences research. Influence upon researchers was tapped by asking, "Who are the people whose ideas have influenced your research since about 1990?" The researcher named up to 20 colleagues, the average being about 12 colleagues. The locations of the colleagues are listed in Table 1.5. The first column shows that the scientists in the United States are influenced largely by compatriots and extremely little by foreign scientists. Japanese scientists are more cosmopolitan in that they are heavily influenced by foreign colleagues. Scientists in Western Europe are influenced by colleagues within their own country, in other West European countries, and in the United States. The center of most influence is the United States, Western Europe is a secondary center of influence, and Japan is rather peripheral in the network of influence.

Influence specifically on the scientists' selection of problematics for research was tapped by asking, "To what extent has each person influenced your choice of problems for research since about 1990?" The extent of a colleague's influence was rated on a scale from 0 for "none," through

TABLE 1.4
Scientists' Travels to Other Institutions and to Conferences Abroad
(in percent)

Destinations	United States	Japan	Western Europe	France	Denmark	Greece
Scientists traveling to other institutions						
United States	81	15	7	5	12	2
Japan	2	61	2	2	3	0
Western Europe	10	14	81			
Scientist's country				73	25	48
Other Western Europe				11	48	40
Other countries	7	10	10	9	12	10
Total	100	100	100	100	100	100
N travels	366	119	472	174	216	60
Scientists traveling to conferences abroad						
United States	NA	37	21	24	16	11
Japan	0	NA	2	3	0	0
Western Europe	52	37	NA	NA	NA	NA
Scientist's country				NA	NA	NA
Other Western Europe			59	55	69	72
Other countries	48	26	18	18	15	18
Total	100	100	100	100	100	100
N travels	286	193	418	244	87	113

TABLE 1.5
Influence upon Scientists from Colleagues around the World
(in percent)

Influencers' Locations	United States	Japan	Western Europe	France	Denmark	Greece
United States	80	29	24	24	21	27
Japan	1	54	1	1	2	1
Western Europe	13	13	68			
Scientist's country				51	47	34
Other Western Europe				18	23	30
Other countries	6	3	7	6	7	3
Total	100	99	100	100	100	100
N influencers	1,820	525	1,790	911	495	382

1 for "little" and 2 for "some," up to 3 for "great." The amount of influence from a place is the sum of the influence from the colleagues in that place, as a percentage of the influence from all the colleagues. This weighted distribution is listed in Table 1.6. The table shows that influence upon selection of problematics is highly — perhaps surprisingly — transnational.

The influence that a scientist receives comes partly from the literature and partly from communication with colleagues. Influence from the literature was tapped by asking, "To what extent has each person influenced your research since 1990 through your reading of the person's publications?" The extent of a colleague's influence was rated on a scale from 0 for "none" up to 3 for "great." The amount of influence from a place is the sum of the influence from the colleagues in that place, as a percentage of the influence from all the colleagues. This weighted distribution of influence through the literature is listed in the top section of Table 1.7. Influence through the literature, as the top section shows, is highly transnational: as much comes from colleagues in other countries.

Influence comes through not only the literature but also personal communication from colleagues. Personal communication was tapped by asking, "To what extent has each person influenced your research since 1990 through personal communication?" This interpersonal influence was also rated on the extent scale. The weighted distribution of influence from personal communication is listed in the bottom section of Table 1.7. Evidently, personal communication from local colleagues is more influential than communication from distant colleagues.

The above analyses show that ideas move extensively. The centers in the networks of influence through publications and personal communication, and specifically on choice of problematics for research, are largely in the United States and in Western Europe. The surging achievement in Japan has not yet become a central source of influence.

COMMUNAL BONDS AMONG CENTERS

Collective cultivation occurs not only through communication and influence but even more intensely through collaboration on joint research. Collaboration was tapped by asking, "To what extent has each person been a collaborator on your research since 1990?" Collaboration was

TABLE 1.6
Influence upon Scientists' Choice of Problems

(in percent)

Influencers' Locations	United States	Japan	Western Europe	France	Denmark	Greece
United States	81	27	23	23	19	26
Japan	1	55	1	1	2	1
Western Europe	12	14	69			
Scientist's country				53	48	34
Other Western Europe				17	23	29
Other countries	6	4	7	6	8	7
Total	100	100	100	100	100	99
N influencers	1,621	500	1,609	803	457	349

TABLE 1.7
Influence upon Scientists from Literature and Communication
(in percent)

Influencers' Locations	United States	Japan	Western Europe	France	Denmark	Greece
Scientists influenced by literature						
United States	78	32	29	27	27	36
Japan	1	48	2	2	3	1
Western Europe	15	15	61			
Scientist's country				44	32	26
Other Western Europe				19	29	27
Other countries	6	4	9	8	10	10
Total	100	99	101	100	101	100
N influencers	1,420	465	1,445	771	360	314
Scientists influenced by communication						
United States	85	19	15	15	16	14
Japan	0	68	1	0	2	0
Western Europe	10	8	79			
Scientist's country				66	55	51
Other Western Europe				15	21	27
Other countries	5	4	6	5	7	8
Total	100	99	101	101	101	100
N influencers	1,390	379	1,338	682	426	230

rated on the extent scale. The weighted distribution is listed in Table 1.8. Collaboration is partly local and partly cosmopolitan. Specifically, the French, Danish, and Greek scientists collaborate extensively with other Europeans. The centers of collaboration are in the United States and Western Europe.

Communality is expressed not only in collective cultivation of the scientific tradition but also in the formation of communal bonds and in the allocation of rewards. Rewards are allocated for performance of a social role. The institutionalized reward for performance of the role of a scientist, contributing to the tradition, is collegial recognition. The desire for recognition was tapped by asking, "To what extent do you care about each person's recognition of your research?" The desire for recognition was rated on the extent scale; the weighted distribution is listed in the top section of Table 1.9. The colleagues that researchers desire recognition from include both local colleagues and foreign colleagues. Notably, the United States and Western Europe are the centers in the network of desire for recognition.

Collegial emulation emerges from the desire for recognition. Collegial emulation was tapped by asking, "To what extent do you feel that the person and you are competing with one another to be first or best in research?" Collegial emulation was rated on the extent scale and the weighted distribution of sources of emulation is listed in the bottom of Table 1.9. The total number of emulators (rated 1, 2, or 3), as listed at the bottom, is about half of the total number of named colleagues, so emulation is substantial but not ubiquitous. The sources of emulation are both local colleagues and colleagues in other places. Notably, the United States and Western Europe are the centers in the network of collegial emulation as well as other relations among scientists. These are centers of bonds that are highly transnational and communal. Cohesion is especially high among scientists within Western Europe, but they are also part of the wider network that binds scientists together among the centers.

CONCLUSION: EMULATION AMONG CENTERS

World science is a communal cultivation of the scientific tradition. The scientific tradition is cultivated by scientists who pursue intellectual intercourse and also communal bonds across long distances in a wide-spanning community. The community, however, is not a free-floating intelligentsia.

TABLE 1.8
Scientists' Collaboration

(in percent)

Collaborators' Locations	United States	Japan	Western Europe	France	Denmark	Greece
United States	87	18	13	13	14	11
Japan	1	72	1	0	2	0
Western Europe	9	8	81			
Scientist's country				69	58	65
Other Western Europe				12	20	18
Other countries	4	2	5	5	6	6
Total	101	100	100	99	100	100
N collaborators	864	284	1,051	555	334	162

TABLE 1.9

Scientists' Desiring Recognition and Feeling Competition from Colleagues

(in percent)

Colleagues' Locations	United States	Japan	Western Europe	France	Denmark	Greece
Scientists desiring recognition						
United States	82	22	22	22	18	28
Japan	0	62	1	1	2	1
Western Europe			70			
Scientist's country	12	12		55	48	34
Other Western Europe				16	25	28
Other countries	5	4	7	5	8	9
Total	99	100	100	99	101	100
N colleagues	1,667	381	1,620	849	413	358
Scientists feeling competition						
United States	79	30	26	27	24	26
Japan	1	49	3	2	3	4
Western Europe			63			
Scientist's country	14	16		43	33	32
Other Western Europe				20	32	27
Other countries	7	5	8	8	7	11
Total	101	100	100	100	99	100
N travels	766	246	719	375	222	122

The scientific tradition is institutionalized in societies that support and guide its cultivation. The recognition that scientists in a nation obtain from colleagues in other countries becomes esteem of the nation among other countries. A nation typically supports science to obtain such esteem among nations. Furthermore, and increasingly salient in the contemporary global system, a society supports science as a means for its innovation of technology to gain a comparative advantage for trade. The pursuit of technological advantages compared to other societies entails some intellectual protectionism that constrains the autonomy and limits the communality of science.

Science is thus an arena in which societies are competing for scientific achievement. Emulation is salient among the United States, Western Europe, and Japan. Each seeks to achieve most in science, both to attain esteem among societies for the achievement and to utilize the scientific knowledge as a basis for innovation that will increase shares on the global market. The economic rivalry among the triadic societies entails some intellectual protectionism and some constraints on the autonomy of science, but the cultivation of the scientific tradition remains a highly communal endeavor.

Scientific achievement was highest in the United States but it has now been surpassed by the growing achievement in Western Europe. Japan has been surging but is not close to the United States or to Western Europe. In the networks among scientists, the United States, despite its declining share of scientific achievement, has remained the main center of deference, of travels, of influence, of collaboration, of collegial emulation, and also the place from which recognition is desired. Western Europe, despite its forging ahead of the United States in scientific achievement, has not become the main center of the networks. Japan, despite is surging achievement, has not yet become central in world science.

NOTE

This study is part of the projects by Professor Schott on International Collegial Ties in Science supported by the U.S. National Science Foundation (NSF INT-9403770) and Science and Technology in Denmark supported by the Danish Social Science Research Council. Appreciation is extended to the surveyed scientists around the world. Self-exemplifying their studied phenomenon, the authors gathered at a U.S. university from Western Europe, Japan, and the United States.

REFERENCES

Ancarani, Vittorio. 1995. "Globalizing the World: Science and Technology in International Relations." In *Handbook of Science and Technology Studies*, edited by Sheila Jasanoff, Gerald E. Markle, James C. Petersen, and Trevor Pinch, pp. 652–70. Thousand Oaks, CA: Sage.

Ben-David, Joseph. 1984. *The Scientist's Role in Society: A Comparative Study.* Chicago, IL: University of Chicago Press.

Clinton, William J., & Albert Gore. 1994. *Science in the National Interest.* Washington, DC: U.S. Government Printing Office.

Council for Science and Technology. 1977. *Chokiteki tenbo ni tatta sougouteki kagakugijutsu seisaku no kihon ni tsuite* [On the basics of comprehensive science and technology policies from a long-term perspective]. Tokyo: Council for Science and Technology.

European Commission. 1994. *Growth, Competitiveness, Employment. The Challenges and Ways Forward into the 21st Century. White Paper.* Luxembourg: Office for Official Publications of the European Communities.

European Commission. 1996. *Green Paper on Innovation.* http://www.cordis.lu/cordis/grnpaper.htm and http://www.cordis.lu/innovation/src/pubresen.htm

Finnemore, Martha. 1993. "International Organizations as Teachers of Norms: United Nations Educational, Scientific and Cultural Organization and Science Policy." *International Organization* 47:565–97.

Fukuzawa, Yukichi. 1985. *Fukuzawa Yukichi on Education.* Tokyo: Tokyo University Press.

Group of Lisbon. 1995. *Limits to Competition.* Cambridge, Mass.: MIT Press.

Martin-Rovet, Dominique. 1995. "The International Exchange of Scholars: The Training of Young Scientists through Research Abroad. I. Young French Scientists in the United States." *Minerva* 33:75–98.

Martin-Rovet, Dominique, & Timothy Carlson. 1995. "The International Exchange of Scholars: The Training of Young Scientists through Research Abroad. II. American Scientists in France." *Minerva* 33:171–91.

McNeely, Connie L. 1995. *Constructing the Nation-State: International Organization and Prescriptive Action.* Westport, CT: Greenwood Press.

Moed, Henk F., & Renger E. de Bruin. 1990. "International Scientific Cooperation and Awareness: A Bibliometric Case Study of Agricultural Research within the European Community." In *Scholarly Communication and Bibliometrics*, edited by Christine L. Borgman, pp. 217–34. Newbury Park, CA: Sage.

National Science Board. 1996. *Science & Engineering Indicators — 1996.* Washington, DC: National Science Foundation.

Ohmae, Kenichi. 1985. *Triad Power: The Coming Shape of Global Competition*. New York: Free Press.

Organisation for Economic Co-operation and Development. 1991. *Technology in a Changing World*. Paris: Organisation for Economic Co-operation and Development.

Organisation for Economic Co-operation and Development. 1992. *Technology and the Economy: The Key Relationships*. Paris: Organisation for Economic Co-operation and Development.

Ostry, Sylvia, & Richard R. Nelson. 1995. *Techno-Nationalism and Techno-Globalism: Conflict and Cooperation*. Washington, DC: Brookings Institution.

Royal Society of London. 1940. *Record of the Royal Society*. London: Royal Society.

Schott, Thomas. 1993. "World Science: Globalization of Institutions and Participation." *Science, Technology & Human Values* 18:196–208.

Schott, Thomas. 1994a. "Collaboration in the Invention of Technology: Globalization, Regions and Centers." *Social Science Research* 23:23–56.

Schott, Thomas. 1994b. "Emerging and Declining Centers of Engineering Science: Japan and the United States." *Knowledge: Creation, Diffusion and Utilization* 15:417–56.

Schott, Thomas. 1997. "The Global-national Nexus in Research: Absorbing World Science in Denmark." *LIBRI* 47: 193–205.

Schott, Thomas, Samuel Kugel, Ruben Berrios, & Keri Rodriguez. 1998. "Peripheries of World Science: Latin America and Eastern Europe. In *American Culture in Europe: Interdisciplinary Perspectives*, edited by Mike-Frank G. Epitropoulos and Victor Roudometof. Westport, CT: Greenwood Press.

Science and Technology Agency. 1991. *White Paper on Science and Technology*. Tokyo: Foreign Press Center.

Servan-Schreiber, Jean-Jacques. 1967. *Le Défi Américain* [The American challenge]. Paris: Editions Denoel.

2

Peripheries in World Science: Latin America and Eastern Europe

Thomas Schott, Samuel A. Kugel, Ruben Berrios,
and Keri L. Rodriguez

A SCIENTIFICALLY SMALL NATION OPTING FOR SELF-RELIANCE VERSUS ATTACHMENT

In the course of the twentieth century, the scientific tradition has become cultivated in every society around the world. The cultivation, moreover, is highly communal. This communal cultivation of the scientific tradition is denoted world science. Participation of nations in world science, however, is not equal. The cultivation is intense in some societies and sporadic in other societies. A few societies have large scientific endeavors and account for much of the cultivation of the scientific tradition around the world. Some of the scientifically big societies have become centers in world science. The current centers are located in the United States of America and Western Europe, as examined in the preceding chapter (Schott, Kanamitsu, & Luther 1998). The typical society is small in its extent of participation. Smallness is indicated by performance of a small fraction of the scientific activity in the world.

Smallness of the scientific endeavor in a country is a condition that is consequential. The condition of smallness implies that a scientist is likely to find few colleagues within her own country (Gaillard, Krishna, & Waast 1997). Smallness may trigger different responses, from an attempt at self-reliance in the country to an outward attachment to a center.

Self-reliance, a reliance on knowledge generated locally rather than on ideas from the outside, was pursued in Japan for several centuries up to the second half of the nineteenth century. Similarly, self-reliance was pursued in China during the cultural revolution in the 1960s and 1970s, when so-called barefoot science was to become an indigenous scholarly tradition detached from the foreign cultivation of the scientific tradition. China opted for such isolation for a decade and then opted for a gradual openness to foreign ideas. Until the end of the 1980s, the communist regime in the East European bloc had a policy of self-reliance. This policy, though, was only partly implemented in the Soviet Union (Schott 1992). Currently, the Islamic region has a movement to cultivate indigenous traditions detached from the cultivation of the scientific tradition outside of the Islamic region. Isolation, though, whether voluntary or imposed, is becoming a rarity and currently the most detached local scientific communities are apparently in Syria, Libya, Iraq, North Korea, and Cuba.

Another response to smallness is attachment to a center. This option involves forming a periphery and pursuing intellectual intercourse with a center. These scientists, who find very few colleagues at home, choose to pursue relations with mainly foreign colleagues. The essential content of the attachment is intellectual transmission, "The selection and promulgation of problems to be studied, the concepts and techniques of their study and the fixation of certain models of achievement exhibit the real links of the . . . system of metropolis and province in the intellectual community" (Shils 1972: 363). Scientists in a periphery often consider attachment to centers beneficial for their research, and the effect of attachment upon research has been estimated as considerable (Schott 1987). Attachment is of course a matter of degree, ranging from one extreme characterized by detachment, isolation, and self-reliance; through loose coupling as a distant periphery and tight coupling as a satellite; to integration at the other extreme. Detached isolation versus attachment as a periphery are thus two polar alternative behaviors in response to the condition of smallness.

This study focuses on such responses to smallness. The questions here are: To what extent is science in a scientifically small country cultivated in self-reliant isolation? To what extent is it cultivated through participation in a more global communal cultivation of the scientific tradition, through peripheral attachment to centers? Are societies different in that some pursue self-reliance and some pursue attachment? Are societies similar in that they mostly attach themselves as peripheries to centers? These questions can be addressed through a comparison of nations. A sample of nations ought to satisfy two criteria. First, the nations should be rather small in science, and, second, they should expectedly differ in their behavior in that some nations expectedly are rather isolated and self-reliant and some nations expectedly form peripheries attached to a center. Therefore, we selected cases on a criterion of expectedly diverse behavior rather than by random sampling. The expectedly peripheral case is Mexico, which has attached itself to the center in the United States. The cases that expectedly are rather isolated and self-reliant are Cuba, Czechoslovakia, and Russia. In selecting these four cases, we are not assuming that they are equal in the sizes of their scientific endeavors. Actually, Cuban science is many times smaller than Russian science, but all of them are actually rather small, as evidenced below. In choosing our cases, we are not postulating that they are equally isolated or peripheral, or that they are even peripheral. Indeed, a scientifically small locality may become a world center of a specialty and some of its scientists may be central in the world scientific community. Actually, some Russian scientists are performing great achievements in scientific research, which attract much deference and recognition, exerting considerable intellectual influence around the world. For example, researchers in mathematical physics around the world know, recognize, and use the contributions by L. D. Faddeev at the scientific academy in St. Petersburg and the city is a center of that field, as he recently chronicled in *40 Years in Mathematical Physics*. St. Petersburg is also the center of some other scientific specialties such as hydrogeology and mass spectroscopy. Within some specialties a center is in Russia, but, in science as a whole, Russia is not a center of world science (Schott 1992). The other countries selected for this inquiry also contain some scientists who are central in the world scientific community. On the whole, however, their smallness prevents them from becoming centers of world science. Our focus is not so much on their attraction of attention but more on their responses to smallness. Their options range mainly from isolation and self-reliance to forming a periphery by attaching themselves to a center.

The four nations will be compared to ascertain their commonalities as well as their individual uniquenesses.

INSTITUTIONAL FOUNDATIONS FOR THE ATTACHMENT OF PERIPHERIES

The scientific tradition involves a faith in invariance of its object, nature, across place and time, and a faith that knowledge has a truthfulness that is independent of place and time. This faith in universal truthfulness has spread and become adopted around the world during the twentieth century. This faith has become institutionalized so firmly — notably in school curricula — that it is taken for granted and occasional doubt is treated as heresy. People's faith that knowledge has a truthfulness regardless of the country in which it was created is an institutional cornerstone for attaching themselves to the center.

The principle that scientific knowledge is a public good, that it belongs to humankind rather than a bounded segment, such as by patenting, is another condition for attachment of a periphery to a center. World public ownership is not inherent but is constructed and contested. The boundary between public science and private appropriation of knowledge is a contested boundary that is negotiated within each nation as well as among states. World public ownership of scientific knowledge, specifically through diffusion between places, is an institutional precondition for the attachment of one place to another.

Another institutional condition for attachment is the conviction that attachment is beneficial, that the benefits of attachment outweigh the costs and are more important than self-reliance. Occasionally, there have been movements advocating self-reliance in scientific activity. Latin America had a movement for self-reliance in the 1970s. Throughout the 1980s, the communist bloc also sought self-reliance. In most small countries, however, priority has been given to attachment. For decades, this option has been advocated by the United Nations Educational, Scientific and Cultural Organization. It is elaborated as part of a doctrine of "internationalization" and is now also promulgated by the Organisation for Economic Co-operation and Development (OECD) and the World Bank.

Another institutional condition affecting intellectual attachment between two nations is the geopolitical relations between the states. Science is not autonomous from geopolitics, although science has some special rights for movement of scientists, interpersonal correspondence, and distribution of publications across geopolitical cleavages (Ziman, Sieghart, & Humphrey 1986). Such autonomy is far from complete, and conflicts between states impede intellectual exchanges. Conversely, a geopolitical alliance between states promotes intellectual attachment between their scientists. The new North American Free Trade Agreement among Mexico, Canada, and the United States promotes scientific exchanges. Earlier the communist bloc was a geopolitical alliance that promoted intellectual exchanges among its nations, including the Soviet Union, Czechoslovakia, and Cuba. In contrast, the geopolitical conflict between the communist bloc and the capitalist bloc hampered exchanges across the cleavage. The cleavage hampered attachments of communist nations to science in the United States, and, although the post-communist nations in Eastern Europe are no longer in conflict with the United States, the conflict has continued between Cuba and the United States. Notably, the United States trade embargo of Cuba includes restrictions on academic travel between the countries (Department of Treasury 1995).

These institutional conditions have been affecting the responses of nations to their smallness in world science, specifically in their opting for attachment as peripheries to centers.

DEFERENCE IN PERIPHERIES TOWARD ACHIEVEMENT IN CENTERS

The first question is, how small are the four selected nations in world science, specifically in contrast to scientific achievement in the centers of world science in the United States and Western Europe? (Western Europe is also differentiated into scientific provinces and metropoles such as Paris and Oxbridge; but can for our purposes be treated as a social entity, as in the preceding chapter.) The scientific size or achievement of a nation can be indicated, albeit crudely, by the volume of scientific publications authored in the nation. The volume, as estimated percentage of the world literature, is listed in Table 2.1 (science here comprises the natural, technological, and medical sciences). A few decades ago, Table 2.1 indicates, the Soviet Union was among the scientifically largest countries, but scientific activity dwindled up to the dissolution of the Soviet Union into Russia and many other independent states. Science continued to dwindle in Russia, and today's Russia is rather small in science compared to achievement in the United States and Western Europe (OECD 1994b). Czechoslovakia was smaller and also dwindled in science. The country split at the end of 1992, and today's Czech Republic is even smaller

(OECD 1992). Mexico is similarly small (OECD 1994a; Saldaña 1996). Cuba is even smaller by this count of articles, but the count underestimates Cuban science because there is little overlap between the journals publishing Cuban research and the journals covered by the source of the count of articles, the Science Citation Index. Cuban science may alternatively be estimated by its number of scientists (Sáenz & Capote 1989, 1993). The number of scientists and engineers engaged in research and development in Cuba is rather similar to both the number in Mexico and the number in the Czech Republic (UNESCO 1997). For our purposes, it is sufficient to know that these three are similarly small and that Russia is larger but still rather small when contrasted with the centers.

TABLE 2.1
Scientific Publications Authored around the World
(in percent)

Authors' Locations	Scientific Publications	
	1975–79	1995
United States	40.9	33.8
Western Europe	33.0	37.4
Eastern Europe	8.5	5.1
Former Soviet Union	5.2	3.0
Russia		2.3
Former Czechoslovakia	0.9	0.5
Czech Republic		0.3
Latin America	1.5	2.2
Mexico	0.2	0.4
Cuba	0.02	0.04
Asia, Africa, Oceania, Canada	16.1	21.5
Total	100.0	100.0

Notes: Western Europe includes Austria, Belgium, Cyprus, Denmark, Finland, France, Germany (both East and West), Greece, Iceland, Ireland, Italy, Luxembourg, Netherlands, Norway, Portugal, Spain, Sweden, Switzerland, and the United Kingdom. Eastern Europe includes the former Soviet Union, the former Czechoslovakia, Albania, Hungary, Poland, Romania, and the former Yugoslavia. Latin America includes all of the Americas except the United States and Canada. The percentages in a column total 100 percent (except for rounding) in this and Tables 2.2–2.9.

Source: *Science Citation Index, 1975–79, 1995*. Philadelphia, PA: Institute for Scientific Information.

Does this achievement in scientific research around the world attract deference? Scientists' deference and other relations were tapped in a survey of a sample of 201 scientists in the four countries, namely 63 scientists interviewed in 1993 in Russia, 24 scientists interviewed in 1991 in Czechoslovakia (in the part that shortly after became the Czech Republic), 77 scientists interviewed in 1994 in Mexico, and 37 scientists interviewed in 1995 in Cuba. The scientists were sampled rather randomly in each site, covering the natural, technological, and medical sciences, and interviewed with a questionnaire that has been validated in other studies (Schott 1992, 1995). The survey in each country was geographically limited so representativeness is not assured; however, survey responses to questions about influence upon research in a country accord with influences indicated by citations in publications authored in the country, and responses to questions about collaboration accord with collaboration indicated by coauthored publications by scientists in the country. This demonstrates that the survey is fairly representative.

Deference from scientists toward scientific achievement around the world was tapped by asking, "Quite apart from any influence upon your own research, who are the five people in the world who have performed the best scientific research in your area of specialization since 1990?" Russian, Czech, Cuban, and Mexican scientists' deference is listed in Table 2.2.

The main center attracting deference is located in the United States, according to Table 2.2. The scientists in all four countries defer extensively to scientific contributions made in the United States and a little less to science in Western Europe (mainly in the United Kingdom, Germany, and France, but the orientation to specific metropoles within Western Europe need not be detailed for our purposes). This similar deference to the United States as the main center and Western Europe as the secondary center is accompanied by some differences. Russian scientists defer extensively to their local contributors (Czechs, Cubans, and Mexicans hardly defer locally), which can be explained partly by some inwardness prevailing in Russia and partly by its large scientific size compared to the other countries. Czech and Cuban scientists also defer to contributors around Eastern Europe (Russians and Mexicans hardly do), which can be explained by their former geopolitical alliance in the communist bloc. Cuban scientists also defer to science around Latin America (Mexicans and others hardly do), which may be explained by the geopolitical

TABLE 2.2
Scientists' Deference to Contributors around the World
(in percent)

Contributors' Locations	Russia	Czechoslovakia	Cuba	Mexico
United States	26	44	46	50
Western Europe	23	38	23	33
Eastern Europe			11	2
Scientist's country	42	5		
Other Eastern Europe	2	5		
Latin America	1	0		
Scientist's country			8	6
Other Latin America			4	1
Asia, Africa, Oceania, Canada	6	8	8	8
Total	100	100	100	100
N contributors	261	79	121	294

squeeze in the form of the economic embargo and political isolation of the island from its mighty neighbor.

These differences among the four nations, however, are minor when juxtaposed to their similarity of deference to the centers. Evidently, all four nations form peripheries deferring to the centers.

PEOPLE MOVING FROM PERIPHERIES TO CENTERS AND BACK

Scientific achievement of centers attracts not only deference but also people. Achievement attracts students who want to apprentice themselves to the creators of the scientific achievements. Educational travel has been institutionalized and is considered to be a credential (Goodman 1984). The educational origins of scientists, which were tapped by asking where they received their highest degree, are listed in Table 2.3.

In all four surveyed nations, as indicated in Table 2.3, scientists have largely been educated within their own country and few traveled abroad for their highest education. This similar tendency for local education is accompanied by some differences. Russia has been nearly self-reliant in higher education. Significant fractions of Czech and Cuban scientists have been educated abroad, especially around Eastern Europe (mostly in the former Soviet Union). Mexico has been far from self-reliant in higher education and many of its scientists have been trained in the United States and Europe (Fortes & Lomnitz 1994). These educational exchanges have been embedded in geopolitical alliances. Cuba, Czechoslovakia, and the other East European countries formed the communist bloc dominated by the former Soviet Union, whereas Mexico has been part of the capitalistic alliance led by the United States and Western Europe, and these two geopolitical regions have contained most educational exchanges during the last decades.

Mature scientists travel to interact with colleagues at other institutions and at conferences. The nature of their travels was tapped by asking, "Which institutions have you visited in the last 12 months for purposes of your research?" and "To which scientific conferences abroad have you traveled in the years 1990 to 1994?" (with slight variations in wording across the surveyed countries, depending on year of interview). The travels are listed in Table 2.4.

TABLE 2.3
Scientists' Education in Own Country and Abroad

(in percent)

Places of Education	Russia	Czechoslovakia	Cuba	Mexico
United States	0	0	0	16
Western Europe	2	4	5	23
Eastern Europe			14	3
Scientist's country	98	92		
Other Eastern Europe	0	4		
Latin America	0	0		
Scientist's country			81	54
Other Latin America			0	0
Asia, Africa, Oceania, Canada	0	0	0	4
Total	100	100	100	100
N scientists	63	24	37	77

In all four surveyed nations, as indicated in Table 2.4, travels have tended to be rather local, within their own country or to proximate centers, and less often to distant centers. The United States and Western Europe have been the centers attracting most travels. This similar tendency of traveling to a proximate center is accompanied by a difference. Cuban scientists travel to other Latin American countries more than to Western Europe and to the neighboring United States. Notably, they hardly visit institutions in Western Europe and hardly attend conferences in the United States. This can be explained by the geopolitical squeeze around Cuba. For example, the United States will not issue a visa to a Cuban to come for a conference in the United States but occasionally does issue a visa to a Cuban to come to visit an institution in the United States (an institution may invite and host a Cuban but may not provide financial support such as an honorarium). The geopolitical squeeze constrains Cuban scientists to travel to the United States less than others and to fewer destinations.

These movements of students and scientists in the four nations show that they, also in this regard, form peripheries attached to the centers. The peripheries differ in their self-reliance versus reliance on centers and they differ in the centers on which they rely. Despite these differences among the four nations in their participation in the global networks of the movement of people, they are similar insofar as they all form peripheries with people moving to centers and back.

IDEAS MOVING TO PERIPHERIES FROM CENTERS

Achievement attracts deference and travels and provides ideas that influence further research. Influence upon researchers was tapped by asking, "Who are the people whose ideas have influenced your research since about 1990?" A researcher named up to 20 such colleagues, with an average among the researchers of a little more than 8 colleagues. The locations of the colleagues are listed in Table 2.5.

The scientists in every surveyed nation, as indicated in Table 2.5, have been influenced largely by colleagues within their country and in the United States and Western Europe, which evidently are the two major centers of influence. Scientists are more influenced by the proximate center than by the distant center. This similar receipt of influence from the two centers is supplemented by some differences. Russian scientists have been influenced by their local colleagues much more than Czech, Cuban, and

TABLE 2.4
Scientists' Travels to Other Institutions and to Conferences Abroad
(in percent)

Destination	Russia	Czechoslovakia	Cuba	Mexico
Scientists visiting institutions				
United States	3	5	24	24
Western Europe	29	64	3	20
Eastern Europe				
Scientist's country	62	0		
Other Eastern Europe	0	14	1	6
Latin America				
Scientist's country			46	37
Other Latin America	0	2	26	8
Asia, Africa, Oceania, Canada	6	15	0	5
Total	100	100	100	100
N travels	93	56	76	157

Scientists attending conferences abroad

United States	12	9	10	41
Western Europe	42	52	25	29
Eastern Europe			15	4
Scientist's country	3*	NA		
Other Eastern Europe	38	31		
Latin America	1	1		
Scientist's country			NA	NA
Other Latin America			47	12
Asia, Africa, Oceania, Canada	4	7	3	14
Total	100	100	100	100
N travels	76	94	60	34

*Russians' travels here denote a few travels to other former Soviet republics.

TABLE 2.5
Influence upon Scientists from Colleagues around the World
(in percent)

Influencers' Locations	Russia	Czechoslovakia	Cuba	Mexico
United States	17	23	20	34
Western Europe	23	32	18	22
Eastern Europe			11	2
Scientist's country	51	28		
Other Eastern Europe	2	8		
Latin America	0	0		
Scientist's country			37	33
Other Latin America			11	3
Asia, Africa, Oceania, Canada	7	9	3	6
Total	100	100	100	100
N influencers	470	235	272	655

Mexican scientists have been influenced by their local colleagues. This rather high degree of self-reliance in Russia can be explained partly by its larger scientific endeavor and partly by an exceptional inwardness in Russia (apart from size). Russian, Czech, and Cuban scientists have been especially influenced by science around Eastern Europe, and Cuban scientists have also been notably influenced by other Latin American colleagues, far more than Mexican scientists have been influenced from science around Latin America. This difference, like their differences in travels, can be explained by their geopolitical alliances and conflicts. The differences among the four nations, however, are minor in juxtaposition to their similarity as peripheries influenced by the two centers.

Influence specifically on the scientists' selection of problematics for their research was tapped by asking, "To what extent has each person influenced your choice of problems for research since 1990?" The respondent rated the colleague's influence on a scale from 0 for "none" through 1 for "little" and 2 for "some" up to 3 for "great" influence on choice of problems. The amount of influence from a place is then calculated as the sum of the influences from the colleagues in that place, as a percentage of the influence from all the colleagues. This weighted distribution of influence from various places is listed in Table 2.6.

Influence upon scientists' selection of problems, as indicated in Table 2.6, comes largely from colleagues within their own country and in the two centers, very much like the overall influence on research (as was listed in Table 2.5). Influence on problem selection, however, has in most countries been more local than overall influence; that is, a researcher is especially receptive to local influence on the selection of problems for research.

Influence on a scientist comes from the scientific literature and from personal communication with colleagues. Influence from the literature was tapped by asking, "To what extent has each person influenced your research since 1990 through your reading of the person's publications?" The respondent rated the influence on the scale from 0 up to 3, as above. The amount of influence from a place is the sum of the influence from the colleagues in that place, as a percentage of all influence. The influence through the literature is listed in Table 2.7. Table 2.7 indicates that the literature has been a medium for influence from local colleagues less than from foreign colleagues; especially from the United States and Western

TABLE 2.6
Influence upon Scientists' Choice of Problems for Research
(in percent)

Influencers' Locations	Russia	Czechoslovakia	Cuba	Mexico
United States	17	23	18	27
Western Europe	23	26	17	27
Eastern Europe			11	3
Scientist's country	51	33		
Other Eastern Europe	2	8		
Latin America	0	0		
Scientist's country			42	36
Other Latin America			9	2
Asia, Africa, Oceania, Canada	7	10	3	5
Total	100	100	100	100
N influencers	408	213	238	325

Europe, which appear about equally central in the network of influence through the literature.

Influence comes through not only the literature but also direct personal communication from colleagues. Personal communication was tapped by asking, "To what extent has each person influenced your research since 1990 through personal communication?" This interpersonal influence was also rated on the scale from 0 to 3. The influence from various places is listed in Table 2.7. Influence through personal communication has been more local than influence through the literature, but it is also highly transnational. In every surveyed country, personal influence has been stronger from Western Europe than from the United States; so Western Europe has been more central than the United States in the network of personal influence. Cuba, unlike the other nations, has been receiving little personal influence from colleagues in the United States, which is explained by the geopolitical conflict between the two states, specifically the U.S. blockade of Cuba. Cuban scientists have been more influenced by communication from colleagues in Eastern Europe and around Latin America.

Scientists in all four countries have been extensively influenced, through the literature and typically also interpersonally, by colleagues in the United States and Western Europe, and thus have been forming peripheries influenced by the two centers. Their differences have been varieties of peripherality.

THE DESIRE IN PERIPHERIES FOR
RECOGNITION FROM CENTERS

Collective cultivation of the scientific tradition is pursued not only through communication and influence but even more intensely through collaboration on joint research. Collaboration was tapped by asking, "To what extent has each person been a collaborator on your research since 1990?" Collaboration was rated on the extent scale. The collaboration with various places is listed in Table 2.8.

Scientists in all four countries, as Table 2.8 shows, have been collaborating more with local colleagues than with foreigners. Indeed, collaboration has been more local than deference and also more local than influence. This, of course, is because collaboration typically is very intense and performed in a team, often around an experiment, yet

TABLE 2.7
Influence upon Scientists from Literature and Communication
(in percent)

Influencers' Locations	Russia	Czechoslovakia	Cuba	Mexico
Scientists influenced by literature				
United States	20	27	21	35
Western Europe	25	31	19	29
Eastern Europe			12	1
Scientist's country	45	22		
Other Eastern Europe	2	9		
Latin America	0	0		
Scientist's country			34	26
Other Latin America			11	2
Asia, Africa, Oceania, Canada	8	11	3	7
Total	100	100	100	100
N influencers	420	214	238	290

Scientists influenced by communication

United States	9	15	6	19
Western Europe	15	26	14	24
Eastern Europe			11	2
Scientist's country	70	43		
Other Eastern Europe	1	7		
Latin America				
Scientist's country	0	0	57	49
Other Latin America			11	2
Asia, Africa, Oceania, Canada	5	9	1	4
Total	100	100	100	100
N influencers	302	181	170	249

TABLE 2.8
Scientists' Collaboration with Colleagues around the World
(in percent)

Collaborators' Locations	Russia	Czechoslovakia	Cuba	Mexico
United States	4	6	8	19
Western Europe	10	22	11	20
Eastern Europe			9	2
Scientist's country	81	60		
Other Eastern Europe	0	7		
Latin America				
Scientist's country	0	0	60	53
Other Latin America			10	2
Asia, Africa, Oceania, Canada	5	5	2	4
Total	100	100	100	100
N collaborators	356	202	150	442

collaboration is actually surprisingly transnational. Scientists in the four countries have been collaborating more with colleagues in Western Europe than in the United States. Western Europe has been more central than the United States in the networks of collaboration.

Cuban scientists, though, have been collaborating extensively with colleagues in Eastern Europe and around Latin America, and have had especially little collaboration with colleagues in the United States. The sparseness of collaboration between Cuban and U.S. scientists is of course explained by the political conflict between the states, a conflict that also makes the Cuban scientists turn toward collaborators around Latin America and in Europe.

Communality is expressed not only in the collective cultivation of the scientific tradition but also in the formation of communal bonds and in the allocation of rewards. Rewards are allocated for performance of a social role. The institutionalized reward for performance of the role of a scientist, contributing to the shared tradition, is collegial recognition. The desire for recognition was tapped by asking, "To what extent do you care about each person's recognition of your research?" The respondent rated the desire for recognition on the extent scale from 1 to 3, which is then used to calculate the weighted distribution. Scientists' desire for recognition from colleagues in various places is listed in Table 2.9. Scientists have been desiring recognition from both local colleagues and foreign colleagues, especially in the centers. Even Cubans, who in other ways have been less attached to the centers, desire recognition from the centers more than they desire recognition from their colleagues in Eastern Europe and around Latin America, with whom they communicate and collaborate. Thus even Cuban scientists attach themselves mainly to the United States and Western Europe as the centers in the networks of desire for recognition.

Collegial emulation emerges from the desire for recognition. Collegial emulation was tapped by asking, "To what extent do you feel that the person and you are competing with one another to be first or best in research?" Collegial emulation was rated on the scale from 0 to 3 and the weighted distribution was then calculated. Scientists' feeling of collegial emulation from various places is listed in Table 2.9. The emulators (rated 1, 2, or 3) are about half of all the named colleagues, so collegial emulation is substantial but not ubiquitous. The emulation is felt

TABLE 2.9

Scientists' Desiring Recognition and Feeling Emulation from Colleagues
(in percent)

Colleagues' Locations	Russia	Czechoslovakia	Cuba	Mexico
Scientists desiring recognition				
United States	17	20	16	27
Western Europe	22	31	16	23
Eastern Europe			11	2
Scientist's country	53	32		
Other Eastern Europe	2	7		
Latin America	0	0		
Scientist's country			41	40
Other Latin America			13	2
Asia, Africa, Oceania, Canada	6	10	3	6
Total	100	100	100	100
N colleagues	432	192	229	318

Scientists feeling emulation

United States	18	23	4	29
Western Europe	32	37	8	24
Eastern Europe			20	3
Scientist's country	42	18		
Other Eastern Europe	3	9		
Latin America				
Scientist's country	0	0	57	34
Other Latin America			8	2
Asia, Africa, Oceania, Canada	5	13	3	8
Total	100	100	100	100
N colleagues	216	149	49	126

partly from local colleagues and partly from colleagues abroad, especially in the centers.

The scientists' attachments are thus not only intellectual exchanges but also communal bonds expressed in desires for recognition and in feelings of emulation from colleagues. These communal bonds, like intellectual exchanges, are highly transnational and are mainly attachments to the centers in the United States and Western Europe.

CONCLUSION: ATTACHMENT OF PERIPHERIES

World science is institutionalized as a communal cultivation of the scientific tradition. It is a social institution in world society. Participation in world science is pursued within a framework of institutional arrangements comprising, first, an institutionalized faith in a time-and-place-invariant nature and an accompanying faith in knowledge with a truthfulness that, likewise, is considered independent of time and place; second, a political-economic principle that scientific knowledge belongs to humankind as a global commons; and third, a principle of autonomy with permission from political authorities to scientists to communicate, travel, publish, and send and receive literature, not only locally but also across boundaries. The institutional framework is rather global but is also affected by other conditions, such as geopolitical alliances and conflicts, that affect participation. Russia, Czechoslovakia, Cuba, and Mexico were here selected as rather small nations in world science that were expected to differ much in their participation. Each nation was analyzed to address the questions of how it responds to its smallness, whether it is self-reliant or relies on participation in more global communal cultivation, and whether it forms a periphery attached to a center.

Russia is a rather small participant in world science, accounting for roughly two percent of the world's major scientific literature in the mid-1990s. Czechoslovakia, Mexico, and Cuba have been far smaller, each accounting for less than half a percent. The smallness of each nation has led it to rely very little on itself and to hardly cultivate science as an indigenous tradition, and instead to rely more on its participation in a rather global communal cultivation of the scientific tradition. The degree of self-reliance in Russia is higher than in the three other countries (partly due to its larger size), but today's Russia is neither self-reliant nor pursues indigenization. Cuba, like Russia, also has some degree of self-reliance, notably more than the Czech scientists. This is mainly a consequence of the geopolitical squeeze around Cuba. Mexico, conversely, is the least self-reliant nation. Mexican scientists are the most outward and integrated into the world scientific community.

The above differences among the four nations in outwardness are minor in relation to their similar participation in the rather global communal cultivation of the scientific tradition. Their differences are essentially differences in extent of participation and in manner of participation.

Mexican scientists attach themselves to the center in the United States and to the center in Western Europe, thus forming a periphery attached to these centers. Cuban scientists defer to and desire recognition from their colleagues in the United States and are influenced by their publications, but have little direct communication and collaboration with them. Their attachment to the center in Western Europe is also modest, but they interact significantly with colleagues in Eastern Europe and around Latin America. They are thus attached to the centers but their attachment is constrained by the geopolitical squeeze. Czech and Russian scientists are attached to the centers in Western Europe and the United States.

The centers in the networks are in the United States and Western Europe. In the network of deference, the main center is in the United States. In the network of influence through personal communication, the major center is in Western Europe. That is, contributions made in the United States attract more deference than West European contributions, but scientists in Western Europe communicate and influence more than scientists in the United States. The United States' centrality is a passive receipt of deference, whereas the West Europeans' centrality is a more active personal communication. The United States is rather inward and self-reliant, whereas Western Europe is more outward and to some extent reciprocating the attachment from peripheries.

In short, the small nations have not opted for self-reliance but have been responding to their smallness by participating in world science, specifically by attaching themselves as peripheries to centers. They differ in their participation and attachments, but their endeavors are merely varieties of peripherality.

NOTE

A research grant to Professor Schott from the U.S. National Science Foundation (NSF INT-9403770) supported the survey in Mexico, and faculty grants to Schott from the University of Pittsburgh supported the surveys in Russia, Czechoslovakia, and Cuba. Appreciation is extended to the scientists interviewed around the world. As a self-exemplification of the examined phenomena the collaboration was anchored on a U.S. institution by authors from Western Europe, Eastern Europe, Latin America, and the United States.

REFERENCES

Department of Treasury, Office of Foreign Assets Control. 1995. "31 CFR Part 515." *Federal Registrar. Rules and Regulations* 60, 203 (October 20): 54194–97.

Fortes, Jacqueline, & Larissa A. Lomnitz. 1994. *Becoming a Scientist in Mexico: The Challenge of Creating a Scientific Community in an Underdeveloped Country*. University Park: Pennsylvania State University Press.

Gaillard, Jacques, V. V. Krishna, & Roland Waast (eds.). 1997. *Scientific Communities in the Developing World*. New Delhi: Sage.

Goodman, Norman. 1984. "The Institutionalization of Overseas Education." In *Bridges to Knowledge: Foreign Students in Comparative Perspective*, edited by Elinor G. Barber, Philip G. Altbach, and Robert G. Myers, pp. 7–18. Chicago, IL: University of Chicago Press.

Organisation for Economic Co-operation and Development. 1992. *Reviews of National Science and Technology Policy. Czech and Slovak Federal Republic*. Paris: Organisation for Economic Co-operation and Development.

Organisation for Economic Co-operation and Development. 1994a. *Reviews of National Science and Technology Policy. Mexico*. Paris: Organisation for Economic Co-operation and Development.

Organisation for Economic Co-operation and Development. 1994b. *Science, Technology and Innovation Policies. Federation of Russia*. Volumes I and II. Paris: Organisation for Economic Co-operation and Development.

Sáenz, Tirso W., & Emilio G. Capote. 1989. *Ciencia y Tecnologia en Cuba. Antecedentes y Desarollo*. Havana: Editorial de Ciencias Sociales.

Sáenz, Tirso W., & Emilio G. Capote. 1993. "El desarrollo de la ciencia y la tecnologia en Cuba: algunes cuestiones actuales." *Interciencia* 18: 289–94.

Saldaña, Juan José. 1996. *Historia Social de las Ciencias en America Latina*. México, D.F.: Universidad Nacional de México, Coordinación de Humanidades: UNAM, Coordinación de la Investigación Cientifica: M. A. Porrúa.

Schott, Thomas. 1987. "Scientific Productivity and International Integration of Small Countries. Mathematics in Denmark and Israel." *Minerva* 25. 3–20.

Schott, Thomas. 1992. "Soviet Science in the Scientific World System: Was It Autarchic, Self-reliant, Distinctive, Isolated, Peripheral, Central?" *Knowledge: Creation, Diffusion, Utilization* 13: 410–39.

Schott, Thomas. 1995. "Performance, Specialization and International Integration of Science in Brazil: Changes and Comparisons with Other Latin American Countries and Israel." In *Science and Technology in Brazil: A New Policy for a Global World*, edited by Simon Schwartzman et al., pp. 227–84. Rio de Janeiro: Fundação Getulio Vargas Editora.

Schott, Thomas, Jun Kanamitsu, & James F. Luther. 1998. "The U.S. Center of World Science and Emulating Centers: Japan and Western Europe." In *American Culture in Europe: Interdisciplinary Perspectives*, edited by Mike-Frank G. Epitropoulos and Victor Roudometof. Westport, CT: Greenwood Press.

Shils, Edward. 1972. *The Intellectuals and the Powers, and Other Essays*, pp. 354–71. Chicago, IL: University of Chicago Press.

United Nations Educational, Scientific and Cultural Organization. 1997. *Statistical Yearbook 1996*. Paris: United Nations Educational, Scientific and Cultural Organization.

Ziman, John, Paul Sieghart, & John Humphrey. 1986. *The World of Science and the Rule of Law: A Study of the Observance and Violations of the Human Rights of Scientists in the Participating States of the Helsinki Accords*. Oxford: Oxford University Press.

3

The Specter of *Amerikanisierung,*
1840–1990

Peter Bergmann

Over the past one hundred fifty years, a specter of *Amerikanisierung* has haunted the German imagination with the 1840s, the 1890s, and the 1940s demarcating the onset of three distinct episodes. From the Young Hegelians through Nietzsche, Americanization was a projection of a looming future; one either to be embraced or rejected with the trend ever more clearly toward repudiation. When *The Communist Manifesto* (1848) announced a specter was haunting Europe, the specter of Communism, an American presence was implied in that apparition, because as Marx and Engels declare in the same document, "socialism and communism did not originate in Germany, but in England, France and North America" (Feuer 1969: 198). The Young Hegelians were less critical than the Young Germans of the 1830s who expressed a strong ambivalence about America (cf. Weber 1966; see generally Moltmann 1973). Seventeen years later, Marx was still pinning hope on the American example when he announced that what 1776 had been for the European middle class the American Civil War would be for the European working class. Within a decade, however, Americanization had come to mean for Marx and Engels the paralysis of the socialist project. When Marx feared Bakunin might gain control of the future of socialism in the Old World, he orchestrated the transfer of the headquarters of the First International from Europe to America. Better the First International die the death of the forgotten in the New World than his rivals control its future in the Old. Marx had abandoned the hope in an American example. Radical enthusiasm for America had run its course. German intellectuals had blown hot and cold; revolutionary romantics were *Europamüde*, "tired of Europe," eager to learn about America; post-revolutionary realists were *Amerikamüde*, bored with Philistine America. Nietzsche's slogan of the 1880s, "No American future!" became the watchword for the international avant-garde of the fin-de-siècle. From the Young Hegelians of the 1840s to the Nietzscheans of the 1890s, the specter of *Amerikanisierung* was an intellectual concern. There were political ramifications, to be sure, before, during, and after the revolution of 1848, but as *Amerikanisierung* became associated with a weakening liberal tradition in Germany, the America discourse of the Bismarckian era (1862–90) became a distancing one.

The specter of *Amerikanisierung* became a more immediate economic and geopolitical "danger" between the Spanish-American War and the fall of Stalingrad. The perception of America as a direct threat to German prospects was fostered within and without Germany. At century's end, the British journalist W. T. Stead's bestseller, *The Americanization of the World or The Trend of the Twentieth Century*, popularized the new insight: "The center of resistance to American principles in Europe lies at Berlin, and the leader against and great protagonist of Americanisation is the Kaiser of Germany" (Stead 1972: 65). Talk of the American danger was common between the Spanish-American War and the Russo-Japanese War (for example, Germanus 1905). One German-American warned that the time was not far off "when the American peril to Europe will be converted into a European peril to America" (Wendtland 1902: 564; see also Schröder 1993; Pommerin 1986; Parsons 1971: 436–52). During World War I the German Right identified Americanism with defeatism, with the conviction that the special German historical path (the *Sonderweg*) was doomed and, consequently, Germany needed to reverse course: the Reich should no longer stave off the "American danger" but rather embrace the American example. World War I ended with a hoped-for Americanization of German defeat. For this reason the Nazis viewed Americanism as a long-range threat that could become an even greater menace than Bolshevism. By the fall of 1943 Hitler declared defeat on the eastern front might be absorbed, but on the western front it could only be fatal. Consequently, a critical element of ultimate victory had to be exclusion of the United States from European politics.

In the last half century, Germans never ceased to associate *Amerikanisierung* with the key formula of World War II: unconditional surrender. The first requirement of unconditional surrender was abandoning any "European Monroe Doctrine." In place of the polarity of

America and Europe came a new duality fashioned of the Cold War and the division of Germany. Americanization came to mean the abandonment of any "third way" between communism and consumerism. By the *Amerikanisierung* debate of the 1980s, the issue was no longer whether Americanization should happen, but how to deal with the Americanization that had happened. The critique of "Americanization" became a form of self-criticism; it involved a questioning of the underlying consensus of what should and should not be imported and adapted for German use.

AMERICA FROM EXEMPLAR TO RIVAL: 1840–1890

Whether the Young Hegelians were the first to pose 1776 as a way station to a world Americanization may still need to be determined, but it is clear that they inaugurated a distinctive German discourse on America. By transferring the Hegelian notion of universal process onto the concept of Americanization, they fused notions of Americanization and globalization, and thereby brought a sense of historical dynamism to their reading of Alexis de Tocqueville's *Democracy in America* (1835–40). They began by correcting "Hegel's error," that is, his disdainful and arbitrary dismissal of the American continent, which they deemed "a blot on his system." Hegel had held the paradoxical view of America as physically and morally impotent and yet representative of the future. The history of "historyless" Americans, however, did not interest Hegel; nor did he have the time, he explained, to concern himself with the "New World and the dreams that are attendant upon it" (Gerbi 1973: 437; also Hennigsen 1973: 224–51; on the American Hegel reception see Pochmann 1948).

De Tocqueville stimulated Hegel's disciples into concerning themseves with those dreams. Emigration to America, the site of utopian experiments, became a Young Hegelian enthusiasm on the eve of the revolution. While de Tocqueville asked why the American and French revolutions had different outcomes (1776 led to a constitutional order while 1789 culminated with Bonaparte), the Young Hegelians focused on the American Revolution as the antecedent to their war of liberation against Napoleon. Just as the Americans freed themselves from the British, so Germans liberated themselves from French hegemony. By 1848 German socialism looked to America. In the Frankfurt Parliament, American republicanism was the inspiration of the Left, and American constitutionalism the model of the moderates. In the wake of the post-1848 revolutionary defeat transplanted Young Hegelians rested their final hopes in a world republic centered in America. Just as America "Americanized" immigrants, so it would reshape the world. All were at least potentially "American."

The number of Forty-Eighter émigrés might have been small (a few thousand), but the 142,000 native-born Germans in New York City and Brooklyn made it the fifth largest urban German concentration after Hamburg, Berlin, Cologne, and Dresden. *Kleindeutschland* lay at the tip of Manhattan, east of the Bowery (Rosenwaike 1972: 51; Spann 1981; Ernst 1949). Its inhabitants were prone to see the New World as an extension of the Old, and anticipated the new politics of the New World unraveling the old states across the Atlantic. For a few years the refugee intellectuals kept alive the vision of a United States of Europe, or at least, United States of Germany. Americanization remained the harbinger of the new, a shortcut to advances nascent within indigenous European tradition (see Levine 1992; Bruncken 1904; Dobert 1958; Easum 1929; Obermann 1947; Zucker 1950; Wittke 1952, 1950, 1945).

The 1852 American presidential campaign provided the opportunity to advance the slogan of the Americanization of the world and rally support for a republican rising in Germany. Delegates at two congresses of German political clubs, one in Philadelphia in January and the other in Wheeling, West Virginia in September, proclaimed the impending Americanization of the world. The American Revolutionary League for Europe resolved to educate the American people to an understanding of their historic mission: a world republic under American leadership. Theodore Poesche and Charles Goepp's *The New Rome; or, the United States of the World* (1853) proclaimed a world republic under American leadership. America was "the new Rome" fusing all nations of all continents into one people. They attributed the failure of the revolution to socialism, or anticapitalism. The United States was destined to undo Czarism and liberate Germany. Americanism, philo-Semitism, and capitalism were presented as a package deal. Embracing Judaism was the route to capitalism for these postrevolutionary antisocialists. "All the world are now Jews; everybody makes money . . . liberty and commerce, which are the characteristics of Judaism and of Americanism, are also those of annexation" (Poesche & Goepp 1853: 105).

The reaction in Germany was harsh. The historian Georg Gervinus was placed in the Heidelberg dock for treason for daring to suggest in his *Introduction to the History of the Nineteenth Century* (1967) that the "people" wanted the American way. The prosecutor's brief focused on a sentence where Gervinus declared not England but America, not constitutionalism but republicanism, was the force of the future (see Boehlich 1967: 51–52, 81–82, 118, 122–23, 129, 135, 138, 153, 225; Gervinus 1967: 169). Gervinus held 1776 up to 1789, and pointed to the mass German immigration of his time (more than one-and-a-half percent of the population between 1852 and 1854) as proof that the "people" favored the republican goals advanced by America (Walker 1964: 157). The book was burnt, the author acquitted, his point of view all but banished from the German academe. In the United States the Know-Nothing backlash of 1853–56 put a different twist on the Forty-Eighter concern with Americanization. The collapse of the "Young America" wing of the Democratic Party precluded American internationalism in the struggle between despotism and liberty, reaction and republicanism. Americanization came to mean only Americanizing the Forty-Eighter. Karl Heinzen warned his fellow emigrants that the Know-Nothings want "us to be 'Be-Nothings.'" His couplet, "Sich amerikanisieren/ Heisst ganz sich verlieren" ("To Americanize oneself is to lose oneself"), was widely quoted (Heinzen 1890: 155–56, 527; see Bergquist 1980: 111–21). Engels complained that those "Germans who are worth anything become easily Americanized and give up any thought of returning" and those "who think of returning home are for the most part only demoralized individualists" (Feuer 1969: 214).

Nietzsche's youthful lecture "The Religious Situation of the Germans in North America," (1865) provides an echo of the Young Hegelian enthusiasm for Americanization. At the end of his three Emersonian years, Nietzsche was shedding his Pietism, but before it faded completely, he addressed the Gustav-Adolf Society, a Pietist missionary society serving the Protestant diaspora, with an extensive commentary on Philip Schaff's *America. A Sketch of Its Political, Social, and Religious Character* (1854) (Nietzsche 1940: 84–97, 401; see Bergmann 1995: 73–84). The historian Perry Miller called Schaff's work "a document of primary importance" in "the history of that mysterious process called 'Americanization'" (Miller in Schaff 1961: xvii). In the 1850s Schaff was a theologian with a message: something was taking place in America that European conservatives failed to understand at their own peril. Schaff postulated a conservative Americanization, the counterpoint of the conservative Grays in German America (that is, the pre-1948 emigrants) to the Greens (Greenhorns, that is, the Forty-Eighters). Nietzsche faithfully echoed Schaff's attacks on the Forty-Eighters as a "godless German-American pest" and "the fearful consequences of German rationalism and infidelity" (Schaff 1961: 224). In *kleindeutschland* there flourished, Nietzsche wrote, "an anarchy of scroundrels, where to one's desire one drinks lager beer, smokes Havana cigars, plays cards and scoffs at princes and priests, mocking all that is holy and openly blasphemous" (Nietzsche 1940: 90–91). The lecture was the swan song of Nietzsche's theological career and his interest in America. One week later he shocked his family with the news he was dropping his theologial studies. He dropped theology in the spring, and by the fall

he had exchanged Emerson for Schopenhauer. Equally important for Nietzsche and his generation of university students was the triumph of Bismarckian policy that precluded the need to further interest oneself in the
American model.

At least for a decade, Emerson's fluent optimism, his sense of a Europe
burdened with tradition, and of an America offering a potential pattern for
the future vanished from Nietzsche's mental horizon. Schopenhauer
shared the conservative rejection of the New World for its hypocritical
legalism and slavery and projected his phobias onto the United States,
castigating its veneration of women. It was Schopenhauer's contempt for
the philistine quality of American cultural life, however, that had broad
appeal in Europe. Schopenhauer's contempt became popular with the
depoliticized avant-garde of mid-century for whom "Americanization"
became synonymous with the vulgarization of life. The avant-garde fed
off a sense of disgust for an impending era of mediocrity. American culture was rejected not simply as insipid or insincere, but as an affront and
as a product of a misbegotten society. Baudelaire transformed Benjamin
Franklin from an Enlightenment icon into the symbol of shopkeeper
morality and Philistine incomprehension, while simultaneously he celebrated Edgar Allan Poe as the martyr of Americanization, the soul mate
of the alienated avant-garde artist. There yawned a gulf between the
morally lazy and the martyrs of alienation, between a self-conscious, self-
important modernism and American popular culture. The avant-garde
held that art had to be difficult and removed, while American popular culture seemed all-too-easy, accessible, and self-infatuated. The distinction
between the avant-garde and popular art, between high and low culture,
sustained the old distinction between aristocratic and peasant culture.
Fear among intellectuals of the consequences of mass democracy fed a
conservative assumption that genuine culture can be sustained only by a
leisure class freed from the burdens of everyday life and labor. A key
move in the history of European modernism was putting a minus sign
before Americanization.

Nietzsche's colleague, Jacob Burckhardt, a Schopenhauer devotee,
evoked the Renaissance as the fountainhead of European individualism.
Burckhardt's and Nietzsche's celebration of the Renaissance despot challenged the vision of American individualism made by de Tocqueville a
generation earlier. The source of European individualism, Burckhardt
argued, lay in the despotism of the Renaissance city-state. The world of
the Renaissance despot became the antithesis of the optimistic, settled
political order de Tocqueville found in America. Burckhardt was attracted to the political world of the Renaissance precisely because it had no

future. Burckhardt's Renaissance reflected Schopenhauer's view of the "world" in all its sinister pointlessness. What redeemed the Italian Renaissance was its art. Artists became the heroes of the new individualism because they created amidst the mindless political violence around them. Emerson's "self-reliant" man was displaced by a rival claiming to be older, bolder, and more creative. American individualism could be dismissed as an immature variety that lacked aesthetic merit. The pathos of a learned individualism making a heroic last stand, defending Renaissance high culture against the tide of neobarbarism, proved irrestistible to the young Nietzsche.

When the crash of 1873 turned the climate increasingly hostile to liberalism, America was degraded into a code word for 1848, "the mad year." German intellectuals raised the specter of Americanization to defend German secondary education. "Hellenism is keeping Americanism from our spiritual borders" became a battle cry of the late 1970s (du Bois-Reymond 1974: 145).[1] Having once believed that they were going to follow the American lead, German liberals had to justify to themselves why they had abandoned that American future. Yet when Nietzsche's health failed, Schopenhauerian pessimism seemed toxic, and Emerson gained another hearing. During the aphoristic period of 1876–82, Nietzsche tired of the cultural war against Americanization. American humorists Mark Twain and Bret Harte were the solace of his convalescence, and his own flight from the German academe became a celebration of experimentation. Americanization was now the infection of the new. The poem, "The New Columbus," charted his voyage to an intellectual New World from which Nietzsche would proclaim "the experimental philosophy" to be "the philosophy of the future (Nietzsche, *Dawn*, Aphorism #327)."

In his last six years of sanity, Nietzsche indulged the placid, anxious, 1880s passion for global political speculations. The future was better seen by looking at America than Germany, one aphorism suggested, because German society remained in a permanent state of emergency (Nietzsche 1984; Nietzsche, *The Wanderer and his Shadow*, Aphorism #287). Nietzsche believed "Germany's temporary political ascendancy" was not to be sustained. It rested too exclusively on the talents and will power of one moody, domineering, and aging individual. The German Empire owed its preeminence to its ascendancy over "tired, old peoples." French decline was symptomatic of European decadence. The former Soviet Union and the Anglo-Saxon powers were the only true protagonists on the world stage. He seemed to favor the former Soviet Union in the coming struggle. His fear was that the Russians would become infected with the mediocrity of British parliamentarianism (p. 237). He consoled himself with the thought that Americans, so involved in haste, would use themselves up before America could become a world power (p. 213). In his notebook he raised the cry: "No American future!" (p. 237).

THE ERA OF CONFRONTATION: 1890–1940

America was largely concealed in German academic discourse between the fall of Bismarck and the suicide of Hitler through the dominance of the Rankean and Marxist traditions. The conservative Rankeans imposed a rigid European great power schema that effectively closed down German historical study of America from the middle of the nineteenth to the middle of the twentieth century. Marxist historians did not question this "Eurocentric" treatment of German history; indeed, they abetted it by viewing America as the anomaly, the country without a working class party (Sombart 1976; Bell 1991: 46–70; Moore 1970; Earle 1992: 400–445; Tyrrell 1986). In the 1890s the mass German migration to America came to an end, the number of returnees fell and the "Uncle from America" became more legendary than real. "Our America is in Germany" was the Social Democratic leader Wilhelm Liebknecht's message to German workers. He argued that the future these workers were seeking could be built in Germany.

With the development of German and American imperialism, however, their rivalry grew. It brought clashes over Samoa and the Philippines; fierce competition for the lucrative Latin American market; and sharp, recurring trade wars. East Elbian agrarians lobbied against the importation of and dependence on American farm products by suggesting German military security was at stake. While Germans protected agrarians, Americans protected industry so that the protectionism of the one targeted the other. Kaiser Wilhelm II declared in 1896 that Europe's only hope lay in "an European Monroe Doctrine," that is, a European customs union that could serve as an economic counterweight to the new American colossus (Vagts 1935: 345–425; Herwig 1976). Julius Wolf, the founder of the Mitteleuropa Economic Society, explained "the two catchwords, *'amerikanische Gefahr'* [American danger] and *'britischer Handelsneid'* [British trade envy] point to the same direction: America 'endangered,' Britain 'envied,' the German advances!" (Fiebig-von Hase 1993: 64). Yet *Amerikanisierung* remained long on specter and short on danger. Germans so relied on American raw materials that any aggressive trade policy became self-defeating, especially because America had also become one of Germany's best customers. German banking and industrial circles recognized a strong American economy as essential to the well-being of world trade. Max Ludwig Goldberger, former head of the Society of Berlin Merchants and Industrialists, was quoted upon leaving New York: "Europe needs to remain awake. The United States is the land of unlimited possibilities." The felicitous phrase, "the land of unlimited possibilities," became the title of his best-seller, and soon a cliché susceptible to irony (Goldberger 1903; Köhler 1908). The Russian revolution of 1905 diverted talk of the American danger, and German interest turned eastward, but like a boomerang carelessly thrown away the American danger reappeared a decade later.

In the "America debate" of 1915–16, America was cast as an arbiter of Germany's fate: could, should America be provoked by undertaking a campaign for unrestricted submarine warfare? No other belligerent debated such a vital strategic issue in public. By 1916 Germany was the one power for whom stalemate could be defined as a kind of victory, but stalemate required that each side pay its own war costs, necessitating the internal concessions the German oligarchy was determined to forestall. The America debate became the one arena where the issue of stalemate could be addressed, and the Right came to identify unrestricted submarine warfare (and possible war with America) as a necessary accompaniment to total war. When the public turned to the educated elite for guidance, it revolved around a subject — America — about which they had been derelict and indifferent for a generation. Max Weber declared it a scandal how readily the German academe discounted American power, while simultaneously bemoaning the Americanization of the German-American community.

Late–nineteenth-century nationalism reinforced a cultural hierarchy (high brow/low brow) by ranking nations as cultures and fostered a view of culture as a war against chaos that also irresistibly became a conflict against other cultures. This reassertion of cultural hierarchies prompted fears that American culture was the inferior among the major civilized nations of the west. Charles Eliot Norton lamented that among the civilized nations, America was the one with the least developed culture. Of all the industrializing societies, Americans had been the most diffident about their culture, while the Germans had made the most of their high culture, their *Kultur*. The war allowed American intellectuals to overturn the old reciprocal relation between the American sense of cultural backwardness and the German sense of cultural superiority by identifying German culture with militarism and barbarism. During the patriotic frenzy between 1916 and 1919 Americanization boards sprung up in many states;

the "hyphenated" German-American *Kultur* became the first target of the purge (Schmidt 1985).

After America's entrance into the war, it was not surprising that "Americanization" was viewed with a certain alarm even by the proponents of a "peace of understanding," such as Prince Max von Baden. In a widely distributed speech in December 1917, Prince Max declared "President Wilson does not want our territory but does want to Americanize our souls." When the Reich concluded a victorious peace with the former Soviet Union and Romania in early 1918, Prince Max wrote a memorandum entitled "Ethical Imperialism" in which he argued the time had come to make peace. The former Soviet Union, the principal foe, was beaten; encirclement was over. Germany could declare its defensive war won. The future looked bright. "England's prestige is being extinguished," declared Prince Max. "The role of moral leader of the world is open. America or we can become England's heir" (Petzold 1964: 204–29; see Gruber 1975; Luebke 1974; Higham 1977; Hartmann 1949). Six months later as Chancellor, Prince Max brought the war to a close by appealing to President Wilson. In defeat, the Germans vainly hoped to use Wilsonianism to save what could be saved.

The Americanization of German defeat faltered on the tension between the appeal of consumerism inherent in the American model and the hold of resentment on the martyred nation. To accept an Americanization of defeat would have required the German Right's acceptance of its culpability for the defeat. Covering for their fatal mistake of underestimating the American factor, the German Right fostered the myth of a deceitful America and Wilson, the trickster, who had unfairly lured Germany into defeat. The battle against an "American peace" defined Hitler's initial political horizon and marked his own Germanization. Hitler was formed and destroyed at those moments when American power came to bear upon European events. The specter of Americanization haunted him from the outset. The great America debate of 1915–16 was the initiation rite of Austrian citizen Hitler as the new *Reichsdeutsche*. The day the Zimmermann telegram was published in America, Hitler was hurrying back to his regiment, cutting short his convalescence in a reserve unit in Munich. No one would more convincingly articulate the stab-in-the-back legend than Hitler, because no one was more eager to deny America's decisive role in World War I. Few on the Flanders Front had believed more fervently in submarine warfare than Hitler. He was determined to believe that the Right had not brought defeat on the Reich by defying the American factor, because "the land of money was bound to enter the war" (Compton 1967: 24).

In the opening stage of his career Hitler drew attention less for his racism than for the anger of the veteran unwilling to accept the Americanization of defeat. Americanism and defeatism became associated in his mind. As an army street orator in counterrevolutionary Munich, he ranted against the defeat. "How could a people that waged such heroic struggles lose its national spirit all at once? Through moral contamination by the Jews. Their systematic undermining of the front and the rear made it possible for the nation to cast aside its tried and proven leaders and throw itself into the arms of a trickster like Wilson" (quoted in Binion 1984: 39; Fraenkel 1960: 66–120). Hitler denounced one man, President Wilson, as he was denouncing one people, the Jews, and one party, the Communists. In September 1919 when he first spoke on the Munich streets, his target was Wilson not Lenin. Wilson's hushed-up stroke a few weeks later, his mysterious disappearance from the public eye, and his subsequent eclipse, were experienced by Hitler, at the very least, as a personal triumph.

Hitler gained respectability on the Right from the vocal way he lamented the shame of defeat. Hitler was convinced the cause of defeat was the lack of ruthlessness on the part of the imperial government; had defeatism been met with terror, had the Prussian military tradition been less correct, and had military planning been bolder Germany would have won. His purpose was not so much to avenge the defeat of 1918 but to retrieve the lost victory of 1917 when Germany controlled Eastern Europe. Hitler's fortunes waned when the American Dawes Plan of 1924 spread prosperity to Germany. With Wilsonianism discredited, Americanization became the metaphor for technocracy, business expansion, and incipient consumerism. The Golden Twenties turned its attention away from the bitter rhetoric of the angry war veteran (Beck 1968; Wette 1985: 71–99; Stoakes 1986). The politician Hitler, marginalized by this Americanization, still upheld the martyrology of defeat and attempted to defuse the promise of Americanization. At the nadir of his career, the threat of America loomed in his imagination. In *Mein Kampf* and his unpublished *Secret Book* Hitler (1961) raised a specter of American "world hegemony": "With the American Union, a new power of such dimensions has come into being as threatens to upset the whole former power and orders of rank of the states" (p. 83). Hitler represented the losers from Americanization — the military desperadoes, the anti-Semites, and the hardcore nationalists. It was only a Nazified Germany that could rally Europe against America, he claimed: "It is again the task of the National Socialist movement to strengthen and prepare our fatherland itself for this task" (p. 106).

When the Great Depression hit, the American model was discredited, and Nazism moved in from the fringe (Trommler 1985). Hitler damned

America for turning Germany into a huge Hooverville, pronounced export capitalism a failure, and proclaimed his policy of *Lebensraum* imperialism the answer. In order to compete Germany needed more territory. Indeed, behind all of Hitler's ideas seemed to be a sense of German weakness, the need to overcome Germany's apparent inability to play the role of a superpower. After the 1929 crash Hitler presented *Lebensraum* as a permanent solution, a guarantee against future economic crises, and a disengagement from a world capitalist system dominated by America. Hitler was convinced that with sufficient *Lebensraum,* one need not worry about economic cycles. Hitler was aiming at a "final solution" for both the economic problem and the Jews. In 1933 Hitler had defeated Americanization for good, or so he thought. America was the land of a failed capitalism, and his identification of America with the Jews became an *idée fixe*. However, America remained a rival, a pedagogic imperialism spreading its "invisible empire" tenaciously and surreptitiously in South America, the Middle East, and China.[2] Hitler told Molotov in 1940 that the American threat was a generation away, materializing "not in 1945 but in 1970 or 1980 at the earliest" (Compton 1967: 247; Friedländer 1967; Rich 1973: 237–46). Anti-Americanism became the ideological cement of the Nazi-Soviet Pact.

The invasion of the Soviet Union allowed reversion to the argument that the United States and the Soviet Union were similar sham ideologies with one proclaiming world democracy, the other world revolution (Ross 1930). The SS propaganda mill responded to Henry Luce's slogan of the "American century" with the formula: "Bolshevism is the Americanism of the 20th century" (SS-Hauptamt 1944: 43). Between Pearl Harbor and Stalingrad a Nazi "Europa-ideology" was out to foil any *Pax Americana* (Halfeld 1941; Wilhelm 1943a, 1943b; Blanke 1944). Hitler ordered propaganda target America's perverse culture: the Hollywood cult of stars, female boxing, mud wrestling, and the sensationalism of American popular culture. This "complete lack of culture," Hitler believed, disqualified Roosevelt from any right to judge Europe. During the last six months of the war, a chasm opened between the population's desire to surrender to the Americans and the Nazi war on defeatism, an insistence on fighting to the bitter end. The unspoken final war aim of most Germans became a preference for defeat to the west: to keep the Russians out and let the Western Powers in, but Hitler's last offensive was against the Americans rather than the Soviets. To turn east to engage the Red Army would have allowed the Anglo-Americans further into Germany, setting off a prairie fire of defeatism. In February 1945, when the Allies launched their final push into Germany, Hitler fulminated against Americanization as

de-Germanization. "Transplant a German to Kiev, and he remains a perfect German. But transplant him to Miami, and you make a degenerate of
him — in other words, an American" (Weinberg 1964: 1020). Hitler
ended his career as he had begun it — futilely combating the Americanization of defeat.

THE REALITY OF AMERICANIZATION: 1940–1990

Theodor Eschenburg, an architect of the West German constitution,
recalled first hearing the formula of "unconditional surrender" on the
radio in the anxious fall of 1944 when Germany's enemies were descend-
ing upon her (Eschenburg 1986: 72). He turned to his library only to dis-
cover that the notion was unknown in international law with usage
seemingly confined to the Spanish civil war, the Russian civil war, and the
American Civil War. The American decision to treat Nazism as it once
treated the Confederacy aroused resentment among Germans who insisted the German situation bore no resemblance to the American Civil War.
Yet every modern war has taken on the characteristics of a civil war, and
from the standpoint of the Americanized exiles, World War II was very
much a spiritual civil war. German émigrés returned to Germany as
"experts," to de-Nazify with an American model. Reorientation, reeducation, and democratization were demanded of the Germans. Almost every
book, pamphlet, magazine, play, film, newspaper, and tract printed
between 1933 and 1945 was banned.

The émigrés of the New School projected the concept of "social conformity" as the essential feature that had immunized American and British
societies during the depression from fascism and totalitarian solutions
(Krohn 1987: 128; Radkau 1971; Lowenstein 1989). The sense of Americanism as a new and superior "modernism" became vital to the selling of
Americanization. Those who had been Americanized tended to reject the
idea that the most modern was latent and borne by an isolated avant garde.
The old quarrel between superficiality and depth was abandoned, and Americanization became what could be seen. The American Left, victimized by
Americanization a quarter century before, embraced Americanization as a
necessary reeducation for the defeated Germans. Americanization had driven out *Kultur* in the first world war; it was now called upon to redeem
Kultur in the second. In Vichy and post-Vichy France, Hegel, Heidegger,
and Husserl became fashionable, but in America exiles tended to blame
the war on the failure of an earlier Americanization. "If the Americans had
better known and understood the Germans in 1918, Hitler and the Second

World War could have been avoided," Emil Ludwig wrote (Köpfe 1987: 81–82; Rupieper 1993).

The American program in 1945 was naive and well-informed, which made it irresistible. American occupation manuals assumed that Germany was a backward country, and to GIs moving through the bombed-out cities, Germany had the look of a backward society. The Red Army soldier, whatever his actions, had the same bombed-out look as the conquered. Russian atrocities and postwar expulsions followed the familiar script, but American affluence seemed new and marvelous to behold. Americans, so recently mired in an isolationism and a depression psychosis, now gloried as the missionaries of a new prosperity. Americanization became defined in Enlightenment verities and involved prosperity, social conformity, fear of subversion, and abandonment of an unhappy past. Nazism was explained as the result of the failed revolution of 1848, and American soldiers were informed that Nazism was a regime run by war criminals with the backing of authoritarian landowners, Prussian militarists, and reactionary coal and steel barons. A "hard" peace called for reeducation, a Europeanization of the German problem, and the maintenance of the east-west alliance. The theory of Germany as the delayed nation fostered an agenda of "catching up."

In the three grim years of military government, opposition to American cultural policy provided the only effective vehicle of protest but this also remained muted. In defeat, high culture was postulated as the inner, indestructible essence of Germany, something that had survived the terrorism of the Nazis. The real Führer was not Hitler but Goethe (Meinecke 1950). Mandarins taught self-purification through the revival of the classics of German literature, and responded to the rebuke of the exiles by declaring the emigrants had lost all "feeling" for the fatherland. The novelist Frank Thiess, claiming to speak for the "inner emigration," accused Thomas Mann of "treason" and of "insulting" the German people (Sontheimer 1961: 145–53). Conservatives viewed Mann as a turncoat after he abandoned the myth of the martyred nation in the 1920s, and he was now denounced as a perpetrator of Americanization. What was particularly resented was that Mann had acquired American citizenship. In the Mandarin view émigrés were a collection of castoffs from real cultures, seeking only comfortable self-preservation in America's nonculture, with its contentment with superficial cosmopolitanism in thought and deed. German thought, in contrast, aimed at reconstituting the rootedness of one's own culture after it had been shattered by philosophical and political cosmopolitanism. A literary tradition that focused on the suffering of the nation could only be hostile toward the United States: America had not suffered enough; the lack of pain and tragedy had impoverished its culture.

The immediate postwar images of underdevelopment made the "miraculous" growth rates of Japan and West Germany in the following quarter century seem doubly impressive. Americanism had come to measure success by the market, and the market rose. The anti-intellectualism of the "economic miracle" had the effect of undercutting Mandarin resistance to Americanization. In East Germany the controlled economic system remained intact and was gradually transformed into a Soviet-type command economy by waves of expropriations. There the cult of the intelligentsia revived the notion of Marxism as the answer to Americanism. The reigning view of the Adenauer era was a fatalistic acceptance of *Amerikanisierung* as punishment for past sins. A frontal attack was, however, avoided in favor of piecemeal critiques. The rightist critic Friedrich Sieburg lamented the flood of American reading matter in the 1950s; a few world-class works might have been washed up in the deluge, he noted, but the great mass of imports had been light confectionery. This was, he fatalistically concluded, fitting punishment for a culture that had long failed to generate passable popular entertainment (Galinsky 1972: 58). Casual American modernization became a means of repressing the memory of Nazism. The elasticity of American mannerisms brought a change of cultural relations in favor of the younger generation vis-à-vis the older, and women vis-à-vis men. By the late 1950s, Americanization was driven by a youth culture eager for a happy, casual modernism. *Bravo* magazine, a propagator of Americanization with a readership that was two-thirds female, mocked Prussian drill and the rule of a gerontocracy, fostering Americanization as the cult of the civilian, as the mark of the young, in contrast to the old military style. Young women were especially sick of talk of the war and its aftermath. "The old got on our nerves with their drivel about the war and the war experience, always glorifying it, even in social democratic cliques. The Americans were the alternative . . . there everything was different: huge country, rich people, big cars, a dominant youth" (Maase 1992: 131).

Americanization became a unifying force among the nations of western Europe, irrespective of whether it had liberated or defeated them. To become "European" was to go through the school of Americanization. Americanization counteracted Europe's perennial fragmentation by creating a common youth culture that in turn could serve as the basis of a new sense of common European identity. The 1960 presidential election was avidly followed as a spectacle of grandeur. Kennedy had the qualities of a hero compared to a Europe of Adenauer and De Gaulle where grey and

unimaginative politicians reigned. In academic discourse, Americanization was eschewed in favor of universals such as democracy, modernization, and the like. Synthetic or overarching cultural critiques of
Amerikanisierung were avoided in favor of concrete denunciations of blue
jeans, teen-age idols, rock and roll, and other cultural imports. In his 1963
article, "The Problem of the so-called Americanization of Germany,"
political scientist Arnold Bergsträsser (1963: 13–23) legitimated Americanization for reasons of state: the Federal Republic required American
support. He countered the East German charge that West Germany had
become "Americanized" by declaring Americanization unavoidable,
although not necessarily desirable.

Americans contemplated West German Americanization with an air of
self-congratulation. *The Atlantic Monthly* sent nine American journalists
in 1967 on a tour of Berlin and major West German cities. "In the Federal Republic, there can scarcely be an aspect of life unaffected by the influence of the United States," Richard Rovere wrote. "Those few Germans
who are critical of their own society begin with the complaint that it
allowed itself to become Americanized. And it has indeed been Americanized, with a vengeance" (Galinsky 1972: 65). Irving Kristol found that
"over the past two decades the style of German life has been 'Americanized' to an almost incredible degree. People read American books, go to
American plays, listened to American music, dress in American fashions,
speak and understand the American language, follow and comprehend
American affairs, are eager to visit the United States, all to an extent without parallel anywhere else in Europe — including, I should say, Britain"
(p. 65).

Yet far more quickly than anybody had supposed Europe was able to
buy all the cars and washing machines it had always wanted. The United
States began to lose its magic aura and, having once towered above all
others, America was gradually cut down to size. Liberals, longtime bear-
ers of the positive *Amerikabild* (picture of America), were driven to active
opposition to the Vietnam War. Radical democrats and socialists attacked
American foreign policy and, increasingly, American culture as well. By
1973 it became a journalistic commonplace to declare the American Century over. "Europe has been Americanized in the last twenty years and the
poor United States Europeanized" (Rossem 1981: 28).

The West German critique was more involuted than it seemed, for it
was inspired by the Frankfurt school, which emerged from its American
exile as "left" defenders of high culture. Theodor Adorno identified
cultural massification with a world-historical event known as "Americanization" (Aronowitz 1993: 88). In the world of "late capitalism,"

Americanism became synonymous with repetition, standardization, and mass production. Far from being democratic, mass culture was manipulative, and Hollywood demonstrated how enlightenment had turned to deception. Genuine art was raised into the last source of resistance. Americanism seemed a mindless juggernaut with designs on everything in sight. The young, in particular, felt compelled to fight the idea that Americanism was historically inevitable, while the "Americanized" generation of the Adenauer years (1949–63) agonized over its own Americanization. The 1960s radical Rudi Dutschke complained in his speech "The difficulty of being a German" that in both parts of Germany, "Americanization and Russification" had gone unchecked; just as the German Democratic Republic did not have "real socialism," the Federal Republic did not have "real democracy" (Herf 1991). What was lacking was "the reunification of the real historical consciousness of the Germans" (Herf 1991). The *Pax Americana* was also increasingly perceived as the *pax atomica*. For Hans Magnus Enzenberger, "the thought that Germany could disappear off the face of the earth due to American actions, without even being at war, as under Hitler, is relatively new — and rather unsettling" (Osterle 1987: 138). In the era of détente, anti-Americanism became a common meeting ground for the two Germanies. Americans had a confrontational policy, while Germans sought détente and relaxation. The German Left felt exposed to a technocratic, heartless American policy intent on threatening a nuclear war that would be limited to Europe. "The American planners can engage in reflection over the nuclear holocaust in Europe with a cool head. The Soviets can do so less. We Germans cannot do it at all" (Eppler 1983). Far from being a model, America had become in the eyes of the peace movement of the early eighties a "deterrence society" based on collectively organized fear, socially organized aggression, a system of mobilized and accumulated *Angst* (Senghass 1969). Deterrence theorists, it was alleged, conjured anticommunism and the Soviet threat to dominate mass consciousness and to guarantee the wealth, influence, status, and power interests of the military-industrial-scientific-education complex.

Much of this anti-American discourse came tumbling down with the Berlin Wall. The role of intellectuals in Marxism had been to defend high culture, but in East Germany anti-Americanism had become identified with cultural stagnation and corruption (Bild 1972). The West-Germanization of East Germany gave a further twist to perceptions of Americanization. "Wessis" found themselves attacked by "Ossis" in much the same vein as "Wessis" had attacked *Verumerikanisierung* a decade before. At the same time postmodernism challenged the modernist cult of an astringent avant garde whose style was one of stress and alienation and whose art was difficult, grasped by a few. The modernist cult of the avant garde heroically blocking the juggernaut of popular mass culture had grown thin, yet, the debate over Americanization is only winded. Current complaints of the rise of an "Amideutsch," a verbal imperialism that had transformed the language so that one can no longer read any trendy German journal without knowledge of English, is a sign that the old concerns have not abated (cf. Pinto 1990: 97–107). If the history of the specter of *Amerikanisierung* is any indication, however, there is reason to believe that much of the threat is the Germans' own doing.

NOTES

1. du Bois-Reymond (1974: 145). The widely-read English translation of this pamphlet omitted the final section (*Der preussische Gymnasialbildung im Kampfe mit der vorschreitenden Amerikaniserung*).
2. "USA koloprtierten, Kultur." *National-Zeitung*, June 14, 1938; Colin Ross. "Amerika greift nach der Weltmacht." *Zeitschrift für Geopolitik* 16 (1939): 414–422; Colin Ross. "Das unsichtbare Reich der USA." *Zeitschrift für Geopolitik* 17 (1940): 153–55.

REFERENCES

Aronowitz, Stanley. 1993. *Roll over Beethoven. The Return of Cultural Strife.* Hannover: Wesleyan University Press.

Beck, Earl R. 1968. *Germany Rediscovers America.* Tallahassee: Florida State University Press.

Bell, Daniel. 1991. "The 'Hegelian Secret': Civil Society and American Exceptionalism." In *Is America Different? A New Look at American Exceptionalism,* edited by Byron E. Shafer, pp. 46–70. Oxford: Clarendon Press.

Bergmann, Peter. 1995. "Nietzsche, Heidegger and the Americanization of Defeat." *International Studies in Philosophy* 27(3): 73–84.

Bergquist, James M. 1980. "The Forty-Eighters and the Politics of the 1850s." In *Germany and America: Essays on Problems of International Relations and Immigration,* edited by Hans L. Trefusse, pp. 111–21. New York: Brooklyn College Press.

Bergsträsser, Arnold. 1963. The Problem of the So-called Americanization of Germany." *Jahrbuch für Amerikastudien* 8(8): 13–23.

Bild, Das Aktuelle (ed.). 1943. *Yankeeism: Tendenzen der americanischen Zivilisation der Gegenwart.* Leipzig: Birnbaum.

Binion, Rudolph. 1984. *Hitler Among the Germans.* DeKalb: Northern Illinois University Press.

Blanke, Gustav. 1944. *Yankeetum: Tendenzen der modernen amerikanischen Zivilisation,* 2d ed. Leipzig: Emil Heinrich [English-language edition *Yan-*

keeism, Aspects and Tendencies of Modern American Civilization].

Boehlich, Walter (ed.). 1967. *Der Hochverratsprozeß gegen Gervinus.* Frankfurt/Main: Insel Verlag.

Bruncken, Ernest. 1904. *German Political Refugees in the United States during the Period From 1815–1860.* Milwaukee.

Compton, James V. 1967. *The Swastika and the Eagle: Hitler, the United States, and the Origins of World War II.* Boston, Mass.: Houghton Mifflin.

Dobert, Eitel Wolf. 1958. *Deutsche Demokraten in Amerika: Die Achtundvierziger und ihre Schriften.* Göttingen: Vandenhoeck & Ruprecht.

du Bois-Reymond, Emil. 1974. "Kulturgeschichte und Naturwissenschaft." In *Vorträge über Philosophie und Gesellschaft,* edited by Siegried Wollgast. East Berlin: F. Meiner.

Earle, Carville. 1992. *Geographical Inquiry and American Historical Problems.* Stanford, Calif.: Stanford University Press.

Easum, Chester Verne. 1929. *The Americanization of Carl Schurz.* Chicago, Ill.: University of Chicago Press.

Eppler, Erhard. 1983. *Die tödliche Utopie der Sicherheit.* Reinbek bei Hamburg: Rowohlt.

Ernst, Robert. 1949. *Immigrant Life in New York City 1825–1863.* New York: Columbia University Press.

Eschenburg, Theodor. 1986. "Die Reaktion der Deutschen." In *Zusammenbruch oder Befreiung? Zur Aktualität des 8. Mai 1945,* edited by Ulrich Albrecht, Elmar Altvater, and Ekkehart Krippendorff. Berlin: Verlag Europäische Perspektive.

Feuer, Lewis. 1969. " The Alienated Americans and Their Influence on Marx and Engels. " In *Marx and the Intellectuals: A Set of Post-ideological Essays,* edited by Lewis S. Feuer. New York: Doubleday.

Fiebig-von Hase, Ragnhild. 1993. "The United States and Germany in the World Arena, 1900–1917." In *Confrontation and Cooperation. Germany and the United States in the Era of World War I, 1900–1924,* edited by Hans-Jürgen Schröder. Providence, R.I.: Berg.

Fraenkel, Ernst. 1960. "Das deutsche Wilsonbild." *Jahrbuch für Amerikastudien* (5): 66–120.

Friedländer, Saul. 1967. *Prelude to Downfall: Hitler and the United States, 1939–1941.* New York: Knopf.

Galinsky, Hans. 1972. *Amerikanisch-deutsche Sprach- und Literaturbeziehungen. Systematische Übersicht und Forschungsbericht 1945–1970.* Frankfurt/Main: Athenäum.

Gerbi, Antonello. 1973. *The Dispute of the New World: The History of a Polemic, 1750–1900.* Pittsburgh, Pa.: University of Pittsburgh Press.

Germanus [Gustav Friedrich]. 1905. *Der amerikanische Gefahr: keine wirtschaftliche, sondern eine geistige.* Altenburg: S. Geibel.

Gervinus, Georg Gottfried. 1967. *Einleitung in die Geschichte des neunzehnten Jahrhunderts,* edited by Walter Boehlich. Frankfurt/Main: Insel.

Goldberger, Max Ludwig. 1903. *Das Land der unbegrenzten Möglichkeiten.* Berlin: F. Fontane.

Gruber, Carol S. 1975. *Mars and Minerva: World War I and the Uses of Higher Learning in America.* Baton Rouge: Louisiana State University Press.

Halfeld, Adolf. 1941. "Der amerikanische Messianismus." *Hamburger Fremdenblatt,* May 20.

Hans-Heinz, Krill. 1962. *Die Rankerenaissance. Max Lenz und Erich Marcks.* Berlin: Walter de Gruyter.

Hartmann, Edward George. 1949. *The Movement to Americanize the Immigrant.* New York: Columbia University Press.

Heinzen, Karl. 1898. *Teutscher Radikalismus in Amerika.* Vol. 1: *Ausgewählte Abhandlungen, Kritiken und Aphorismen aus den Jahren 1854–1879.* Milwaukee: Freidenker.

Hennigsen, Manfred. 1973. "Das Amerikabild des Hegel, Marx and Engels." *Zeitschrift für Politik* 20(20): 224–51.

Herf, Jeffrey. 1991. *War by Other Means: Soviet Power, West German Resistance, and the Battles of the Euromissiles.* New York: Free Press.

Herwig, Holger H. 1976. *Politics of Frustration: The United States in German Naval Planning, 1889–1941.* Boston, Mass.: Little, Brown.

Higham, John. 1977. *Strangers in the Land. Patterns of American Nativism 1860–1925.* New York: Atheneum.

Hitler, Adolf. 1961. *Secret Book.* New York: Grove Press.

Köhler, Erich. 1908. *Ludwig Max Goldberger.* Charlottenburg: Virgil Verlag.

Köpfe, Wulf. 1987. "Die Bestrafung und Besserung der Deutschen. Über die amerikanischen Kriegsziele, über Völkerpsychologie und Emil Ludwig." In *Deutschland nach Hitler: Zukunftsplane im Exil und aus der Besatzungszeit, 1939–1949,* edited by Thomas Koebner, Gert Sautermeister, and Sigrid Schneider, pp. 81–82. Oplade: Westdeutscher Verlag.

Krohn, Claus-Dieter. 1987. "Let Us Be Prepared to Win the Peace. Nachkriegsplanungen emigrierter deutscher Sozialwissenschaftler an der New School for Social Research in New York." In *Deutschland nach Hitler: Zukunftsplane im Exil und aus der Besatzungszeit, 1939–1949,* edited by Thomas Koebner, Gert Sautermeister, and Sigrid Schneider. Oplade: Westdeutscher Verlag.

Levine, Bruce. 1992. *The Spirit of 1848: German Immigrants, Labor Conflict, and the Coming of the Civil War.* Urbana: University of Illinois Press.

Lowenstein, Steven M. 1989. *Frankfurt on the Hudson: The German-Jewish Community of Washington Heights, 1933–1983.* Detroit, Mich.: Wayne State University Press.

Luebke, Frederick C. 1974. *Bonds of Loyalty, German-Americans and World War I.* De Kalb: Northern Illinois University Press.

Maase, Kaspar. 1992. *BRAVO Amerika. Erkundigungen zur Jugendkultur der Bundespreublik in den funfziger Jahren.* Hamburg: Junius Verlag.

Max von Baden, Prinz. 1928. *Erinnerungen und Dokumente*. Stuttgart: Deutsche verlagsanstalt.

Meinecke, Friedrich. 1950. *The German Catastrophe*. Cambridge, Mass.: Harvard University Press.

Moltmann, Günter. 1973. *Atlantische Blockpolitik im 19. Jahrhundert. Die Vereinigten Staaten und der deutsche Liberalismus während der Revolution von 1848/49*. Düsseldorf: Droste Verlag.

Moore, R. Laurence. 1970. *European Socialists and the American Promised Land*. New York: Oxford University Press.

Nietzsche, Friedrich. 1940. *Werke und Briefe: Historisch-Kritische-Gesamtausgabe*. Munich: Beck.

Nietzsche, Friedrich. *The Dawn*, Aphorism #327.

Nietzsche, Friedrich. *The Wanderer and His Shadow*, Aphorism #287.

Nietzsche, Friedrich. 1984. *Human, All-Too-Human: A Book for Free Spirits*. Lincoln: University of Nebraska Press.

Obermann, Karl. 1947. *Joseph Weydemeyer: Pioneer of American Socialism*. New York: International Publishers.

Osterle, Heinz D. 1987. "Interview with Hans Magnus Enzenberger on German-American Relations." *New German Critique* 42 (Fall).

Parsons, Edward B. 1971. "The German-American Crisis of 1902–1903." *Historian* (33): 436–52.

Petzold, Joachim. 1964. "'Ethischer Imperialismus': Eine Studie über die politische Konzeption des Kreises um den Prinzen Max v. Baden am Vorabend der deutschen Frühjahrsoffensive von 1918." In *Politik im Krieg 1914–1918*, edited by Fritz Klein, pp. 204–29. East Berlin: Akademie.

Pinto, Diana. 1990. "The French Intelligentsia Rediscovers America." In *The Rise and Fall of Anti-Americanism. A Century of French Perception*, edited by Denis Lacorne, Jacques Rupnik, and Marie-France Toinet, pp. 97–107. New York: St. Martin's Press.

Pochmann, Henry A. 1948. *New England Transcendentalism and St. Louis Hegelianism*. Philadelphia, Pa.: Carl Schurz Memorial Foundation.

Poesche, Theodore and Charles Goepp. 1853. *The New Rome: or, the United States of the World*. New York: G. P. Putman.

Pommerin, Reiner. 1986. *Der Kaiser und Amerika: Die USA in der Politik der Reichsleitung 1890–1917*. Köln: Böhlau Verlag.

Radkau, Joachim. 1971. *Die deutsche Emigration in den USA. Ihr Einfluss auf die amerikanische Europapolitik 1933–1945*. Düsseldorf: Bertelsmann.

Rich, Norman. 1973. *Hitler's War Aims*. New York: Norton.

Rosenwaike, Ira. 1972. *Population History of New York City*. Syracuse, N.Y.: Syracuse University Press.

Ross, Colin. 1930. *Die Welt auf der Waage*. Leipzig: F. A. Brockhaus.

Ross, Colin. 1939. "Amerika greift nach der Weltmacht." *Zeitschrift für Geopolitik* 1616: 414–22.

Ross, Colin. 1940. "Das unsichtbare Reich der USA." *Zeitschrift für Geopolitik* 17: 153–55.

Rossem, Maarten van. 1981. "Le Defi Européen." In *Image and Impact: American Influences in the Netherlands since 1945*, edited by Rob Kroes. Amsterdam: Amerika Institut.

Rupieper, Hermann-Josef. 1993. *Die Wurzeln der westdeutschen Nachkriegsdemokatie. Der amerikanische Beitrag 1945–1952*. Opladen: Westdetuscher Verlag.

Schaff, Philip. 1961. *America. A Sketch of Its Political, Social, and Religious Character*, edited by Perry Miller. Cambridge, Mass.: Belknap.

Schmidt, Henry J. 1985. "The Rhetoric of Survival: The Germanist in America from 1900 to 1925." In *America and the Germans*, edited by Frank Trommler and Joseph McVeigh. Philadelphia: University of Pennsylvania Press.

Schröder, Hans-Jürgen (ed.). 1993. *Confrontation and Cooperation. Germany and the United States in the Era of World War I, 1900–1924*. Providence, R.I.: Berg.

Senghaas, Dieter. 1969. *Abschreckung und Frieden: Studien zur organisierten Friedlosigkeit*. Frankfurt/Main: Europaische Verlagsanst.

Sombart, Werner R. 1976. *Why is There No Socialism in the United States?*, translated by P. M. Hocking and C. T. Husbands. London: Macmillan.

Sontheimer, Kurt. 1961. *Thomas Mann und die Deutschen*. Munich: Nymphenburger.

Spann, Edward K. 1981. *The New Metropolis. New York City, 1840–1857*. New York: Columbia University Press.

SS-Hauptamt. 1944. *Amerikanismus eine Weltgefahr*. Berlin: SS-Hauptamt.

Stead, William Thomas. 1972. *The Americanization of the World or The Trend of the Twentieth Century*. New York: Garland.

Stoakes, Geoffrey. 1986. *Hitler and the Quest for World Dominion: Nazi Ideology and Foreign Policy in the 1920s*. Leamington Spa: Berg.

Trommler, Frank. 1985. "The Rise and Fall of Americanism in Germany." In *America and the Germans* (2 vols.), edited by Frank Trommler and Joseph McVeigh. Philadelphia: University of Pennsylvania Press.

Tyrrell, Ian. 1986. *The Absent Marx: Class Analysis and Liberal History in Twentieth-Century America*. New York: Greenwood.

Vagts, Alfred. 1935. *Deutschland und die Vereinigten Staaten in der Weltpolitik*, Vol. I. New York: Dickson and Thompson.

Walker, Mack. 1964. *Germany and the Emigration 1816–1885*. Cambridge, Mass.: Harvard University Press.

Weber, Paul C. 1966. *America in Imaginative German Literature in the First Half of the Nineteenth Century*. New York: Columbia University Press.

Weiberg, Gerhard L. 1964. "Hitler's Image of the United States." *American Historical Review* 69, p. 1020.

Wendtland, Wilhelm. 1902. "A German View of the American Peril." *North American Review* (174).

Wette, Wolfram. 1985. "From Kellog to Hitler (1928–1933): German Public Opinion Concerning the Rejection or Glorification of War." In *The German Military in the Age of Total War*, edited by Wilhelm Diest, pp. 71–99. London: Berg.

Wilhelm, Theodor. 1943a. "Missionare der Weltdemokratie. Die Kulturpropaganda der USA im Dienst des Imperialismus." *Westdeutscher Beobachter*, March 5.

Wilhelm, Theodor. 1943b. "Unter dem Deckmantel der Kultur. Die Kulturpropaganda der USA im Dienste des Imperialismus." *Westdeutscher Beobachter*, March 3.

Wittke, Carl. 1945. *Against the Current. The Life of Karl Heinzen (1809–80).* Chicago, Ill.: University of Chicago Press.

Wittke, Carl. 1950. *The Utopian Communist: A Biography of Wilhelm Weitling, Nineteenth Century Reformer.* Baton Rouge: Louisiana State University Press.

Wittke, Carl. 1952. *Refugees of Revolution: The German Forty-Eighters in America.* Philadelphia: University of Pennsylvania Press.

Zucker, Adolf Eduard (ed.). 1950. *The Forty-Eighters.* New York: Columbia University Press.

4

The Colonization of the Russian Political and Legal System

David Lempert

In the past, they would show us pictures of American demonstrations with police controlling crowds with force, and say, "Look what they do to stop dissent in America." Today we see the same thing and they say, "This is how democracies keep order."

> — a Russian law student in 1990, three years before
> President Yeltsin sent troops against the elected
> Parliament with U.S. government encouragement
> and five years before sending them into
> Chechnya with little U.S. government protest[1]

Two hundred seventy million customers; five hundred forty million shoes; billions and billions of hamburgers. No wonder corporate eyes light up when Mikhail Gorbachev stresses the need for doing more business with the United States.

> — Lowenstein et al. 1989: 21[2]

Three years ago, if I had predicted that the majority of major U.S. firms in Moscow would be doubling their sales and revenue every year and that Russia would be home to over 700 American firms . . . people would have politely called me a visionary to my face and a crackpot behind my back. . . . Let me predict that within three years Americans will be able to travel to Sochi and Samara as easily and as regularly as they now travel to Chicago and Cleveland. And that when they travel there, they will be able to stay in more than three-star hotels, eat at

McDonald's and better and rent American cars, and will be able to call home without all of the traditional difficulties.

— Thomas Pickering 1996[3]

The international bourgeoisie, deprived of the opportunity of waging open war against Soviet Russia, is waiting and watching for the moment when circumstances will permit it to resume the war.

— Lenin 1921[4]

For most of the twentieth century, as in much of its previous history, Russia and its empire remained closed to the West, allowing only carefully selected visitors, symbols, products, and ideas to enter.

In the mid-1980s, with the inability of the Russian empire to further expand and with its economic system unable to adapt quickly to meeting its needs from within, the floodgates opened.

In came a wave of American films and symbols: of vigilantism and violence, Rambo films and Bruce Lee Kung Fu movies, Freddie Krueger massacres, Tom and Jerry cartoon mayhem. In came works of Dale Carnegie, Henry Ford, and Lee Iacocca as best sellers. In came televised music videos, MTV. In came images of gangsters and robber barons as symbols of prosperity, alongside children's board games modeled on America's Monopoly™.

Along with them came the Western consultants, the corporate lawyers, the Wall Street investment bankers, the politicians, and the established scholars with what they proclaimed as visions of "democracy" and "markets" for the Russians. The end of the Cold War generated a sudden interest both in Russia and in America for a transfer of the forms of the American economic, political, and legal systems to Russia. The losers of the Cold War were looking to the winners in the hope of finding renewed prosperity. The winners looked to the losers to recreate their image on those they had defeated and to reap the early spoils of peace; the chance for new markets and materials.

This was the beginning of an export wave; of symbols and slogans in law and politics as in other fields. From a joint conference in the Kremlin for U.S. and Soviet lawyers, to scholarships and internships, to government projects designed to restructure the Russian constitution and legal institutions, what amounted to a small invasion began in the mid-1980s and continues despite growing disaffection with the results of the policies of the new pro-Western governments.

What is being transferred by those with the greatest resources to transfer their vision — government leaders and business interests — has less to do with concepts of justice, accountability, and access than with establishing a particular kind of order favorable to particular players.

The process former Soviet President Mikhail Gorbachev began created élite-élite networks between Soviet Communist Party (now, ex-Party) officials and their deal-making younger assistants — the "Red Managers" — and Western élites. The political and legal changes they have sought are predominantly those that create procedural rules beneficial to both élites; rules to favor processes of resource extraction and the opening of the Soviet market to Western products.

The process is not a one way exchange of ideology of law and politics but a different mix of Russian and Western traditions as resources and ideas flow in an uncertain environment. Indeed, the Russian legal system as a set of political institutions and a codification of political relations — including the organization of the profession, its legal codes, and legal culture — has long retained the characteristic features of Roman civil law and European traditions mixed with its own peculiar variants. These now shape the advice, money, and symbols coming from the United States and they interact to create something altogether unlike anything reflecting Anglo-American concepts of fairness or justice.

The reforms in the Russian legal system that have been the key concern on both sides are mostly about property rights — about freeing Russian property for sale, about letting billions of dollars of resources flow illegally across the borders into Western banks with justice systems on both sides turning a blind eye to the consequences — and about securing the interests of Western capital in Russia's new "market." Much is changing in the law of property and little in the law of rights and accountability. In the profession, the change is about who has access to lawyers and who can purchase them — including foreign businesses with interests opposed to those of Russian citizens — rather than about increasing access or improving the workings of the profession.

As the story unfolds, it is slowly being documented elsewhere — the billions of dollars flooding out of the country to Western banks (an amount as much as several times what the West has proposed in real aid and certainly much more than has been given);[5] the spoils taken by organized crime; and the effect on the Russian populace of policies under the veneer of Western concepts, which have been used to transfer much of the Russian economy into the hands of a few at the expense of the many.[6]

This chapter tells the beginning of the tale, fitting it into the context of the theory of interaction between powerful and weak states in the global economy. In an ironic confirmation of the theory, it is a tale that proved impossible to tell in any major media in the United States as the events were unfolding. It is only now being reported piecemeal, after the fact, when the results of an overall process have been achieved.

This is an excerpt from the early history as it has been recorded through field observation in Russia and participant observation in the United States, and pieced together with other documented sources.

It begins with a discussion of the history of Western contact in order to set the context for recent events, exchanges, and influence. The types of processes that have been at work in other interactions between First World industrial cultures and Third World, mostly traditional, societies also describes what is occurring in the new relationship between Russia and the West.

As an example of relations between nations or even between the United States and other countries, the processes occurring in Russia are not new to historians or social scientists. The events in Russia are merely the latest addition to a lengthening list of what some would call "developing client states."[7] Social scientists have long depicted the processes of dependency, describing the tie between class structure and underdevelopment as a successor form of mercantile economics and colonialism,[8] as a process of world systems theory,[9] or in terms of the "secession of the rich" from within the first world.[10] The addition of Russia to the picture is new only because it is so rare that modern empires engulf one another, and it has been difficult to transcend the ideological descriptions imposed on Russian society by the West in order to clearly see the fall of the Soviet Union as fulfillment of the predictions of these theories, rather than as confirmations of mythologies of various "isms" ("communism" or "capitalism").[11]

This chapter summarizes the findings of one of the first American anthropologists to study in urban Russia. It draws but a few examples of one particular process from several volumes of material collected in the field in 1989–90 following social experimentation, participant observation, interviews, surveys, and historical research in Moscow, Leningrad/St. Petersburg, and Yakutsk in 1989–90,[12] as well as first hand participation in the processes of assistance for the World Bank and the U.S. Agency for International Development (USAID), and related activity in the scholarly communities and media between 1990 and 1994. The full story of the changes and the different processes that are at work to describe relations between victors and vanquished — "diffusion," "cultural imperialism," and "dependency" — is described therein. Along with it is a more theoretical discussion of changing American models of "democracy" and the rejection of the social contract participatory view of the eighteenth century in favor of the more statist view as the model to transfer to the Newly Independent States.

WESTERNIZATION AS AN HISTORICAL
PART OF INTERNAL CONTROL

The history of Russian cultural borrowing from the West has a double edge. On the one hand, there were advances in legal and political forms that introduced limited protections for citizens. Many of these reforms occurred shortly before the 1917 revolution. On the other hand, scholars have noted ironically how Western ideologies and exchanges were also used as means of increasing control.

Westernization as an imperial policy objective dates back to 1698 when Peter the Great began his transformation of Russia in copying Western norms by requiring men to shave their beards and adopt Western clothes. From the Tsar to Lenin to Stalin to Gorbachev, facial hair and special clothing disappeared to be replaced by the forms set in the nineteenth century by British tailors. By 1990, Russia's leaders were almost perfect mirrors of their Western counterparts, with short hair and shaven faces, Western suits, collared shirts, and ties.

Western style "rights" were introduced first during the nineteenth century. The copying of Western legal codes, the introduction of the jury system, and the development of the *advokatura* (defense lawyers) and *procurator* (government prosecutor) from Roman legal traditions were not only drawn from ancient practices but also were contemporary borrowings from French and German legal forms. Even the concept of glasnost, which Gorbachev repeated as a basis of his perestroika reforms, was a translation from German. It was part of the 1864 judicial reforms[13] and had been part of Tsar Alexander II's rhetoric from as early as the late 1850s.

At the same time that these concepts were introduced, they were interpreted to benefit the same élites and to fit into Russia's existing political culture. One scholar calls the introduction of Western economic concepts into Russia part of "repressive modernization," explaining that "the West takes on a rather strange appearance when reflected in the Russian mirror. In the pre-Emancipation era, educated Russians were disquietingly eager to cite Western economic theory in support of a variety of coercive schemes instead of the liberating traditions that we are more accustomed to consider part of the Western legacy."[14] In the 1850s, the doctrines of Adam Smith and private property rights were purged of their links to human freedom and used to strengthen the institution of slavery. Because serfs were classified as "property," laissez-faire policies meant that the master had the private property right to do as he pleased with his serfs.[15]

The elimination of slavery (serfdom) in 1861 did not change the relationship or the way that Western concepts were used. Although the peasants were able to obtain some forms of private property (their land) in the nineteenth century, the gentry also used its new private property rights to increase control over the landholding peasants under their aegis. Under the guise of peasant "ignorance" and inability of the peasants to effectively manage their property, they took advantage of the ideology of "privatization" to claim freedom from government controls.[16] Indeed, it has been argued that the abolition of serfdom was not a redistribution of rights but merely a prelude to industrialization[17] and that the élites continued to direct changes even though the technology of production had changed.[18]

In more recent history, Communist Party General Secretary Nikita Khrushchev presided over a period of Westernization and liberalization as well, leading to some speculation that the Khrushchev era reforms (and the Kennedy era reforms in the United States) would have brought an end to the Cold War and allowed for the increase in political and economic rights in both countries, had the United States been able to support Khrushchev in his attempts to reduce the Soviet military.[19]

The impetus for increased business transactions with the West, echoing the joint ventures and foreign investment in Russia in the late nineteenth century, that occurred in greater frequency during the perestroika period, occurred early under Soviet rule, with antecedents dating back to the New Economic Policy of the 1920s. The Soviet government had major business dealings not only with Armand Hammer but also with Henry Ford and heads of other major corporations. Although transactions slowed during the Stalinist period and the Cold War, they began to accelerate several years before perestroika at the instigation of Soviet leaders. One author described the treatment that Soviet élites extended to American business executives, even before perestroika, as "The Red Carpet." As early as the 1970s, Pepsi-Co signed contracts for sales of bottled flavored carbonated beverages, while banker David Rockefeller, Kaiser Industries Chair Edward Kaiser, W. Averill Harriman, and others were treated like royalty in Moscow.[20]

The difference between the diffusion during the perestroika period and during the eighteenth and nineteenth centuries was that during the earlier periods, central authority remained firmly in place. Russian leaders invited Westernization through selective borrowing rather than from a position of weakness.

During perestroika, it was the "reformers" in Russia who increasingly sought contact with the West as part of an internal intergenerational struggle. Seeking Western help was viewed as a means of helping dislodge an older generation of élites who had been inattentive to the country's economic and spiritual decay and whose ineffective military spending in a contained empire was moving the country toward famine. These reformers, the privileged children of the privileged, did not seem to have a clear idea of what they wanted from the West or any real knowledge about it. In opposing the older generation, the younger "reformers" had more than a ready set of slogans and a vision of higher living standards in rallying support that would bring them to power. In the West they also had an ally against the old élites that could supply them with a means of affluence in uncertain times.

Indeed, in both countries in the 1970s, industrial enterprises were subject to more effective controls and were still very much a part of the cultures in which they were created. Few Russian enterprises had yet become international or multinational institutions operating outside of nation-states and with their own norms, as had U.S. enterprises. These developments were soon to come, however, as their young leaders began to seek freedom from the state along with a more international outlook.[21]

By early 1990, American popular culture had already arrived in Russia, with a new ideology soon to follow. Russian children went to video arcades to watch Tom and Jerry cartoons. They posted Sylvestor Stallone and Arnold Schwarzenegger on their walls. They played with Mickey Mouse toys and purchased calendars with Snow White and the Seven Dwarfs. For amusement, they played American computer games in special computer rooms or arcades. In the bookstores, among the best sellers were Henry Ford's autobiography, out in 200,000 copies on first printing as a manual on capitalist accumulation, along with Dale Carnegie's psychology manual, *How to Win Friends and Influence People*, copies of American books on sexual techniques, and Chrysler Chairman Lee Iacocca's newest book, referred to in the *New York Times* as one of the books "celebrating greed."[22]

All of this was merely a prelude to other selected imports in politics, law, and economics and for the resource transfers that were beginning to occur as the economy was opened to foreign penetration.

U.S. GOVERNMENT AND BUSINESS AIMS AND THE MECHANISMS OF INFLUENCE AND DEPENDENCY

Leading up to perestroika and continuing through it, the contacts that existed for economic exchanges were at the élite levels. Élites of the two societies merged into a network of their own, similar in some ways to the monarchical élite networks that existed throughout Europe before the nineteenth century.

Before perestroika, even if managers had suggested entering into joint venture or trade agreements, they would have to have been approved by the Kremlin. During 1989–90, the approval process was disappearing. With the move toward a "market" system, managers making joint venture agreements were not responsible to anyone. The national resources they managed were under their control. Any blame for the country's economic problems would fall on the elected officials. The greater freedom of managers in both countries and the Soviet Union's economic collapse offered the promise of a larger number of contracts with terms more favorable to the Western corporations and with the cooperation but not the strict oversight of Western governments.

The dynamics of the business deal between corporate and enterprise managers in both countries were quite simple. The salary of a Russian enterprise manager in 1990 was about 600 rubles per month. At the black market rate, this translated to about $40 per month. Indeed, $100 per month was already more than Soviet President Gorbachev or Russian President Yeltsin's salaries. The potential for Western influence was enormous. A foreign company seeking special access to raw materials or markets would have expected to spend, in the United States, at least $50,000 per year ($4,000 per month) on the salary of an executive to manage an operation abroad. It could pay the Soviet manager — or even the Soviet President — anywhere from one to one hundred times what the Soviet President was earning if it saw a potential business opportunity. To this was added the potential for other perquisites — trips abroad, copying and FAX machines, special products.

This, indeed, is what began to happen, with the sale and purchase of lawyers, law professors, managers, and cohorts of government officials. The managers' incentives were, clearly, to seek these joint venture agreements. The only constraint on the terms of the contracts that they would make was their own ability to remain in the positions of management. Because there were no laws on management responsibility and accountability, and because the access to Western resources and power gave them additional advantages, there was little reason to assume that they would lose their positions if they chose to participate. Because they were the ones creating the reforms with Western help, the ultimate outcome could be no surprise. Thus, the real incentives — favored by the Soviet managers and by their Western partners — were to create legal and political mechanisms that would give managers controlling interests in their companies.[23] Management control, however, also meant management unaccountability to the enterprise, with benefits reaching the public only when the incentives to the manager began to coincide with incentives for greater productivity and concern for the ability of consumers to keep buying. This, in a sense, was the U.S. model, though with many fewer controls or regulations. In the absence of controls, some elected officials were combining their positions in business and in the legislatures for personal fortune as part of what they described to the public as "reform" and for which there were no standards to condemn their behavior.[24]

What was happening throughout the legal profession was no different, even in places like the law schools, where the next generation of the country's lawyers was being trained. As early as 1990, in Moscow, law professors were already taking on foreign firms as clients, and were paid $2,000 per month or the equivalent of 100 times their salaries.[25] Indeed, the financial incentives to represent foreign interests over those of Russia in their teaching of law and rights was now on the magnitude of 100 to 1, and there were no efforts by the law schools even to raise the issue of how the purchase of their skills by foreigners would affect the law curricula, their ability to teach objectively, and the future of the Russian people and their resources.

What held true for interactions between Western and Russian cultures at the level of government, economic actors, and cultural symbols was reflected on a small scale in all legal institutions, making the relationship as a whole easier to see. It seemed as if Western institutions were linking with their counterparts in Russia in a direct one-to-one mapping and were trying to impose their organizational forms and values onto them.

Most of the interaction was between the élites in the two cultures who held power in major institutions. It began with lawyers in government circles — President Mikhail Gorbachev (the first lawyer to head the country since Vladimir Lenin) and his Deputy and former law school classmate Anatolii Lukianov (a participant in the 1990 failed military coup, granted amnesty in 1994 after his election to Parliament) and worked its way down through the profession and into public consciousness. Because the contacts were based on the material gain of the different groupings of actors reflecting their particular needs and values rather than some overall guiding policy or ethic, the political and legal values transmitted and the institutional changes made had little to do with establishing a system of rights of individuals and their access to the law. It was mostly about creating the legal structure necessary for Western business to invest and extract profits.

The formal contacts that occurred in 1989–90 between the legal professions of the two countries were easy to map and to see as a starting point for how they would develop over time. At the highest level, the Bush Administration sent a delegation of élite American lawyers and justices who were met by the élites in the profession in Russia. American police and sheriffs came to meet with Russian police. The heads of the American Bar Association came to meet with the newly formed Association of Advocates and the Union of Lawyers. Political leaders and lawyers like Leningrad Mayor Anatolii Sobchak, on the Russian side, were invited to the United States by their counterparts. Corporate lawyers came seeking business contacts through Soviet lawyers. Consumerist lawyer Ralph Nader came to try to find public interest lawyers. The effect each group had seemed to be proportional to the power and resources they commanded in the United States.

The connections different institutions and individuals made and the influence they had matched the structure of resources in the United States and the West. Institutions with power and wealth had the most opportunities to make contacts in Russia — through visits, invitations, and gifts. They were also those most highly regarded by the Russians.

To see the process is to view it at its different levels — political institutions, economic institutions, and legal institutions — and then to consider its effects.

U.S. GOVERNMENT PROGRAMS

In 1990, Soviet President Gorbachev sought expert advice on economic reforms for the Soviet economy. The place he sought it was directly from the Bush Administration.

As Wendell Willkie, III, an official in the Department of Commerce, described the Bush Administration's policy in a speech to U.S. and Soviet lawyers in the Kremlin, "[The Soviet Union] is one of the world's largest unexplored and undeveloped markets [with] huge deposits of resources. [The United States wants] access to the domestic market [and] Soviet officials are disappointed that there is not greater interest in the U.S. in investing here. . . . Major changes are still needed to improve the investment environment to enhance prospects."[26]

In the spring, Secretary of Commerce Robert Mosbacher had brought Chief Executive Officers of 15 of the top U.S. corporations to Moscow to discuss trade, foreign investment, and what Willkie described as "sound economic development." The companies also proposed to bring several Soviets to work as interns in their businesses in order to prepare them to work as managers for their companies in the Soviet Union.

On another trip, Bush's Chief of Staff, John Sununu, was in the country to present U.S. plans for investment. Following Sununu's visit, Republican leader Senator Robert Dole arrived. A rumor spread in Leningrad that Dole was signing an agreement to send 1,000 American managers to work in Soviet enterprises and train Soviets in American management techniques, as part of developing business-to-business contacts.

The major U.S. government program for building "rule of law" in Russia in 1989–90 was a seminar arranged by the Bush Administration in which the Administration hand-picked a number of lawyers for a trip to the Soviet Union. The initiative began after a trip by Attorney General Richard Thornburgh to Moscow in October of 1989, whose visit received national attention. Thornburgh was shown on national television on the evening news, telling students at Moscow State University's Law Faculty about "the future of the U.S.S.R." and the importance of "rule of law." Following his trip, he arranged for seminars in the spring in Moscow and Leningrad.

The first American delegation arrived in Leningrad in late March, with copies of the U.S. constitution and of speeches they had written, in English. The head of the group was Donald B. Ayer, Deputy Attorney General of the U.S. Department of Justice. He described the group as a "broad range of lawyers" the variety of which was "deliberate — to share with you an accurate perspective of the range of views in our system" because "significant disagreements are essential." Of the eleven members of the group, ten were men and ten were white. Six worked for the U.S. government — four from the U.S. Department of Justice, one from the State Department, and one U.S. District Judge. There was one state supreme court judge and four professors. Only one of the lawyers defended individuals against the state, defense lawyer and New York University Professor Burt Neuborne, who described himself as a token among the group.

On the Soviet side, meetings were scheduled by the Association of Lawyers. Of the 40 or 50 Soviet lawyers at the seminar, several had been members of the *nomenklatura*. Others were second-level administrators who had learned of the conference through them.

Although Ayer framed his opening address in terms of "help we are providing" to the Soviet Union for "genuine protection for all citizens . . . and limitation and order for the activities of the state," none of the talks addressed issues of how the people could hold government or economic bureaucracies accountable or how laws would be enforced. There were no explanations of public access to courts or legal systems, of challenging the prosecutor, of avoiding monopolization of legal services by élites, or of civil disobedience as an historical path to achieving rights in the United States. There was nothing about distribution of wealth or opportunity as a key step to political equality and free markets. Instead, the focus was on the coordination of officials; of political, economic, and administrative authority.

In a sense, because these meetings were so short and Americans knew little about the system they were visiting or the people they were dealing with, for the dialogues to continue and for the diffusion of ideas to have been successful, it became important that the people whom the American lawyers met in the seminars stay in power. The very group who needed to be removed and whose authority needed to be challenged if "rule of law" were to occur suddenly became an important set of contacts.

The Embassy's explanation was that after the seminar, substantial programs would follow and that this was a necessary step for preliminary contacts.

As of 1990, the only major project underway was to bring 50 Soviet graduate students in law who were planning careers in teaching to take courses at American law schools on constitutional law. At $20,000 per student per year, that would have run about $1 million.

Two years later, the program reappeared under the direction of the U.S. Information Agency — 160 Benjamin Franklin Fellows were to be selected in each of two years in the categories of business administration, economics, and public administration. The cost of the program was estimated at $7 million; $45,000 per student per year; enough to have paid the salaries of 160 American teachers to reach several thousand Soviet students. At 1990 exchange rates, if the money were used for training new Soviet lawyers, it could have been used to educate 3 million lawyers, increasing the number of lawyers in the country by twentyfold and reaching 20,000 times as many Russians as the exchange program. In contrast, according to one of the coordinators of the program, the goal was to "stimulate future contacts" with the belief that many of the students would "assume leadership roles upon their return home, as future policy makers."[27]

Four years later, however, nine years after the start of perestroika, most other projects were still awaiting development, with the focus shifting to education of "privatization" rather than oversight of accountability.[28] Of the $900 million allocated for USAID projects to "build democracy" in the former Soviet Republics, only 5 percent was set aside for the "rule of law." The lion's share went to privatization efforts.[29] Money set aside for education projects was used to transport an élite group of Russians to the United States for training for short seminars; a way to develop contacts for Americans but a far cry from initiating any real reform.[30]

QUASI-GOVERNMENTAL CONTACTS

The first major conference of U.S. and Soviet lawyers, from political figures to professionals, took place in 1990 as part of a commercial effort arranged by the Center for International Cooperation focusing on potential business opportunities. The event, titled "Moscow Conference on Law and Economic Cooperation" was soon endorsed by the government, bringing together both the American Bar Association and the newly formed Union of Soviet Lawyers. It featured a dinner in the Kremlin with President Gorbachev and a speech by Prime Minister Ryzhkov, as well as a personal message from U.S. President Bush and speeches by U.S. Ambassador Matlock and U.S. Commerce Department Official Wendell Willkie III.

The organizing and executive committees and the participants on both sides (700 American lawyers and 3,000 Soviets) included high government officials, past and present, and economic élites. On the U.S. side, the organizing committee included three American Bar Association presidents, two former Secretaries of State, and several corporate attorneys. Of 19 members, there were two women and one black. "The diversity of opinion found in the U.S. is not represented on this platform," explained Talbot D'Alemberte, then President-Elect of the American Bar Association.

On the U.S. side, the American lawyers self selected on ability to pay and, for many, invest in future business opportunities. The conference was advertised through the American Bar Association and open to anyone who paid the $1,200 conference fees plus the additional expenditures of travel.

Soviet lawyers were hand picked. On the Soviet side were 3,000 lawyers organized by the Union of Lawyers, a new organization linking the élites in the profession and starting to model itself on the monopoly practice of the American Bar Association. In Leningrad (St. Petersburg), conference participants were said to be hand picked by the Union. In order for Soviet lawyers to attend, they needed to arrange the formal permission required to take the days away from work and to be able to command hotel space in Moscow.

The conference began with prepared absentee statements from Presidents Bush and Gorbachev stressing the linkage between a market economy and "rule of law." President Bush remarked that "we Americans have always believed the rule of law protects the rights of individuals and guides the workings of the market system. Free enterprise leads to freedom and self determination includes the right to determine economic destiny." This was almost exactly the same as a statement made by Gorbachev and cited in the Soviet press two weeks earlier.

Willkie then outlined the Bush Administration's policy on providing assistance, noting that, "We Americans must further the process of bringing the Soviet Union into the world economic system."

The first major address on law at the conference was made by former U.S. Secretary of State and corporate attorney, William Rogers. Rogers noted that this was the first meeting ever of its kind and that U.S.-Soviet cooperation in opposing Iraq's takeover of Kuwait marked the first time that the two nations had acted together to combat acts by an international outlaw. "Even leaders now will face imprisonment for their illegal acts," he asserted. The audience applauded, with the irony of the statement unquestioned. Although there were more than 2,000 lawyers in the hall, none called for bringing Rogers to answer for any of his own actions under international law. No one queried why he remained silent about previous alleged violations of international law by his superiors; acts that many critics found to be similar to those he was condemning. Rogers was Secretary of State in the Nixon administration, which had been involved in efforts to overthrow (and potentially had been implicated in the death of) the elected president of Chile, Salvador Allende, in violation of Chile's state sovereignty and of the nonintervention treaty approved by the countries of the Americas. Although Rogers was on record as having opposed, for political and legal grounds, U.S. military operations in an undeclared war in Indochina and the secret bombings of a neutral country, Cambodia, he was a spokesman for the policy and never pursued legal action against Kissinger, Nixon, or any other administration officials for their role.[31]

Rogers then turned to his vision of economic reform. He told Soviet leaders and lawyers how "shopkeepers, small business, small farmers, and privatization of large companies will require new laws and totally different attitudes towards profit," drawing imagery from an eighteenth century model that no longer described the United States. In contrast to the view he presented, more than half of all Americans in the 1980s worked in businesses of more than 50 people and only about 7 percent worked for themselves.[32] "Most investment in the U.S. is made by private individuals, . . . banks and companies," Rogers continued. The order was deceptive. Even in the early 1970s, two-thirds of all privately owned stock in the United States was owned by 2 percent of America's families.[33]

"Democracy is alive and well in the U.S.," former U.S. Secretary of State under President Carter Edmund Muskie also remarked at the conference. Muskie's speech was also shaded to present an illusory ideal. Nowhere did Muskie mention that by 1990, the majority of American citizens no longer voted even in presidential elections once every four years, let alone participated in other forms of political activity. "We have found a way to separate powers so that they cannot be and are not abused," the former Secretary of State added, in the midst of Iran-Contra investigations confirming foreign policy making beyond popular or congressional control.

The distribution of the panels that followed was divided between issues of "rule of law," joint ventures, and other economic ties; individual rights and criminal law issues; and global issues (environment, disarmament, etc.). Attendance was disproportionately high at the panels on economic issues.

On a panel on Freedom of Information, Soviets saw American speakers from the Central Intelligence Agency (CIA) and a corporate lawyer outnumber a public interest lawyer. On a panel on Economic Crimes, the Soviets saw three corporate lawyers. Similarly, many of the Soviet speakers were élites and former *nomenklatura*, presenting the new ideologies of forming a "new business class" and trading currency on international markets.

"Stock ownership includes the right to vote," American securities lawyers told Soviet lawyers. "Widows have no fraud to fear from securities markets . . . there are thousands and thousands of widows in the U.S. with stock and retired people living very well off of dividends and stock."

"Widows are defrauded in stock sales," a state attorney general argued, challenging a panelist's view of stock markets. The audience represented a much larger cross section of lawyers, which actively asked questions and corrected the panelists, both on the U.S. and Soviet sides; but their voice was relegated to reacting defensively. "Home rule cities is an idea we have for giving more power to cities," the Mayor of Austin explained in a supplement to a panel on federalism.

"This is very good theater but we are economically illiterate," complained one Soviet lawyer at a presentation on Soviet economic reforms that she believed painted a utopian view the Americans wanted to hear, but which had nothing to do with Soviet reality. In another session, a Soviet lawyer who headed a society for two million poor families and had started a lawsuit spoke about how General Prosecutor Sukharev, one of the conference's keynote speakers, had never answered his pleas for assistance.

In many cases, the average lawyers in the audience listening to the panels realized that there were two groups of high status lawyers, each presenting what appeared to be a distorted view of reality, with both being rewarded with new status and prestige by the conference. At the same time, there was no way for the average Soviet and American lawyers to talk with each other or to have an exchange on common problems. They knew little about each other. They did not have their own translators. Their only times and places to exchange ideas were during the last few minutes of the panel presentations, which were reserved less for discussions than for questions of the panelists.

CORPORATE LAWYERS AND FOUNDATIONS

American foundations and law firms echoed government and quasi-governmental efforts to "assist" in legal reform in Russia. It appeared that most of that effort also directly rebounded to the benefit of large institutional clients of those firms rather than toward promoting governmental accountability or individual rights in Russia.

The largest program of assistance for training Soviet lawyers was conducted by the American Bar Association with financial support from the Soros Foundation, headed by George Soros, a Hungarian-born millionaire. In 1989–90, there were 17 Soviet lawyers in the United States working alongside American lawyers. The *New York Times* reported that the goal of the program was "to aid Soviet systemic change." The places that the lawyers worked represented one type of change. Interns worked in corporate law firms — Cleary, Gottlieb, Steen and Hamilton; Arnold and Porter; Millbank, Tweed; and others. The *Times* noted that "several hinted that they would put their new skills to use . . . in easing business dealings between the two countries."[34] Few, if any, worked alongside consumer lawyers or civil rights lawyers, in class action suits, or in other types of law where there were holes in the Soviet legal system.

Weyman Lundquist of Heller, Ehrman, White and McAuliffe, indicated openly that his firm's hope was "to develop and groom interns to represent its clients in the Soviet Union." They were considering keeping their intern on retainer upon his return to Moscow.

Like government monies, the more than $100,000 spent annually on this program, if applied directly in the Soviet Union, would have been enough to build several new law schools and educate thousands of lawyers. Instead, it went for business contacts for American firms. Although Soros gave money to be allocated directly in Leningrad (St. Petersburg) for purposes identified by individuals there, the money went for theaters, visiting delegations, and charities but not for structural changes. It was not until 1996 that the foundation first began even to make contacts with the law schools, and the programs it had in mind had yet to address the range of needs of Russia's citizens and community groups.

Besides conferences, there were also more long-term interactions as the early contacts began to turn into more permanent activities. Several small branches of major U.S. corporate law firms were beginning to open in Moscow. By 1990, the U.S. Embassy estimated that there were about 20 to 30 American lawyers working in the city. Coudert Brothers, the largest, opened the first U.S. legal office at the beginning of 1988.

Although it is difficult to estimate the influence these lawyers had from the beginning, they did have some in areas where there were potential conflicts of interest. Despite Coudert's representation of large multinational corporate clients, the government turned to them for advice in drafting antitrust laws.

PUBLIC INTEREST LAWYERS

In comparison to the status and economic power that government and corporate lawyers commanded, public interest lawyers visiting Russia with warnings for the Russian public had little chance to be heard.

Consumer advocate Ralph Nader visited Moscow in June of 1990. In introducing him, Nader's hosts described him as "the last person of any importance to be invited to the U.S.S.R."

The message that Nader brought was a strong one, and in stark opposition to those being delivered by U.S. government lawyers, by corporate lawyers, and by the Russian media. "The market system is just another system of power. . . . More accountability through competition [is only partially true. Shared monopolies are likely to arise in which the only competition is] psychological excitement generated by advertising," he told small audiences in Moscow and a televised audience in an interview with Vladimir Posner (then working in Russia for Soviet television). "Ownership does not mean control," he warned, and pointed to the powerlessness of most shareholders, pension fund owners, and bank depositors. "People who already have power gain experience in concentrating it because they work at it every day."

Nader's words seemed to make little or no difference to his audience. Nader told those who were benefiting most from the new market reforms and joint ventures that they should oppose them for the good of their society. "Do not become an imitative culture," Nader told researchers who were wearing Western business suits and receiving invitations for meetings that paid in hard currency that were sponsored by foreign corporations and offered travel abroad. One researcher who listened to Nader jumped up afterwards to denounce him to a colleague.

In a sense, Nader was really just another part of the one-to-one mapping of what he termed "mass consumer culture" onto Russian culture.
Instead of calling for structural reforms that would have changed the
nature of the system toward which Russia was moving, Nader called for
the addition of a new lobbying group representing consumers and the
introduction of referenda, a direct but low-content form of participation.
He presented no advice on how Russians should defend themselves
against the "organized and sensual appeals — color, sight, sound, sex" of
mass consumer culture.[35]

THE IMPACT OF THE WEST — TWISTING
THE MYTHS OF "DEMOCRACY" AND
THE "FREE MARKET" FOR CONTROL

The impact of these contacts and those that have followed was to begin
to replicate features of the American system within the mold of Russian
authoritarianism. Besides facilitating the process of foreign investment
and the flight of capital and intellectual resources (a brain drain of scientists and professionals) to the West, the myths of America that were being
presented within Russia and the particular pieces of the American system
that were copied in the Russian context had the effect of strengthening the
control of local élites and of newly emerging élites rather than building
democracy. Because America had its own control system in place —
though a different one from that existing under Soviet rule — areas in
which Western "market" and political controls were more effective
became areas that élites could adopt for social control in Russia and still
claim legitimacy on the international scene and within Russia.

Federalism, separation of powers, the shielding of the secret police and
the military from direct scrutiny, the use of government force, the shielding of economic institutions under the guise of "privatization," and the
selling of the justice system to the highest bidders as part of the "free market" ideology were all means by which American concepts of democracy
and law were copied into the Russian context and used, ironically, as blud-
geons of control.

At the national level, though much of their authority had already disin-
tegrated, Russians used the American concept of federalism as a means of
justifying military action to prevent the Republics from becoming independent, of continuing Russian influence within them once they were, and
of maintaining Russia's grip on its own minority regions. "The United
States did not allow secession of the southern states," was the argument
that many Russians began to offer as early as 1989 and later when it

declared war on the Chechens. "Keeping the union together was necessary for its economic strength." Other Russians pointed to Abraham Lincoln as a major American hero because of his use of the United States' military to destroy the Confederacy of southern states and to assert central authority. In the Russian context, federalism was not a philosophy of autonomy and protection of difference, but a means of legitimizing the bringing of minority peoples into the dominant society.

The second bedrock of American twentieth century political ideology, that of separation of powers, was used in the Russian context not to define new powers of citizens and controls over military, political, or economic bureaucracies. Instead it was used only by the leaders of those institutions to justify their attempts to coordinate their own power with new legitimacy. The new Russian constitution of 1993, as well as those of the former Soviet republics, was based on Western constitutional models developed at a time when power and wealth were widely distributed among citizens (for example, eighteenth-century America), in which it was enough to detail government powers without addressing the powers of citizens. Like the Stalin constitution of 1936, the new constitutions merely listed a series of unenforceable rights.[36] What made them different from the Stalinist constitutions was that they did so using the Western rhetoric.

The renamed KGB and other security organs also used the symbol of the United States to justify their existence. "What's bad about working for the KGB?" one KGB lawyer elected to a regional Council was quoted in the local press as saying. "President Bush worked for the CIA." Similarly, those who favored retaining the almost unlimited powers and secrecy of the Russian secret police pointed to the United States, where accountability of the CIA and FBI was limited to oversight by committees of the U.S. Congress. Shortly after the Iran-Contra investigations, in which it became public knowledge that these organizations conducted their own operations with little Congressional oversight, the KGB proposed the same oversight from the Supreme Soviet, based on the U.S. model, as an indication of its willingness to be "subject to" civilian authority.[37] As early as 1989, when KGB officials were challenged, they would point to the United States, set up a public relations office, and agree to meet with elected officials as the extent of their responsibility. The police state apparatus in Russia remains immune from public control and monitoring, and is as strong or stronger than before. It is now responsible only to a leader elected in a single vote of some 100 million Russians and legitimized by law.

Similar to the justification of an unaccountable secret police is justification for use of the regular Russian police forces in maintaining public order. The day before an expected demonstration in 1990, Leningrad television news ran a story on procedures in America for the right of assembly, explaining how obtaining permits from the police, having the police at demonstrations, and being subject to arrest for being out of order were consistent with "democracy." This was said to be a radical reversal from stories in the past that had condemned actions of the U.S. government and police forces as violations of human rights. Earlier footage had shown American police beating up or shooting demonstrators in the late 1960s and early 1970s, sometimes at the order of the U.S. Attorney General or state governors and city mayors, without being subject to sanction despite claims of a democratic process. Indeed, these activities only presaged President Boris Yeltsin's disbanding of and military attack on the elected Russian parliament and on political demonstrators who opposed him in 1993, resulting in the deaths and jailings of hundreds of Russians but having little effect among U.S. leaders, the U.S. press, or Western lending institutions in continuing to call him a champion of democracy and Russia's best hope and to do everything possible to promote his hold on power.

Although violent crime in the United States is ten times that in Russia, even now, and the "State" has become outwardly nonviolent (Soviet police did not carry guns; in 1991 there were almost twice as many inmates per 1,000 citizens in American prisons than there were in the Soviet Union), recent popular films and television commentaries began in 1989 to use the example of the death penalty and the heavy arming of U.S. police as justification to a return to police state enforcement in the country. Indeed, this was the message of one of the most popular films in 1989–90, "Tak Zhit Nelzya" (No way to live) narrated by one of the country's most popular nationalist television personalities, Alexander Nevzorov, and opening with a discussion with New York city police.

Within the legal profession itself, market concepts quickly took hold, but to the detriment of rights. The Russians quickly introduced the concept of "privatization" of justice into the one place where it was most inappropriate, access to lawyers, which had before been viewed as a public good. Legal services are now being sold in the Russian marketplace rather than equitably allocated to the citizenry, while legal reformists in St. Petersburg are moving to change legal education in order to create a legal system that will convince Western business that their investments will be secure. Those that have the most money — institutions, foreign businesses, and organized crime — can now purchase the most justice, while ordinary Russians have little access.

This, and the model of regulating legal services through a professional monopoly, was also justified by reference to the United States, particularly to the monopoly on legal services of the American Bar Association. "There is a rich historical soil in Russia for helping the poor," the Deputy Chair of the Union of Soviet Defense Lawyers and of the Moscow Kollegiia explained in 1990. "There were many pre-Revolutionary lawyers who fought for justice. We don't want to impose any standards that would require lawyers to serve the poor and needy." How they were doing this was not clear. His model for providing legal services was the United States, where in the previous ten years, the amount of legal services provided for the poor, either by government or by private initiative, had almost disappeared. "There will be lawyers like in America, like in the Dustin Hoffman movie, 'Justice for All,' who defend clients without an interest in salary but out of a belief in justice." The Defense Bar, however, would take no steps to encourage them.

CONVINCING THE PUBLIC

Although these new structural changes, linkages, and élite activities, coupled with a new set of myths, were presented to the public by those who most benefited from them, they were believed because they fit with the public's deepest hopes, despite the reality.

A national survey in the Soviet Union in 1990 found that the public favored "capitalism" to "communism" by 51 percent to 32 percent, and when asked to name their favorite country, 32 percent picked the United States.[38] Of those majorities, it is unlikely that more than 1 percent had ever visited the countries they named, spent any time in any countries called "capitalist," or knew what it really was in a modern industrial system, yet they believed that life in a capitalist system could be a kind of paradise and that prosperity awaited them if they had faith in it.

With the acts of Western influence came not just passive acceptance but active belief. The Russians adopted a new set of beliefs and heroes from the West, from Henry Ford to Ronald Reagan. These beliefs reached the status of myth and magic, replacing direct experience and rational thought. Russians had little objective basis on which to make judgments because they had never been to the West and had little contact with it. They knew little about economics or Western cultures. What little they knew was what was presented to them on television or in movies or in their press — mere images. Although they had learned a set of concepts and facts about the West in their education that focused on the West's inequities and problems, it was the idealized positive image of the West they sought to justify.

In a short time, America, Germany, and Japan — once Russia's enemies — suddenly became its great source of hope. "In America, human
rights are openly trampled," was a slogan many remembered learning in
school. In 1990, they laughed that they could have been taught such
things. Russians ridiculed the 1930s children's rhyme about "Mister
Twister," the American millionaire, banker, friend of presidents, and
bigot, who came for a holiday in Leningrad and was a stereotypical rich
imperialist. They believed that such Americans no longer existed and
never really had. Everything had changed. The fear of talking with Americans or even marrying one (the fear that one's relatives might lose their
jobs) was starting to give way. Everything Russians saw in the media or
were taught about the West was a reversal of what had come before.

In a sense, the new belief was much like the "cargo cults" of Pacific
Islanders. In the Pacific, the "great birds" (planes) had once landed and
disgorged white men with fire sticks, carrying gifts. Years later, islanders
would still go out to the landing sites and pray for the return of the great
birds, to leave gifts. During the perestroika era, decades after most Western capitalists had left Russia, their return was eagerly awaited. "Let's
become a free economic zone," said an old man in Siberia. "Sell the
forests. Sell the coal, the minerals, the gold, the diamonds. Let the West
take what they want. Let them come in and give us what we need to start
over. Bring us medical services for the old."

Russians continually queried visitors (generally upwardly mobile,
well-to-do white Americans with the resources to travel to Russia or affil-
iated with organizations with the resources to pay their way) about the life
of the "average American." They sought to justify a view of how much
better the "average American" lived than the "average Russian," and to
link that with a kind of magic formula that the Russians could copy.

Among the comparative statistics about private homes and private
automobiles and consumer goods were others that Russians liked to cite.
They talked about how polls showed that Americans were "happier."
They quoted an economic statistic that showed that 80 percent of production costs in the United States went to workers while only 30 percent of
production costs in the Soviet Union did, and used this to make the infer-
ence that workers were more valued.

Certainly, the standard of living (consumer goods, leisure, life
expectancy) was higher in the United States than in the Soviet Union.
Any statistic made clear that it was, in the same way that the living stan-
dards under Scandinavian socialism were higher than in the United States.
The difference between the comparison between Russia and the United
States, and the United States and Scandinavia, was that for the Russians,

the comparison with the United States contained a belief that there was some way just to wish for improvement and to get it, or that leaders or outsiders would bring it, or that "capitalism" and "white, middle, and upper middle class America" were somehow one and the same and part of a magic formula.

The questions never moved on to the steps necessary to achieve the vision; that is, what government or individuals could do on a microlevel. They never asked about the other America; the capitalist economies of Guatemala or Honduras or Mexico or El Salvador and their histories with the United States or even about "the other America" within U.S. borders. Conversations repeated the limited vision they had, over and over, and linked it to simple slogans like "private property," without explanation of who would have ownership and control, and how they would use it, or what the individual would do to produce more than before. "We wish we had your problems in the United States and would gladly trade ours," they would say.

Part of their belief was that improvement was inevitable because Americans and Russians, or Russians and Europeans, in general, were of the same "soul." "Americans are the same as we are, and we have always loved them, more than any other peoples," Russians would say. The British were said to be cold, the Asians were said to be detail oriented, the Africans were viewed as primitive. When Russians referred to Americans, it was a pristine vision of peoples of European origin. Russians never really defined what the commonality of soul was that they felt with Americans, though they pointed to MTV, films, rock music, authors like Salinger, and to America's military power. The commonality some seemed to find was in military strength and alienation.

The Russian belief in mutability — that they could change into "Americans" merely with the change of leadership — was symbolized best in the film, "We Can't Live Like This." To draw the comparison between the material poverty of Russia and the availability of consumer goods in the West, the film switches scenes between the Exhibit of Achievements of the People's Economy (V.D.N.Kha.) in Moscow and the everyday exhibit of economic achievements in what was West Germany — a typical urban shopping district. At the end of the film, when the Berlin wall is chiseled away and East Germans run across into West Germany to the audience's cheers, the impression created is that the two sides of the wall, stretching from America on the one side to Siberia on the other, are really the same. As a brick wall determined that one half of Germany would become economically weaker than another though the people on both sides were the same, the film echoes the belief that removing the wall and changing a few policies would make Russians as prosperous as Americans were in the 1980s, a belief they were eager to hear.

It was this mythical view that allowed surface changes to occur without any appropriate legal or regular safeguards; with a new found belief in the myth of private ownership in a country that had no mechanisms for giving those without capital (non-Party and non-Mafia) access to ownership or oversight; a belief resulting in adoption of a political economy of positive wage incentives for the more than 90 percent who have no private property and no access to capital and who can find work, in a structure of coordinated monopolies, and whose legal and political rights reflect the same distribution.

This was the new Russian system of law and politics; one in its essence increasingly similar to the American model, but in terms of rights and accountability, also not that different, qualitatively, from what had existed in Russia in the previous thirty years. Although there are harsher terms to describe what was occurring, they are probably justified. The process was similar to those that had occurred in Latin America, something that one scholar referred to in a series of case studies as "legal imperialism."[39]

This was the process of "Pepsi-Stroika" — American influence in the restructuring of Russia.

NOTES

This research was conducted on a fellowship from the University of California in 1989–90 as part of an exchange with Leningrad (St. Petersburg) State University. Support for initial write-up of the material was provided by the Harvard University Russian Research Center and by the Harvard Ukrainian Research Institute.

An earlier version of this chapter, "Pepsi-Stroika: American Cultural Influence on the Russian Political and Legal System" appeared in the *Legal Studies Forum*, 20(3) (Fall 1996).

1. From field observations and interviews conducted between 1989 and 1990. Much of the material in this chapter is original ethnographic research taken from larger studies described below.

2. Andrew Lowenstein, David Brody, Gowen H. McCoy, and Janice Arthur McCoy, "Doing Business Under Perestroika," *The Stanford Business School Magazine*, October 1989, p. 21.

3. From a speech by Thomas Pickering, U.S. ambassador to Russia, at an American Chamber of Commerce luncheon in Moscow, "For the Record," *The Washington Post*, October 22, 1996.

4. V. I. Lenin, Third Congress of the Communist International, 1921.

5.   The net effect of Western policy of economic and political "reform" of the former Soviet Union has been to drain capital from the former Empire into Western banks with little notice. At the same time, great attention has been given to the little that has been sent back in return in the form of "aid."

Izvestia reported that already in 1992 between $55 and $180 billion — as much as half of Russia's annual gross national product — had already been taken out of the country. (*Izvestia*, April 7, 1992, p. 3, in Current Digest of the Soviet Press 44:14 [17:1].) This was said to include 90 percent of the country's historical treasures. (*Izvestia*, February 12, 1993, p. 5, in Current Digest of the Soviet Press 45:6 [12:1].) The *Washington Post* reported that $11 to $15 billion was placed in Swiss Bank accounts in 1993 and confirmed that the amount in Swiss banks was at least $30 billion. (Hobart Rowen, "Lending Agencies Should Shift Focus to Eastern Europe, Old Soviet Empire," *Washington Post*, February 27, 1994, p. H 13.)

Compare this benefit to Western economies with the amount going in the form of loan and grant assistance; what Harvard economist and World Bank consultant Jeff Sachs estimated at only $3 billion (Jeff Sachs, "The IMF's Phony Figures on Aid to Russia," *Washington Post*, March 4, 1994, p. A 23) and which by World Bank accounts is no more than $38 billion — most of it in "debt relief" rather than in actual transfer of funds! (S. J. Anjaria, "The IMF's Financial Flow to Russia," *Washington Post*, March 11, 1994.)

By 1996, major U.S. publications were no longer making a pretext that the World Bank and the International Monetary Fund were using their leverage to influence the country's politics in a way that would be favorable to Western economic interests. A story in the *New York Times*, for example, boldly reported that "A large I.M.F. loan [of more than $1 billion before the June 1996 Russian presidential election] is designed to give Yeltsin an election year boost" (Michael R. Gordon, "Russia Drops Big Tariff Increase, Clearing Way for an I.M.F. Loan," *New York Times*, March 26, 1996, p. 1). Several weeks after the election, the loan disbursements slowed to a trickle.

6.   See, for example, Louis Uchitelle, "In the New Russia, an Era of Takeovers," *New York Times*, April 17, 1994, Section 3, p. 1; Paul Klebnikov, "Russia — the Ultimate Emerging Market," *Forbes*, February 14, 1994, p. 88, for an explanation of how Western advice on privatization without any safeguards, has reconcentrated power under the guise of "privatization."

For a more detailed explanation of the process, see *The New Republic*, April 4, 1994.

7.   Noam Chomsky, *Deterring Democracy*. London: Verso, 1991.

8.   Andre Gunder Frank, James D. Cochroft, and Dale L. Johnson, *Dependence and Underdevelopment: Latin America's Political Economy*. Garden City, N.Y.: Anchor Books, 1972.

9.   Immanuel Wallerstein, "An Historical Perspective: The Emergence of the New Economic Order," in *The Capitalist World Economy*. Cambridge: Cambridge University Press, 1979.

10.   Robert Reich, *The Work of Nations: Preparing Ourselves for 21st Century Capitalism*. New York: Alfred Knopf, 1991.

11.   See David Lempert, "Changing Russian Political Culture in the 1990s: Parasites, Paradigms, and Perestroika," *Comparative Studies in Society and History*, 35(3) (July 1993): 628–46.

12.   See David Lempert, *Daily Life in a Crumbling Empire: The Absorption of Russia into the World Economy*, Eastern European Monograph Series. New York: Columbia University Press, 1996.

13.   Harold J. Berman, "Gorbachev's Law Reforms in Historical Perspective," in Albert Schmidt, ed. *Impact of Perestroika on Soviet Law*. Boston, Mass.: Martinus Nijhoff, 1990.

14.   Esther Kingston-Mann, 1991. "In the Light and Shadow of the West: The Impact of Western Economics in Pre-Emancipation Russia," *Comparative Studies in Society and History*, 33(1): 86–105.

15.   Esther Kingston-Mann, seminar at Harvard, November 7, 1991.

16.   Kingston-Mann, 1991, p. 96.

17.   Alexander Gershenkron, "Problems and Patterns of Russian Economic Development," in Cyril Black, ed., *The Transformation of Russian Society: Aspects of Social Change Since 1861*. Cambridge, Mass.: Harvard University Press, 1960, pp. 42–71.

18.   D. Von Laue, *Why Lenin? Why Stalin?: A Reappraisal of the Russian Revolution, 1900–1930*. New York: Lippincott, 1971.

19.   Alexander Yanov, *Drama of the Soviet 1960s: A Lost Reform*, Stephen P. Dunn, ed., Berkeley, Calif.: Institute of International Studies, 1984. Current revisions of American history of the early 1960s suggest that almost parallel developments in the two countries resulted in military backlashes against reformist leaders, prolonging the Cold War for a generation and severely depleting the resources of both countries and much of the Third World. (See Peter Dale Scott, Paul L. Hoch, and Russel Stetler, eds., *Assassinations: Dallas and Beyond*. New York: Random House, 1976.) As I. F. Stone wrote the week of President Kennedy's assassination, "Khrushchev, like Kennedy, seems to suffer from an internal opposition in his own bureaucracy which would like to trip up better Russian-American relations" (*I.F. Stone Weekly*, November 25, 1963).

20.   Joseph Finder, *The Red Carpet*. New York: Holt, Rinehart and Winston, 1983.

21.   Richard J. Barnet and Ronald E. Müller, *Global Reach: The Power of the Multinational Corporations*. New York: Simon and Schuster, 1974.

22.   See *New York Times*, April 25, 1990, for this characterization of the work.

23.   For an explanation of how the process worked on the Soviet side, see Simon Johnson and Heidi Kroll, "Managerial Strategies for Spontaneous Privatization," *Soviet Economy*, 7(4) (1991): 281–316.

24.   One lawyer and deputy in the Ukrainian Parliament even went so far as to advertise his business services combined with his political position in open

letters to Harvard scholars.

25. Letter to author from Peter Maggs, December 10, 1990.

26. Wendell Wilkie, III, Moscow Conference on Law and Cooperation, Kremlin, July 1990.

27. Paul Desruisseaux, "U.S. Plans Fellowship for Graduate Students from Former U.S.S.R.," *The Chronicle of Higher Education*, March 11, 1992, p. A. 35.

28. For the paper trail of how U.S. government policies and those of the World Bank continued to support rapid privatization, long after the results of the policies of privatization — as a wholesale theft of the Soviet economy — were not only clear but were even being reported in the Western press, see the U.S. Agency for International Development's "Requests for Proposals" for "Democratization," "Rule of Law," and "Economic Restructuring" through which the millions of dollars of assistance were allocated (mostly to Western consultants).

A recent RFP, OP/CC/N-94-2 (beginning in late 1994), for Technical Assistance in Support of the Privatization and Economic Restructuring Program for Europe and the New Independent States, supposedly designed to "strengthen the legal, fiscal, regulatory and institutional policy framework" for economic restructuring, sought only three legal specialists for every seven investment bankers, financial analysts, or accountants who would encourage privatization and outweighed lawyers with support for the propaganda role to "encourage the general public to support and participate actively in the privatization programs" through "media campaigns" rather than through oversight or judicial mechanisms.

Earlier USAID contracts in 1991 noted that if there were conflicts between rapid privatization and privatization only after anti-monopoly safeguards, that privatization should go ahead without the safeguards.

29. See the "Peace, Prosperity and Democracy Act of 1994" or the Congressional Presentation of the USAID Fiscal Year 1995 budget. as summarized in Society for International Development, "USAID Offers Perspectives on Foreign Assistance Act and FY95 Budget," *Development Connections*, 14(8) (April 1994): 1.

30. In 1994, a major USAID contract for civic education was given to the Academy for Educational Development whose ideas for in-country training, in order to have greater impact, were changed by USAID.

31. William Shawcross, *Sideshow: Kissinger, Nixon and the Destruction of Cambodia*. New York: Simon and Schuster, 1979.

32. U. S. Bureau of the Census. *Statistical Abstract of the United States*. Washington, D.C.: U. S. Department of Commerce, 1990.

33. John Gardner, *In Common Cause*. New York: W. W. Norton, 1972, p. 66.

34. Felicity Barringer, "Soviet Lawyers in Odyssey Through U.S. Law," *New York Times*, December 8, 1989, p. B. 24.

35.   In more recent speeches in Eastern Europe (for example, an address to the Law Reform Programs Workshop at the Constitutional and Legislative Policy Institute of the Soros Foundation's Open Society Institute in Budapest, Hungary, October 14–16, 1995) and in his 1996 presidential campaign, Nader has seemed to recognize the need for more effective structural reforms.

For an example of such a model, see David Lempert, *A Return to Democracy: The Modern Democracy Amendments*, unpublished book manuscripts, 1987, 1993, and 1996.

36.   See David Lempert, "The Proposed Constitution of Ukraine: Continuity Under the Banner of Change, With a Model for Authoritarian to Democratic Transitions," *Demokratizatsiya*, 2(2) (Spring 1994): 268.

37.   Seymour Martin Lipset, "Politics and Society in the U.S.S.R.: A Traveller's Report," *P.S.: Political Science and Politics*, March 1990, p. 23.

38.   Lipset, "Politics and Society in the U.S.S.R."

39.   John Gardner, *Legal Imperialism: American Lawyers and Foreign Aid in Latin America*. Madison: University of Wisconsin Press, 1980.

Young Hungarians, Then and Now. A Hungarian teen sporting a Native American Mohawk haircut gives a thumbs up sign on a site of Roman ruins in Buda. At right, the depiction of one of his ancestors, during the time of the Roman conquest. Courtesy of David Lempert.

Ronald McDonald Engulfs the Children of Pest. To capture the Hungarian food service market, McDonald's begins with the children, enveloped here in a play cage outside a McDonald's eatery as their parents look on. Courtesy of David Lempert.

All Roads Lead to . . . American Fast Food. In the middle of Vorosmarty tér in central Pest, American multi-nationals have taken over public spaces and communications with directions to their services. Courtesy of David Lempert.

Competing Ideals of Womanhood. A feminine ideal, according to the American "Eskimo" ice cream company, vies for attention with the German frau in a beer ad, on billboards outside an abandoned warehouse in Pest. Courtesy of David Lempert.

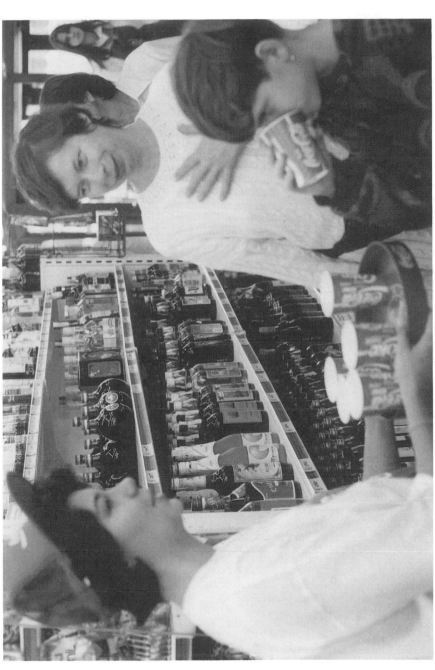

Hooking the Next Generation. Coca Cola pushes its non-nutritive carbonated water to Hungary's children in Pest's groceries, before parents can weigh the consequences. Courtesy of David Lempert.

High Rises. Highest on the Buda landscape, above Roman ruins and socialist tenaments are American advertisements and billboards like these, on apartment houses. Courtesy of David Lempert.

Role Models? A Hungarian girl, in an American flag design jacket, looks at the latest display of toy adult figures in Pest's "Royal" store: Barbie and Ken dolls and action figures. Courtesy of David Lempert.

5

Youth Culture and Lifestyle in Modern Greece

Mike-Frank G. Epitropoulos and Victor Roudometof

The proliferation of U.S. cultural influence has raised issues concerning the extent to which it signifies a movement toward a "global culture" (Featherstone 1990) or, alternatively, whether the world becomes increasingly "Westernized." The most sinister of these scenarios claims that the cultural distinctiveness of particular locales is under siege by the forces of Western "cultural imperialism" (Greenwood 1972: 80–91; 1977: 129–38; Schiller 1976; see Tomlinson 1991 for a critical assessment). In this chapter we will address an issue that these debates most often ignore, namely the possibility of a degree of *cultural syncretism*. By doing so, we do not imply that the aforementioned concerns are not valid, but rather we attempt to exemplify the complex nature of issues surrounding cultural contact and social transformation.

We use the domain of Greek youth culture as a site that makes it possible to observe the effects of American (and more generally Western European) cultural products on Greek society and also the interaction between American and indigenous culture, as well as the fundamental ambivalence that characterizes the outcome of this interaction. It should be clear from the outset that our investigation aims to inquire into the "Western" aspects of Greek culture and as such, it pertains only to a limited domain. Modern Greece has been characterized by a lively indigenous national folk culture with its own symbols (singers, poets, literary figures, and very distinguished leisure patterns), and the reader should not interpret our discussion as an attempt to describe the totality of the Greek lifestyle (for a general discussion see Chouliaras 1993). Instead, we have decided to focus on that domain of cultural activity that most prominently displays the signs of an American cultural influence. Our attempt is to render this phenomenon accountable in the context of modern Greek experience and demonstrate the various uses of American and Western European culture in the Greek context.

THE POST–WORLD WAR II TRANSFORMATION OF GREEK SOCIETY

Traditional Greek society has been marked by the absence of an industrial working class, with small shopkeepers, civil servants, professionals, the self-employed, and peasants constituting the majority of the population (Lambiri-Dimaki 1983; Mouzelis & Attalides 1971: 165–97; Mouzelis 1978; Tsoukalas 1987; Petmezidou-Tsoulouvi 1987; Diamantouros 1983: 43–69). Until 1945, peasantry was the dominant segment of the population and the basic institutions shaping individual identity were, and to some extent still are, the kinship structure and the Greek Orthodox religion (McNeill 1978). During the post–World War II period, Greece has been transformed from an agricultural to an urban society, a change mainly achieved through nontraditional sources of wealth — that is, tourism and the flow of foreign currency from the Greek immigrants in West Germany, Australia, or the United States (McNeill 1978; Ioakimidis 1984: 33–60; McNall 1974a, 1974b: 46–63, 1976: 28–42). The resulting increase in the standard of living led to a prevailing consumerism (Vergopoulos 1985: 92–130; Karapostolis 1984).

During the same period, a great wave of internal migration altered the traditional setting resulting in a population explosion of the metropolitan areas of Athens and Thessaloniki (the two major cities of the country). This wave of urbanization altered the traditional spatial division from one between rural areas versus metropolis to one among rural areas, provincial towns, and metropolises (Lambiri-Dimaki 1983: 184–86). The metropolitan areas of Athens and Thessaloniki are excluded from the current discussion because their size and cosmopolitan character differentiate them significantly from the rest of the country. Instead, attention is focused on the smaller provincial towns and the rural areas affected by urbanization. Many rural areas were deserted and only a minority of them have been revitalized as tourist resorts (especially the islands of Corfu, Mykonos, Crete, and Rhodes).

Concommitant with these spatial and socioeconomic changes, a process of cultural change occurred as well. The key feature of the traditional Greek culture has been a powerful ingroup versus outgroup division in which all those who fall within the group are "our" people (*dikoi mas*) whereas all those who fall outside the boundaries of the group are foreigners (*xenoi*) (Campbell 1964, 1983: 184–207; de Boulay, 1974; Dimen & Friedl, 1976; Pollis 1965: 29–47; Vassiliou & Vassiliou 1973: 326–34; Triandis & Vassiliou 1972: 299–335; Dubisch 1986; Kataki 1984). The key concept linked with this form of collectivism has been that of *philotimo*, the sense of one's family honor and esteem (Herzfeld 1986: 215–34). Loyalty is reinforced only within the group where the value of *philotimo* is upheld. In the post–World War II period, the Greek family has continued to be the dominant institution, thus remaining "a rather passive agent in social change and in most cases, a conservative one" (Gizelis et al. 1984: 131). In Greece, the state and other public institutions operate on the basis of particularistic criteria (clientelism) that reinforce dependency upon kinship. The family constitutes a socioeconomic unit that assumes the responsibility of finding suitable employment for its offspring even if this requires a prolonged period of time (Tsoukalas 1986: 163–204). Traditionally, very few young people used to live on their own, and in the postwar period students have been the only group of young people that has the opportunity of living outside the family household. The economic and emotional dependency on the family and its patriarchic structure are factors that contribute to the perpetuation of the traditional value system. The family is the main agent responsible for the transmission of the traditional values from one generation to another. The key difficulty in the life cycle of young people is making the transition to a state of maturity, and this difficulty is attributed to their chronic dependency upon the kin group (Tselika 1991; Lipovatch 1988: 86–107; Petmezidou-Tsoulouvi 1987).

During the past thirty years, Greek society, as other semiperipheral states in the world system, has become increasingly enmeshed in a process of globalization that brings different cultures and communities into close contact with each other (Robertson 1992). Tourism, the impact of immigrants returning home after being exposed to Western culture, and the impact of mass media have contributed to the society's increasing cultural contact with American and Western European cultural items (music, clothes, varieties of food and drink, and attitudes). Leisure is the area where cultural changes of this type can most easily be identified. As more young people gain a degree of economic independence from the kin group, they tend to demonstrate it in their leisure time. In fact, during the past twenty years, a distinctive "youth culture" manifested itself rendering visible a "generation gap" between the older World War II generation and the new generation that grew up during the transformation period following the war (Lambiri-Dimaki 1983: 32–44). By youth culture we mean "the particular pattern of beliefs, values, symbols, and activities that a group of young people are seen to share" (Frith 1984: 8). In terms of beliefs and values, in recent years a shift has occurred in the values of the youth from collectivism toward individualism (Kataki 1984; Georgas 1989: 89–98; see also Gardiki et al. 1987, 1988). For our purposes, attention is focused on the symbols and the activities of the youth. The issue is whether this distinct youth culture that revolves around Western cultural artifacts and modes of leisure reflects a pattern of growing Westernization of lifestyle (for a theoretical discussion, see Featherstone 1991).

In the following, we describe the cultural transformation of two settings, an urban and a rural one, in an attempt to explicate the social changes involved in the emergence of Greek youth culture and account for the fascination a significant number of the Greek youth display toward Western cultural artifacts. Studies of Western European and American youth culture focus on the relationship between class and subculture (Hall & Jefferson 1976; Brake 1985; for critiques, see Marsland 1982: 305–22; Allerbeck & Rosenmayr 1979: 7–16; Smith 1981: 239–51). Although the relationship between class and youth culture remains an important one, our research aims to investigate different kinds of problems than the subcultural approach.

Specifically, we examine the places youth have come to spend their leisure time during the past two decades, which in our case are cafes, pubs, video arcades, and discos. These are not the only places where young people go, because there is a lively indigenous folk culture with its own settings. However, according to recent nationwide research by the Greek Center for Social Research (Gardiki et al. 1987, 1988), the majority of teenagers and young adults prefer Western forms of music and entertainment. This tendency is stronger in the metropolitan and urban areas and weaker in rural settings. Moreover, the number of these establishments has increased dramatically during the past two decades. For both rural and urban contexts the methods utilized were participant observation of the leisure sites and in-depth interviewing of participants of the youth culture. In order to compare the 1950s and 1960s settings with current leisure patterns, interviews with older people (over 50 years old) were also conducted as a means to inquire into their own experiences as young adults.[1]

KAVALA: SOCIAL CHANGE
IN AN URBAN CONTEXT

Kavala is one of the provincial towns that has been transformed during the post–World War II period. Kavala is located in Northeastern Greece, a three-hour ride from Thessaloniki. It is the largest city in Northeastern Greece and its population rose from 44,978 in 1961 to 55,390 in 1981 (National Statistical Service of Greece 1963, 1984).

Its 1950s urban context displayed the "traditional" society's typical features, especially with respect to the family's strong authoritarian control over the youth. Schools were segregated and gender communication was officially prohibited and sanctioned. High school teachers were responsible for enforcing these rules and making sure that any deviants would be punished. The main form of leisure, the "walk" (*volta*) in the city's main commercial street, was closely related with the institutions of marriage and family. This activity was related with what the local people called the "brides' bazaar" (*nifopazaro*). In the evenings after closing time, the main commercial street (Omonia Street) became the gathering place of the youth. Four cinemas were located there and also a couple of pastryshops. Movies were a much more important source of entertainment in the 1950s than in the later days because there was no television or recreational establishments with the exception of the restaurants and coffee shops. Going to the movies, however, was not a high priority of the youth in either the 1950s or the 1980s (see Cowan 1990 for an analysis of traditional modes of leisure). Groups of young boys and girls would come down dressed in their Sunday best to walk up and down the street, to exchange looks, and to flirt with each other. Weekends would be the peaks of these activities whereas working days tended to have less "action." In the early 1960s, the native author Vassilis Vasilikos (1966) wrote about the walk and the brides' bazaar: "As night falls, the new portside which is not finished yet — the space has been filled but not leveled up — fills with people who come, next to the docked boats, to take a walk. Formerly . . . the walk took place at the 'brides' bazaar' of Omonia Str. This is Kavala's center street, full of showcases, shops, and pastryshops. The walk always started from Fessas' bakery up to the courthouse. Up and down, up and down, and outside this street, darkness, deserted, and silent tobacco warehouses" (pp. 60–61).

This used to be the place for relations to be created and to flourish, the legitimate place for males and females to meet members of the opposite sex. The young people who would participate in this leisure activity were mainly high school graduates or working young people. Teenagers could not participate in the walk "because it was inconceivable . . . to dress up and go to Omonia at an age of 17 or 18. . . . It was remote . . . out of reach." The following quote summarizes the situation: "When I was 21 years old and had a relationship I did not dare tell my own mother because she would rip out all of my hair, she would abuse me, argue with me, . . . and I was forced [to] say [that I would go] to the cinema or out with a girl-friend . . . and [instead] I was going to see my buddy up in the mountains . . . so my brother would not see me . . . so my neighbor would not see me, and tell my brother or my mother and [then they would] abuse me . . . and then they would beat me to death."

Usually, social control operated in more subtle ways and by and large behind the household's closed doors. The consequences of this system were hypocrisy and secrecy. "We were forced to go to the forests . . . to the rocks on the seashore, to restrooms," an interviewee said to us. To get together with a male companion "a girl would have to tell a lie" in order for the social conventions to be upheld. For the teenagers of the era, especially females, making up an excuse was the only way they could attend a party, the only form of leisure available to them. The practical goal of all these efforts was to impose a norm of sexual morality. A double standard prevailed because females carried the burden of virginity, and young teenagers (especially females) were forbidden to participate in the local brides' bazaar. Once out of high school, however, the status of a person changed from teenager to young adult and one could walk freely on Omonia Street. The walk constituted an activity associated with adulthood, romance, and flirtation. The relationships between the genders were typically male dominated. To sum up, the 1950s urban context demonstrated all the features of the traditional society and did not allow youth to participate in activities other than those designated as the suitable steps toward marriage. The walk and the brides' bazaar were leisure activities that legitimized marriage as a goal in life for young adults, especially females. All activities that assumed a degree of independence from this pattern were sanctioned and social control was rigidly enforced by family members, friends, and persons of authority.

From 1960 to 1980, the urban landscape was dramatically altered as new streets were opened and electricity, water, and telephone services were made available to every household. The construction of a new port in the 1960s was also accompanied by the construction of a new park that came to be the new "hot spot" leisure place. Tobacco warehouses in Kavala were gradually replaced by apartment complexes that came to dominate the urban landscape. Following the rise of the tourist industry in the early 1960s a number of hotels were built in the area close to the park.

These developments marked the beginnings of a spatial differentiation in the leisure patterns of older and younger generations, whereas at the same time there was a rapid decline in the prohibitions imposed upon young people. This establishment of a social space allocated mainly to the youth was a necessary prerequisite for youth culture (Rojek 1989: 191–204). The process accelerated after the fall of the Greek dictatorship in 1974 and reached its peak during the late 1970s and early 1980s. To cite one example, during the dictatorship students were prohibited from wearing blue jeans in high school. The rise in the standard of living offered young people the opportunity to have enough pocket money from their families to enable them to become consumers. In just a few years, from 1979 to 1986, Red Cross Avenue, the street where most of the city's hotels are located, was transformed from a commercial street to a leisure place associated almost exclusively with youth. Pubs, modern-style cafes, video arcades, and other similar establishments flooded the area, which — to borrow a term from Goffman (1967) — became the place "where the action is," which led to the total desertion of Omonia Street. There are at least forty modern-style cafes (*kafeteries*) and pubs within the city, of which the majority are concentrated in the vicinity of Red Cross Avenue. This change in leisure patterns was simultaneous with the establishment of freer communication between the genders and it created a district that thrives off the pocket money of teenagers and young adults.

Establishing a realm of freedom for young people created conflicts between the adults entrusted to enforce the old rules, mainly high school teachers, and the young people. The battleground of this conflict concerned the youths' social activities and promiscuity: "Until 1975 if the principal would see you with a girl, you got expelled. . . . But even until 1978 if you were [seen] on a date you got expelled . . . . A teacher saw one couple [walking] down a small street . . . and [they] got expelled. . . . [Until 1975], if they would see you smoking outside the school you got expelled, then [the prohibition] was only within school limits."

This conflict about the right to do something was previously considered out of reach. Doing something prohibited by the adult world is typical of teenagers; the important aspect of the phenomenon is that the consumption of cultural goods was one of the means employed in this struggle. Thereby, the right to get into a movie theater, the right to meet a girl or a boy, the right to "hang out" together, the right to smoke and consume certain goods such as the right to purchase blue jeans, the right to go to a disco on Saturday night, all became small battlegrounds between teenagers and adults. Most of these small battles were won by the youth in just a few years, a development that indicates a lack of resistance by the adult world. The established "leisure district" is located 200 meters from the port side and occupies approximately a kilometer of Red Cross Avenue alongside the local park. Modern-style cafes and pubs are the establishments that characterize the district.

The distinction between the two is vague. In practical terms, both of them serve liquor and coffee. Contrary to the U.S. experience (Cavan 1966), there are no physical, legal, or social barriers imposed on establishments that serve liquor. Beer is available even from local kiosks and age restrictions do not seem to be enforced. The establishments of the district extend their presence out onto the pavement of the avenue and this feature creates the sociability of the area. Most of the sidewalk in front of each establishment is occupied by tables and chairs that transform the public space into an extension of the establishment. The typical arrangement involves four chairs around a small round table. These outlets are usually covered by a kind of plastic ceiling thus protecting the customers from possible rain. From April until late October, customers can sit either inside the establishment or outside at the aforementioned tables. Typically during the summer season, from May until September, it is the exterior of these places where most people prefer to sit. This practice is referred to as putting "tables outside" the shops (*trapezakia exo*). Because most of the pavement of the district is occupied by these establishments, there is only a short aisle left for those who walk on the street. The conditions for close proximity are thus created.

A modern-style cafe's interior typically consists of a small bar and a number of tables and chairs in an arrangement similar to those outside. Decorations on the walls emphasize bright colors in combinations of red and white. Soft lighting is typical, whereas on the walls, abstract art paintings, reproductions of classical paintings, or pictures of early twentieth century European cafes prevail. Most of these cafes have predominately American popular music in the background. The typical drink in the cafes is not the traditional Turkish coffee but, especially during the summer season, Néscafé frapé, an icy blend of American instant coffee poured over two ice cubes. All the aforementioned features set these places in sharp contrast to the traditional Greek rural cafe (*kafenio*). The traditional cafe is a place where *men* go to drink the traditional Turkish coffee, to chat, and to play cards and backgammon. The modern-style cafes, however, are open to both genders and their overall orientation stands in a sharp semiotic contrast vis-à-vis the traditional establishments. As Cowan (1991: 180–202; 1990: 70–74) suggests, this opening up of the public space to women does not imply the acceptance of women's status as equal to that of men, but, rather that the substitution of the traditional cafe by the

modern-style cafe signifies the intrusion of modernity in places previously untouched by it.

Since 1979 when they first appeared, the cafes of Red Cross Avenue
have acted as an attraction for youth. An interviewee recalls the late 1970s
and early 1980s: "We used to go to the cafe and drink . . . ginger ale or
. . . soda . . . something we considered to be very 'modern.' I mean simple things . . . we considered them very important . . . we did not have the
opportunity to have them on an everyday basis or to consider them something easy."

Weekends were the peaks of this leisure pattern because females had
the opportunity to participate more freely in these activities. In addition to
cafes, discos gained popularity among the youth. There were three discos
in the city during the late 1970s, and two of them were located in the base-
ments of two hotels on Red Cross Avenue. On weekends, they became the
"hot places" for high school students and helped bring together teenagers
of the opposite sex. This does not mean that going to the disco was an
established and acceptable activity. A conservative father might go into
the disco in order to pick up his daughter and reprimand her in public for
being there. These kinds of incidents gradually became less and less common. The obligation of wearing uniforms to school had been abolished
but the restrictions in interaction remained. In the words of an interviewee: "[If] you would see a boy and a girl walking in the port side . . . that
was it . . . [you immediately thought that] . . . he is involved with her."
Communication restrictions between the genders were formally abandoned in the early 1980s with the desegregation of the schools. Desegregation altered the whole pattern of interaction and communication among
teenagers. This change corresponds with the expansion of the cafes on
Red Cross Avenue where more and more teenagers were able to go.
Simultaneously with the expansion of the cafes and the use of discos as
meeting places for the youth, the first pubs opened in the area. By
1980–81 there were already three pubs in the area. These places differed
from the cafes because they targeted a more mature audience. A pub
owner said to us: "The crowd that was gathered there was of all sorts . . .
because everybody wanted to get to know the new, the newly created,
. . . the different . . . this did not have anything to do with the cafe. It was
associated with something 'alien' (xenoferto). . . . When these places
opened they did not know the term 'pub.' . . . This term did not exist in
Greece."

The attraction of the "new," the different, the "alien," targeted a different audience. Young people over twenty, but under thirty-five, have com-
prised the clientele of these places. The pubs have been meeting places for

young people who are not under the control of their families, such as students from the newly-created, local technical school or young people working on their own who are looking for places to socialize. Each pub has developed its own circle of regulars, but a common characteristic of pubs has been the tendency to feature rock and pop music. Pubs tend to open later than the cafes, targeting the over–twenty-five male crowd. Most of them come in peer groups (*paréa*) and tend to develop preferences for this or that establishment. Quality of service, the general environment, the kind of music, and the number of females that show up in a particular establishment are all factors that determine the number of people that will show up in a particular place. Some of them play loud rock music with people hanging around in a way similar to American pubs, whereas others specialize in offering a place more suitable for conversation. Alcohol is the typical drink in these establishments, with hard liquor (whiskey, vodka, or cocktails) being far more popular than beer. The age of the customers ranges from sixteen to thirty-five and it is related to the type of establishment. Teenagers and young adults (around twenty) tend to cluster around a number of cafes located in the center of the district whereas older folks (over twenty) tend to group together in pubs that are located next to them. Although the pubs serve coffee, their clientele tend to show up relatively later than the teenagers and are more likely to order hard liquor than the teenagers.

Pubs and cafes constitute the main places where the everyday sociability of the youth is expressed.[2] Neither of them has equivalents in the traditional Greek context. They are almost exclusively oriented toward the youth — thereby making youth a socially distinct category — and their intrusion into the public space signifies the impact of modernity (and economic development) in the local community. It is not accidental that the first customers of the pubs were young people with a degree of economic independence from their families or students who were far from home. The pub and its adolescent version, the cafe, are places that offer the opportunity for close association among one's peers away from direct family control. They also have the connotations of promiscuity outside the context of marriage and thus defy the traditional norm that sexual relationships and marriage are linked. Not surprisingly, the rise of these establishments did not totally alter the gender roles within the society because the majority of customers continue to be males. Females show up in large numbers during the weekends and usually they do so in the presence of a peer group consisting either exclusively of females or of a mixed composition. However, these establishments signify the acceptance of modernity as a cultural condition that becomes part of the society itself. The young people who were attracted to these places acted under the impulse to familiarize themselves with the modern, a setting that is not traditional and represents a break with former modes of leisure. The speed of this process has been extraordinary. In just a few years, modernity established itself as a permanent condition of everyday life.

The organization of leisure space represents an effort to reproduce Western forms of leisure, but the outcome is a mutation that fuses Western and local elements. The spatial arrangement has been altered from revolving around the traditional piazza, the central square of the city, to that of a four-lane highway along which establishments are located next to one another, a feature that creates the impression of a parody or a caricature of the American architectural form (see Venturi, Brown, & Izenour 1977). Every night, usually between 8:30 and 11:30 P.M., the area is filled with young people with their motorbikes and motorcycles, cars crossing the avenue, neon lights, and the constant sound of the crowd. Most people come down in peer groups of four or five, or they might go to the area by themselves and meet their friends there. There is a communal sense in their sociability; people tend to sit in the company of others and it is extremely rare to see a person alone. People come in to "see and be seen," that is, they are both the audience and the players in the theater of leisure. By sitting in a cafe, there is the possibility of watching the people walking up and down the pavement while the observer is visible to the pedestrians. The metaphor of the theater is suitable for understanding this process and it helps explain the special attention to clothes and the general presentation of oneself that participants, females more often than males, exhibit. Especially during weekends, this mode of sociability represents a modernized, upgraded version of the brides' bazaar. An older interviewee implicitly emphasized this continuity between the two settings by saying to us that "the communication between the sexes did not change . . . [but] the means have changed."

During the summer season, more establishments open up in the city's suburbs and some of the clientele move to them. For example, the two discos located in the area close down and two others, located on the outskirts of the city, take their place. During the past five years, more seasonal establishments have started operating in the city's suburbs during summer months, displaying a temporal character in their infrastructure. Their important advantage is that most of them are located in places that offer spectacular views of the beach and some of them are right on the seashore. The principle that seems to have dictated their creation is the idea of making an establishment as spectacular as possible. Access to these places is somehow restricted because some of them cannot be reached by public transportation. This, however, does not appear to have an impact on the number of young people that show up; there is a constant flow of cars and motorcycles heading out to the suburbs nearly every night from 10:00 P.M. and later.

Both the Red Cross Avenue district and the seasonal establishments are constructed in a way as to offer as much view as possible. This process has led to the transformation of the urban context or the seashore into a "spectacle." The influence of tourism is to be found underneath this process. A "tourist gaze" (Urry 1990) has successfully transformed these sites to places socially defined as "tourist resorts." This has been the case with Red Cross Avenue and the seasonal establishments, with the additional characteristic that these places are targeted not toward outsiders but toward local customers and especially those of young age. For youth, tourism and consumerism have been closely associated with modernity and their "taste" has been shaped by these factors.

KARPATHOS: SOCIAL CHANGE IN A RURAL CONTEXT

Tourism and contact with "foreigners" are also influential factors in the rural context. The Dodekanese island of Karpathos will serve as an example of a rural setting. One of the approximately 3,000 Greek islands in the Aegean sea, Karpathos lies between Crete and Rhodes. The total permanent population of the island is approximately 5,000 inhabitants, but during the summer season this number can swell to even 15,000. Karpathos City (Pigadia) and the villages of Aperi and Menetes, all of them in the south of the island, are the most populous. The island can be seen as characteristic of rural regions of Greece that have not been influenced up until very recently by the tourist industry (for an assessment, see Loukissas 1982: 523–41; for some case studies of particular islands, see Stott 1988: 187–206; Buck-Morss 1987: 200–35). Immediately following World War II, Karpathos, like many other parts of Greece, experienced an exodus of many of its inhabitants to the United States, Australia, Canada, Rhodesia (Zimbabwe), and the Republic of South Africa. This exodus resulted in the expatriates being familiarized with Western culture. Because many of the expatriates did not abandon their communities permanently, continuing to have family ties with the island, they became agents of social change for the traditional context.

In the 1950s, Karpathos was characterized by traditional island lifestyle with agriculture and fishing serving as the main sources of income for the majority of the population. Families' control over youth was strict, and for

young women it was authoritarian in most cases. The traditional conduct
and modes of communication between the genders were policed, with
only the sanctioned social events — saints' feast days (*panigiria*), engage-
ments, weddings, and occasional parties at private homes — providing a
"legitimate" leisure space. As in Kavala, the most common form of day-
to-day leisure was the walk through the traditional piazza, where all of the
rules of the brides' bazaar apply. In the traditional setting, flirtation, physical contact, or sex were carried out in subtle ways and under a veil of
secrecy. Flirtation occurred (and still does) by eye contact, and, given the
historically strict policing of the youth's interpersonal relations, it has
evolved into an art form. To this day, one can observe examples of this
practice at dances and local feasts in which one would dance next to a
male or a female in the traditional line dances. A man would signal his
intentions to a woman by getting close to her in the traditional local
dances and attempting to squeeze her tightly and rub his arm as high up
on her breast as he could. Of course, for any relationship to occur there
would have to be a positive response from the woman (a return squeeze,
a lean into the man, or deep eye contact). Obviously, if the woman cut out
of the dance line, it either meant a hard-to-get attitude or a flat-out rejection of the implied flirtation.

Sexual intercourse and long-term nonmarital relationships were established at great costs of secrecy, logistical planning, confidence, and time-
accountability. The risks were correspondingly high. Typically any such
relationships would have to occur in the fields or stables of this agricultural island society. Many men shared great tales of their secret sexual
exploits in stables and windmills. In those cases where sexual exploits led
to pregnancy, the woman paid a heavy price in terms of social ostracism
as well as verbal and physical abuse.

By the early 1960s, the young men had been exposed to various forms
of European and American culture (such as the waltz, early forms of rock-
and-roll, and so on) through radio, newspapers, and most importantly
through expatriates periodically returning to the island. In an attempt to
experiment with the new lifestyle, one group of men from the village of
Othos attempted to organize a European-style party. They envisioned a
ballroom-style affair with exclusively young people dancing as couples.
This was culturally radical in the Karpathian context because it meant the
exclusion of the older people and because dancing as couples was foreign
to the local culture. In the traditional context, dances always had been
communal. Additionally, dancing as couples implied an intimate contact
between unmarried young people, an activity socially sanctioned by the
local society. Realizing the challenges they faced, this group of young

men discussed the matter with the elders and, based on their advice, they scheduled the party. In order to avoid suspicions of promiscuity, they arranged to hold the party right in the middle of the street, in the heart of the village with bright lights serving as testimony of their good intentions. A phonograph and a collection of European records were the musical entertainment, and wine and soft drinks accompanied the appetizers at the refreshment table. The young men dressed up in their finest clothes and nervously proceeded to the heart of the village. The disc jockey began the musical program while the others poured themselves drinks and snacked as they waited for the party to begin. However, not a single female attended this "gala" event. "It was humiliating," said the man who conveyed this story to us, "here you are in the middle of the village — with all of the eyes on you — waiting for the women. . . . It was as if we raped them or [as if] we were crazy." Although this event was a memorable failure, it set the basis for later developments in leisure patterns.

Whereas Kavala's landscape developed and urbanized from 1960 to 1980, Karpathos lagged behind and did not change dramatically until the early 1980s. The onset of the 1980s brought with it two important politicoeconomic developments that changed the infrastructural and social landscapes of the island. First, the election of a socialist government in 1981 significantly benefited the island. The socialists catered to the Greek periphery and Karpathos' overwhelming support for them yielded a political economic windfall in terms of party-based patronage (including the construction of a new port, new roads, and the foundations for further airport development). Second, the government's enactment of Law #1262, an incentive program for investments in the nation's tourist industry and a number of investment incentive packages offered by the European Community's Integrated Mediterranean Programs greatly impacted upon the island. These programs helped the island toward tourist development resulting in a rapid proliferation of hotels, restaurants, bars, and discotheques. Corresponding to these socioeconomic changes, from the early 1980s and thereafter, a surge in repatriation occurred, leading to an intensification of the social transformation. Consequently, not only have the labor market needs changed dramatically, but also the locals' consumption habits, modes of interaction with foreigners, and interpersonal relations have been impacted. Agriculture and fishing have been almost entirely abandoned in favor of construction and service jobs mostly catering to tourists. The number and types of workers needed to fill jobs in the tourist industry has necessitated female participation in the labor force, often in positions that would have been unacceptable for women in the not so distant past. Women, especially young women, work at hotel reception desks, travel agencies, restaurants, shops, bars, and discotheques. Young men dominate the construction market, and many of them leave the island for university studies upon high school graduation, a passage that offers them their first taste of independence from the local community.

Because of the island's small size and its growing dependency upon the tourist industry, the traditional agricultural distinction between the winter and summer seasons has been further reinforced (Cohen 1984: 373–92; Lafante 1980). Flows of tourists are prevalent from May through September while diaspora Karpathians vacation primarily between June and August. This translates into seasonal operations for businesses of all kinds and especially for hotels. For the locals this seasonal dichotomy bears a significant impact in group affiliation and socialization. During the winter (which is off-season and a low point for tourism) the society preserves its communal character. Parties are family-oriented in the traditional *kathisto* style, taking place in packed warm homes with local wine and appetizers accompanied by native instruments (lyra and laouto) until the early hours. Almost all of the bars and discotheques are closed during this season and relationships tend to be more personal and as many interviewees called them more "authentic." As a young Karpathian put it: "You see, in the winter . . . the island is one peer group . . . in the summer, they break up looking for tourists, sex, etc. . . . and lately, since so many locals have opened up businesses, a tension has come about among them [the locals] . . . The winter is more authentic."

In the summer, local youth have more choices and many winter-time friends may not even speak to each other in the summer because each may join a different peer group. Where do these summer peer groups come from? They are diaspora Karpathian youth (mainly American or Australian, but also some are from the capital, Athens, as well). Essentially, these youth are tourists. The locals, however, differentiate between "tourists" (*touristes*) — implying stereotypically "back-packing blond Europeans" — and "our (diaspora) children," referring to Karpathian generations born, raised, or living outside of the island or abroad. Because of the strong family ties that characterize the local community, the expatriates and their offspring are seen as part of the Karpathian society and not as "foreigners." In fact, annual summer vacations to Karpathos by diaspora youth serve as a means for them to demonstrate their love of their own homeland to the immediate kin group. To the eyes of the kin group, this activity is prestigious and reaffirms the devotion of the young adults to the local society. As a repatriate Karpathian said: "You kids make us proud . . . we're proud that you come here every year . . . to see and live the traditions . . . you should get married here to carry on the traditions and customs . . . don't end up with an American or a Puerto Rican [woman] . . . you'll die [in the U.S.] and nobody will remember you . . . your family name will be lost."

Although a minimum level of direct interaction between local and diaspora youth exists, only in few villages is there a high degree of interaction between diaspora and local youth. Generally, there is more interaction between local and diaspora youth in the villages with more seasonal establishments whereas there is less contact between them in the more traditional villages. The summer season revolves around beach time, parties, local saints' feast days, and romances.

Young American Karpathians are typically called "frisbees" by the local population — as a mocking characterization of their "typical, flamboyant, and shallow American ways" — and tend to be more cliquish than other groups. Frisbees are usually the loudest (and "proudest") group on the beach, exhorting cursing phrases with New Jersey accents while they play volleyball, American football, or *kamaki* (the act of flirting with or "picking up" girls) at the feet of nature-seeking Danes, Germans, and Austrians. Within Greek culture, *kamaki*, the art of seducing "foreign" women, is a honorable activity because it adds to a male's masculine image. His partner, meanwhile, is considered a woman of "inferior status," a "street woman," because she does not conform to the norm of female virginity (see Buck-Morss 1987: 200–35; Zinovieff, 1991: 203–20). "Frisbees" are also most often the hosts of house or community center parties, and the primary clientele at the seasonal establishments. Of course, this is not to say that all, or only, American youth are "frisbees." There also exist "frisbees" from Canada and Australia, and less flamboyant ("cool") youth from the United States and elsewhere.

Overall, the island has eleven villages. Its topography provides a natural geographic separation between the northern and southern villages. There are seven villages in the south (*kato xoria*), where most of the population and development are found, and there are four villages in the north that are less accessible by transportation and more traditional. Karpathos City is the hot spot of the island's night life, although there is also significant activity in the villages of Othos and Arkasa and in the seaside resort area of Amoopi (Menetes). In these places, one finds the majority of modern-style cafes, pubs and bars, and discotheques. The remaining villages have few or no establishments to speak of.

Let us now concentrate on the establishments that local and diaspora youth frequent, that is, modern-style cafes, pubs, and discos. Modern-style cafes are generally similar to the ones in Kavala, and their peak

business times are from 7 to 10 P.M. These establishments are overwhelmingly dominated by youth and all young women can frequent
them with little or no problems from their families. Youth typically
dress casually with emphasis on attractiveness, because the modern-style
cafes are the most accepted establishment. Again, noteworthy is that the
traditional cafe is not typically frequented by youth when compared to the
new establishments.

Meanwhile, American-style pubs and bars are busiest between 11 P.M.
and 2 A.M. In some of these establishments the American influence is
more pronounced with whiskey and beer being the typical drinks, a pattern that closely follows the American "shot-and-a-beer" culture. This
style replaces the more traditional, Greek "ouzo-and-meze" culture. Eat-
ing is part of the Greek ritual of entertainment whereas the American style
puts a heavy emphasis on the consumption of large amounts of liquor. In
the Greek mode, leisure tends to be relaxing and "laid back" versus the
dynamic and fast-paced style of the American mode.

Although many young women do go to pubs and bars in the summer,
they have to go with peer groups or be subjugated to more gossip and
character assassination. In general, typical dress is semiformal, although
female dress is "sleazier" (imitating American standards). It is more difficult for young women to get permission to frequent pubs than cafes. In
these places, music is typically American rock-and-roll, especially from
the 1960s era, although more contemporary rock and Greek neotradition-
al "folk" music (*bouzoukia*) are gaining more attention. The specific share
of time any one type of music gets depends heavily on the type of bar or
the type of clientele the bars attract (or would like to attract). Discos and
theme bars are generally similar to the American ones — just like the discos in Kavala — and attract the biggest crowds. The theme bars combine
"authentic" architecture and decor with modern entertainment and feature
a blend of American and *bouzoukia*. They constitute characteristic examples of staged authenticity aimed toward the tourists.

Their clientele is mixed, including both local and diaspora youth and
tourists. Significant numbers of customers do not show up until midnight
to 2 A.M., and these places are commonly open until dawn. Again, Western (particularly American) influences are especially strong, affecting not
only the musical program but also the establishment's drink selection,
menu, architecture, art, and spatial arrangement. The "sleaziest" appearances are saved for discos, as the traditional brides' bazaar is being
replaced by an individualistic hunt for instant, carnal gratification More
women (most of them tourists) are found at discos and theme bars than at
either pubs or modern-style cafes.

In the villages with night life activity — Othos, Arkasa, and Amoopi — parties constitute a mode of leisure that is most clearly geared toward the local youth. These parties have come a long way from the earlier, failed attempt at European-style parties. In sharp contrast to the earlier anecdote, typical parties in the villages are dimly lit in the courtyards of homes, or more commonly at community centers and exclusively oriented toward the youth. In these parties, disc jockeys follow similar musical formats to those of their professional counterparts at pubs or discos, but may play more slow songs or blues to maximize couple dancing (another original intent of the "early pioneers" of the early sixties). Typical drinks include alcoholic punches or screwdrivers. Here, too, the young women usually have to attend with their peer group, and rarely are tourists found at these parties. Frisbees' parties almost always have the implicit goal of hooking up with a member of the opposite sex.

After spending the evening at such a party or disco, many of the local and diaspora youth — especially those successful in their "carnal hunt" — may go to a theme bar or pub for a night cap. Obviously, some couples end up enjoying sexual intercourse in fields, cars, hotel rooms, or on the beach. As in the past, those young men who do "score" sexually attain higher status or prestige in their peer group. However, female tourists, diaspora Karpathian, and Greek "liberated" women are many times considered whores because they are perceived to "give it up" more easily (being easier prey for sexual exploits). Hence, the leisure activity has preserved the male-oriented character of earlier leisure patterns and the double standard vis-à-vis females. Within Greek culture, *kamaki*, the art of flirting or seducing foreign women, is an honorable activity because it adds to a male's masculine image. His partner, meanwhile, is considered a woman of inferior status, a "street woman," because she does not conform to the norm of female virginity (cf. Zinovieff 1991).

Despite this feature, women continue to be the most significant benefactors in terms of gains in autonomy and "acceptable" gender roles and conduct. Now they are more socially aggressive and participatory in decision making in both public and private spheres.

Owing in large part to the extraordinarily close ties with significant numbers of diaspora Karpathians of the West and the repatriation surge of the past fifteen years, Karpathos is heavily influenced by American fads and artifacts. As such, the island is an extreme example of a local community coming under the strong influence of American and Western cultural forms. As we have described, American culture has affected the youth more than the society at large. Local youth generally accept modern American fads and culture, albeit in altered forms. There does exist a strong resistance to the Americanization and xenomania, however. The strongest such resistance lies in the older generations and with more traditionally-oriented young people. In like fashion, the intensity of American culture and its presence are greater in the summer season when frisbees and Karpathians from Greece's metropolitan centers join local youth in peer groups.

To a considerable extent, diaspora frisbees and local youth embody the forms American culture takes (Nash 1977: 33–47; McCannell 1990). Echoing the resistance to the rapid proliferation of American cultural forms, many older locals expressed antifrisbee sentiments, which, however, rarely amounted to hatred. They identified frisbees and local youth as the two main agents of social change, though immigrants vacationing from the West and pop culture definitely deserve honorable mention. They also placed the responsibility of the deterioration and decline of local customs and traditions on these two groups. One older prominent local artist said, "the problem is that the youth are no longer touched by or emotional to the Karpathian music, and thus the Karpathian identity."

CONCLUSION

In this discussion, we explored the emergence of Greek youth culture during the past thirty years. We studied only rural and provincial town settings, and hence, our conclusions pertain only to them. In our view, these settings exemplify the cultural changes associated with the post–World War II transformation even more clearly than the two metropolitan areas. We surveyed the cultural changes of an urban (Kavala) and a rural (Karpathos) context to present an image of the social transformation in both of them.

Of the socioeconomic and cultural factors that transformed Greek society in the post–World War II period, the development of tourism and increasing contact with outsiders provided the important impetus for the rise of the modern Greek youth culture. Key features in its development were the creation of a number of establishments oriented toward the youth, the availability of pocket money for the youth that elevated them to the status of potential consumers, and the gradual liberalization of the family environment allowing for more freedom of movement and more interaction between the genders. All three factors were absent in the 1950s and early 1960s social context and their emergence in the following decades signifies the impact of modernity in the local societies. Both in Kavala and Karpathos the emerging leisure environment has been constructed as an imitation of American and Western forms of leisure (pubs, rock music, discos, and so on). However, some traditional features such as the emphasis on close proximity as well as the communal character, the theatrical nature, and a good portion of the male-oriented character of leisure have been preserved.

The rural lifestyle that characterized the traditional agricultural communities of Karpathos is the one that has been most directly influenced by the recent development of tourism. The American influence is more strongly felt than in other places in Greece because it signifies the transition from an agricultural to a tourist-oriented community and demonstrates the impact of new cultural forms into the community's life. In contrast, Kavala displays more continuity with its past, mainly because in this urban context the impact of American forms cannot be confused with other social changes.

Greek youth culture is the result of the emerging awareness of the modern as distinct from the traditional. The elevation of youth into the status of consumers has led to a situation that can be labeled as the "consumption of modernity." Young people appear to be especially likely to consume all kinds of symbolic images associated with the modern as it is being filtered and presented in the world around them, hence, their fascination with pubs, modern-style cafes, or establishments that demonstrate the impact of the "tourist gaze." The symbolic features of these establishments and the symbolic media employed by the youth (clothes, music) set the youth culture apart from the adult world that still displays the signs of tradition. Greek society has been characterized by gerontocracy (Lambiri-Dimaki 1983: 9–48) and the spatial and symbolic separation of youth by the rest of the social environment manifests a gap between them and the older generations. To some extent, it is reasonable to argue that the dividing lines between tradition and modernity largely overlap with the boundaries between the older and younger generations. In this context, modernity becomes a matter of signification: the symbolic display of Western forms represents one of the means that youth employ in order to present themselves as Western and modern (as distinct from traditional or peasant). These presumed Western (most often American) artifacts represent an idealized version of U.S. culture and often times are far from being truly foreign.

Greek youth culture centers around a number of artifacts that serve as symbolic markers of Western cultural presence, with the pub and the modern-style cafe being the most prominent ones and the discos somewhat less prevalent. These establishments are far from simple imitations of their Western counterparts. Although not radically different in their appearance, the Greek pubs and modern-style cafes are neither identical to nor do they fulfill the same functions as the American or British pubs and the European cafes. The first feature that sets them apart is that they are almost exclusively oriented toward youth. Second, they operate as symbols that manifest the modernity of the urban space. Also, the spatial arrangement within them and the atmosphere is, for the most part, unlike those of their U.S. counterparts. Their customers always show up in the evening, and they all tend to sit together with their peer group. In fact, it is extremely rare to see people sitting by themselves because, in a society with strong collectivist tendencies, this indicates a degree of social deviance. Furthermore, these activities, repeated mechanically over and over every night, are meaningful only in terms of the assumption that this social space is contrasted against the background of the operation of family as a key factor determining their lives. This argument accounts for their overwhelming popularity. To some extent, the modern establishments fulfill for the youth the same function that the traditional cafe fulfills for the older generations: a space for sociability to be expressed and social relations to flourish. The key difference between the two is, of course, that the new establishments integrate both genders as more or less equal partners in the consumption of the social space.

Moreover, the adoption of the new lifestyle does not mean that the traditional forms of leisure are destroyed; for example, the walk continues to function albeit in a new manner that makes it compatible with the changed social environment. There is evidence to support the thesis that Western cultural forms are fused with local traditions resulting in a form of cultural syncretism. The new settings and modes of interaction provide a cultural context that young adults use creatively in order to assert their own individuality versus the family-oriented structure of Greek society. In a sense, the newly constructed social space offers a degree of freedom vis-à-vis the family environment (Kelly 1987). Its use by youth manifests the ability of young people to use cultural objects of their surrounding world to articulate a common culture of their own (Willis 1990) and assert their own identity. This might not appear to be extremely subversive, but it is important in terms of shaping Greek society's future orientation with respect to modernity itself.

In theoretical terms, cultural imperialism theorists often ignore processes of cultural syncretism and tend to argue that local cultures are displaced by Western commercial culture. Of course, the cultural imperialism thesis is based on a set of assumptions guiding one's research efforts with no common agreement regarding their exact interpretation. In its most vulgar form, cultural imperialism can be defined as the assertion that the adoption of American (and more generally Western) cultural forms by another culture signifies the adoption of the peculiar cultural content present in the form in its original cultural milieu. To the extent that this vulgar form of the cultural imperialism thesis stands up in the case of Greece, the evidence suggests a form of cultural syncretism. Cultural syncretism stands for a fusion of American cultural forms with local traditional practices. This is not to reject wholly the idea of cultural imperialism, but rather to suggest that alternative formulations of it might be more plausible. Because although social change has been occurring at an extremely rapid pace and traditions have undergone analogous changes, they have not been eliminated.

NOTES

1. Participant observation in Kavala was employed during Victor Roudometof's four month stay in the city during the summer of 1991. In Karpathos, Mike Epitropoulos followed a similar technique during the summer of 1992. In both cases, it consisted of observations of the daily routines of the youth and their places (cafes, pubs, etc.) during evenings and nights from 8:00 P.M. until 1:00 A.M. Additionally, a number of interviews were conducted with young adults and pub owners. Both researchers have a very close and personal relationship with the settings and this helped them establish a good rapport with the people. In this chapter, all quotations unless otherwise indicated are from the interviews. Finally, the authors point out that this chapter is published without significant revisions nearly five years after it was completed. Consequently, post-1993 changes in modern Greek popular culture (and recent literature on these issues) are not discussed here.

2. Another feature of the whole process was the expansion of video arcades in the area. Around 1982–83 video arcades expanded rapidly and became standard meeting places for the teenagers. Contrary to U.S. experience, video games are not normally sold as software. Instead, a shop owner can purchase a number of machines, install a software, and open a shop with these machines. The video games fad faded away but the establishments kept a good portion of their audience and up to this day are parts of the teenage life. The low cost of this sort of entertainment contributes to their longevity (in 1991, one game costs 20 drs, approximately 200 drs = $1).

REFERENCES

Sources in Greek are indicated by (G).

Allerbeck, Klaus and Rosenmayr, Leopold. 1979. "Failures and Achievements of the Sociology of Youth." *Current Sociology* 27(2–3): 7–16
Brake, Michael. 1985. *Comparative Youth Culture*. London: Routledge.

Buck-Morss, Susan. 1987. "Semiotic Boundaries and the Politics of Meaning: Modernity on Tour — A Village in Transition." In *New Ways of Knowing: The Sciences, Society, and Reconstructive Knowledge*, edited by Marcus G. Raskin and Herbert J. Bernstein, pp. 200–35. Totowa, N.J.: Rowman and Littlefield.

Campbell, John Kennedy. 1964. *Honour, Family, and Patronage: A Study of the Institutions and Moral Values in a Greek Mountain Community*. Oxford: Clarendon Press.

Campbell, John Kennedy. 1983. "Traditional Values and Continuities in Greek Society." In *Greece in the 1980s*, edited by Richard Clogg, pp. 184–207. New York: St. Martin's Press.

Cavan, Sherri. 1966. *Liquor License: An Ethnography of Bar Behavior*. Chicago, Ill.: Aldine.

Chouliaras, Yiorgos. 1993. "Greek Culture in the New Europe." In *Greece, the New Europe, and the Changing International Order*, edited by Harry J. Psomiades and Stavros B. Thomadakis, pp. 79–122. New York: Pella.

Cohen, Erik. 1984. "The Sociology of Tourism: Approaches, Issues, and Findings." *Annual Review of Sociology* 10: 373–92.

Cowan, Jane K. 1990. *Dance and the Body Politic in Northern Greece*. Princeton, N.J.: Princeton University Press.

Cowan, Jane K. 1991. "Going out for Coffee? Contesting the Grounds of Gendered Pleasures in Everyday Sociablity." In *Contested Identites: Gender and Kinship in Modern Greece*, edited by Peter Loizos and Euthymios Papataxiarchis, pp. 180–202. Princeton, N.J.: Princeton University Press.

de Boulay, Juliet. 1974. *Portrait of a Greek Mountain Village*. Oxford: Clarendon Press.

Diamantouros, Nikiforos P. 1983. "Greek Political Culture in Transition: Historical Origins, Evolution, Current Trends." In *Greece in the 1980s*, edited by Richard Clogg, pp. 43–69. New York: St. Martin's Press.

Dimen, Muriel and Friedl, Ernestine (eds.). 1976. *Regional Variation in Modern Greece and Cyprus: Toward a Perspective on the Ethnography of Greece*. New York: New York Academy of Sciences.

Dubisch, Jill (ed.). 1986. *Gender and Power in Rural Greece*. Princeton, N.J.: Princeton University Press.

Featherstone, Mike (ed.). 1990. *Global Culture: Nationalism, Globalization, and Modernity*. London: Sage.

Featherstone, Mike. 1991. *Consumer Culture and Postmodernism*. London: Sage.

Frith, Simon. 1984. *The Sociology of Youth*. Lancashire: Causeway Books.

Gardiki, O., Kelperis C., Mouriki A., Mirizakis G., Paradellis Th., and Teperoglou A. 1987. *Youth: Time Allocation — Interpersonal Relations* (vol. 1) (G). Athens: National Center for Social Research.

Gardiki, O., Kelperis, C., Mouriki, A., Mirizakis, G., Paradellis, Th., and Teperoglou, A. 1988. *Youth: Time Allocation — Interpersonal Relations* (vol. 2) (G). Athens: National Center for Social Research.

Georgas, James. 1989. "Changing Family Values in Greece: From Collectivist to Individualist." *Journal of Cross-Cultural Psychology* 20(1) (March): 80–91.

Gizelis, G., Kautantzoglou, P., Teperoglou, A., and Filias, V. 1984. *Tradition and Modernity in the Cultural Activities of the Greek Family: Changing Patterns* (G). Athens: National Institute for Social Research .

Goffman, Erving. 1967. *Interaction Ritual*. New York: Doubleday.

Greenwood, Davydd J. 1972. "Tourism as an Agent of Change: A Spanish Basque Case." *Ethnology* 11 (1): 80–91.

Greenwood, Davydd J. 1977. "Culture by the Pound: An Anthropological Perspective on Tourism as Cultural Commodification." In *Hosts and Guests*, edited by Valene L. Smith, pp. 129–38. Philadelphia: University of Pennsylvania Press.

Hall, Stewart and Jefferson, T. 1976. *Resistance through Rituals*. London: Hutchinson.

Herzfield, Michael. 1986. "Within and Without: The Category of 'Female' in the Ethnography of Modern Greece." In *Gender and Power in Rural Greece*, edited by Jill Dubisch, pp. 215–34. Princeton, N.J.: Princeton University Press.

Ioakimidis, P.C. 1984. "Greece: From Military Dictatorship to Socialism." In *Southern Europe Transformed: Political and Economic Change in Greece, Italy, Portugal, and Spain*, edited by Alan Williams, pp. 33–60. London: Harper & Row.

Karapostolis, Vasilis. 1984. *The Consumer Behavior in the Greek Society 1960–1975* (G). Athens: National Center for Social Research.

Kataki, C. 1984. *The Three Facets of the Greek Family* (G). Athens: Kedros.

Kelly, J. R. 1987. *Freedom To Be: A New Sociology of Leisure*. New York: Macmillan.

Lafant, Marie-Francoise. 1980. "Introduction: Tourism in the Process of Internationalization." *International Social Science Journal* 32 (1): 16–43.

Lambiri-Dimaki, Jane. 1983. *Social Stratification in Greece 1962–1982: Collected Essays*. Athens: Sakkoulas.

Lipovatch, Thanos. 1988. "Theses for the Political Psychology of Greeks. Prospects for the year 2000." In *Greece towards 2000* (G), edited by Il. Katsouris, T. Gianitsis, and P. Kazakos, pp. 86–107. Athens: Papazisi.

Loukissas, Philippos J. 1982. "Tourism's Regional Development Impacts: A Comparative Analysis of the Greek Islands." *Annals of Tourism Research* 9: 523–41.

Marsland, D. 1982. "It's my Life: Young People and Leisure." *Leisure Studies* 1: 305–22.

McCannell, Dean. 1990. *The Tourist: A New Theory of the Leisure Class*. New York: Shocken Books.

McNall, Skott G. 1974a. *The Greek Peasant*. Washington, D.C.: The American Sociological Association.

McNall, Skott G. 1974b. "Value Systems that Inhibit Modernization: The Case of Greece." *Studies in Comparative International Development* 9 (3): 46–63.

McNall, Skott G. 1976. "Barriers to Development and Modernization in Greece." In *Regional Variation in Modern Greece and Cyprus: Toward a Perspective on the Ethnography of Greece*, edited by Dimen Muriel and Ernestine Friedl, pp. 28–42. New York: New York Academy of Sciences.

McNeill, William H. 1978. *The Metamorphosis of Greece since World War II*. Chicago, Ill.: University of Chicago Press.

Mouzelis, Nicos. 1978. *Modern Greece: Facets of Underdevelopment*. London: Macmillan.

Mouzelis, Nicos and Attalides, Michael A. 1971. "Greece." In *Contemporary Europe: Class, Status, and Power*, edited by Margaret Scotfort Archer and Salvador Giner, pp. 165–97. London: Weidefeld & Nicolson.

Nash, Dennison. 1977. "Tourism as a Form of Imperialism." In *Hosts and Guests*, edited by Valene L. Smith, pp. 33–47. Philadelphia: University of Pennsylvania Press.

National Statistical Service of Greece. 1963. Census of March 19, 1961. Vol. I. Athens: National Statistical Service.

National Statistical Service of Greece. 1984. Census of April 5, 1981. Vol. II. Athens: National Statistical Service.

Petmezidou-Tsoulouvi, Maria. 1987. *Social Classes and Mechanisms of Social Reproduction* (G). Athens: Exantas.

Pollis, Adamantia. 1965. "Political Implications of the Modern Greek Conception of Self." *British Journal of Sociology* 16 (March): 29–47.

Robertson, Roland. 1992. *Globalization: Social Theory and Global Culture*. London: Sage.

Rojek, Chris. 1989. "Leisure Time and Leisure Space." In *Leisure for Leisure: Critical Essays*, edited by Chris Rojek, pp. 191–204. New York: Routledge.

Schiller, Herbert I. 1976. *Communication and Cultural Domination*. New York: M. E. Sharpe.

Smith, David M. 1981. "New Movements in the Sociology of Youth: a Critique." *British Journal of Sociology* 32 (June 2): 239–51.

Stott, Margaret A. 1988. "Property, Labor, and Household Economy: The Transition to Tourism in Mykonos, Greece." *Journal of Modern Greek Studies* 3(2): 187–206.

Theory, Culture, and Society. 1990. Special issue on Nationalism, Globalization, and Modernity 7. London: Sage.

Tomlinson, John. 1991. *Cultural Imperialism: A Critical Introduction*. Baltimore, Md.: Johns Hopkins University Press.

Triandis, Harry C. and Vassiliou, Vasso. 1972. "A Comparative Analysis of Subjective Culture." In *The Analysis of Subjective Culture*, edited by Harry C. Triandis, pp. 299–335. New York: Wiley and Sons.

Tselika, Ilektra. 1991. *Youth and Social Dynamic* (G). Athens: Odisseas.

Tsoukalas, Constantine. 1986. "Employment and Employed in the Capital: Opacities, Questions, Hypotheses." In *Greece in Evolution* (G), pp. 163–242. Athens: Exantas.

Tsoukalas, Constantine. 1987. *State, Society, and Occupation in Post-war Greece* (G). Athens: Themelio.

Urry, John. 1990. *The Tourist Gaze: Leisure and Travel in Contemporary Soceties*. London: Sage.

Vasilikos, Vasilis. 1966. *Outside the Walls* (G). Athens: Themelio.

Vassiliou, Vasso G. and Vassiliou, George. 1973. "The Implicative Meaning of the Greek concept of Philotimo." *Journal of Cross Cultural Psychology* 4 (September 3): 326–41.

Venturi, Robert, Scott Brown, Denise, and Izenour, Steven. 1977. *Learning from Las Vegas: The Forgotten Symbolism of Architectural Form*. Cambridge, Mass.: MIT Press.

Vergopoulos, Kostas. 1985. "Economic Crisis and Modernization in Greece and the European South." *The Greek Review for Social Research*, 92–130.

Willis, Paul. 1990. *Common Culture: Symbolic Work at Play in the Everyday Cultures of the Young*. Milton Keynes: Open University Press.

Zinovieff, Sofka. 1991. "Hunters and Hunted: Kamaki and the Ambiguities of Sexual Predation in a Greek Town." In *Contested Identities: Gender and Kinship in Modern Greece*, edited by Peter Loizos and Evthymios Papataxiarchis, pp. 203–20. Princeton, N.J.: Princeton University Press.

6

African-American Images in German Advertising, 1987–1992: The Uses of Imagined Diversity

Steve Fox

In the late 1980s and early 1990s, a remarkable concentration of nonwhite figures appeared in Germany's advertising. Most of them were black males, identifiable as German perceptions of African-American types. The ads were concentrated in two venues: in Germany's booming outdoor billboard sector, which dominated the urban light-rail stations, bus stops, and streets; and in publications serving the 14- to 34-year-old youth market, especially music and film magazines. Dramatized versions of these print ads also appeared in packages of commercials shown in cinemas before the main features. The advertisers using these images were mostly cigarette companies targeting the youth market, under the heavy influence of an American tobacco industry looking abroad to replace its declining domestic consumer base. Another heavy user of these racial and ethnic images was the cable television division of Telekom, the federally controlled German mail and communications conglomerate.

In the 1980s, advertising engulfed all sectors of society, using the techniques of art to seduce our souls. Germans, like all industrialized citizens, witnessed nearly 16,000 commercial messages per day, counting logos, labels, and announcements. No facet of experience could not be "sponsored."[1] At the time the proliferation of black images appeared across Germany, U.S. imagery in general was at a peak in all sectors of German advertising. It was the period when German society began dealing with the two most profound cultural crises since World War II: one was the rapid increase in German anxiety about "foreigners" in their midst, and the other was the unification of East and West Germanys, separated by Cold War rivalry for 40 years. Both crises forced Germans to confront the narrow, ethnicity-based definition of German citizenship. To confront that meant to confront also its complement — the sets of popular stereotypes of all who are non-German, stereotypes that are rooted in German experiences of isolation, homogeneity, and, since World War II, their consumption of modern mass media images with heavy U.S. influence. The ads featuring black and other ethnic types, having few links to the actual clashes of difference taking place daily in German society, usually portrayed difference as opposition.

This chapter argues that Germany's flirtation with "others" in its late 1980s to early 1990s advertising was a significant public comment on the conflicts pulling at the society, but that the ads were more likely to reinforce the status quo than to help bring about the pluralism they seemed to represent. The ads were a continuation of racial representation themes more than a century old in Europe, as well as a new variation tailored to the late–Cold War German predicament of immigration and globalization. The images of whites and nonwhites in these ads had many voices, some progressive, some status-quo, some reactionary. In the final analysis, the ad campaigns, despite their ubiquity and popularity, could be expected to add little to the German ruminations on difference. As ads, they are rooted in a symbol system that portrays social relationships strictly on the level of appearances, using commodified images as signs of meaning and encouraging us to commodify and fetishize ourselves to achieve the effects implied in the pictures. Advertising has always depicted difference (mostly male-female until recent years) as based on subordination, as Erving Goffman has made clear.[2] As depictions of racial and ethnic difference proliferated in advertising in the 1980s, whites and nonwhites in Germany, seeing not a Turk or Moroccan or Vietnamese in their ads, found themselves engaged in a heightened meditation on envy, desire, and power — made abstract by its use of off-the-shelf images from the United States.

BACKGROUND: EUROPE'S IMAGES OF OTHERNESS, GERMANY'S 1980S IDENTITY CRISIS, AND TODAY'S "LIFESTYLE" AND "NON-AD" ADVERTISING

Since the days of the slave trade and colonial plantations, blacks have played an important role in the European imagination — representing the primitive. African-American dance scholar Brenda Dixon Gottschild is married to a German and has traveled extensively in the country during its recent unification period. She writes,

The "seduction of the primitive" is a trope that has played havoc with the European psyche since the Age of Enlightenment. It is a love-hate relationship of binary opposites, with the black body as the screen upon which Europe projected its fears and phobias, along with its fantasies and desires. It is the primitive trope which defines the European concept of the "other," be it the Hottentot Venus in nineteenth-century London, Josephine Baker in twentieth-century Paris, "Ashanti Fever" in turn-of-the-century Vienna, or the consciously non-European influences in the revolutionary work of artists like Picasso, Matisse, and Gauguin.[3]

Europeans, like white Americans, have used the image of blacks to comment on whatever was dangerous, illicit, or hip in a white context. Thus blacks became prominently associated, in the white mind, with sexuality, violence, emotional extremes, and death. Sander Gilman writes that, for Germans, blacks have a particularly abstract symbolic use, because there have been almost no blacks in Germany until a trickle in the past few decades. In Germany, blacks are mythic figures linked with other liminal types — Jews, Gypsies, madmen, and women — as protean screens on which the dominant white culture projects images meant to illuminate and clarify white ideals by depicting their imagined opposites (Gilman 1982: xi–xiv, 2).

AMERICANIZATION AND BLACK IMAGES

After World War II, the presence of many blacks in the U.S. armed forces and Europe's desire to clear the rubble and return to normalcy combined to offer dissenting European youth a strong, new image of blackness: the hipster. Especially in Britain, whose Commonwealth system allowed blacks from the Caribbean to fly into London cheaply and without visas, white youth adopted traits (or imagined traits) of American blacks and West Indian immigrants to create an extensive system of subcultures: Teddy Boys, Mods and Rockers, Beats and Hippies.[4] Dick Hebdige sees these complex British alternative scenes as having a common origin: they were built on U.S. black images the English teens thought were "untouched by dreary conventions of white, higher-class people" (1988: 47). "At lilac evening I walked with every muscle aching among the lights of 27th and Walton in the Denver colored section, wishing I were a Negro, feeling that the best the white world had offered was not enough ecstasy for me, not enough life, joy, kicks, darkness, music. . . . I wished I were . . . anything but what I was so drearily, a 'white man' disillusioned."[5]

Wherever war had reduced cities to rubble and introduced modernization in the U.S. mold, people saw their generations-old working class cultures being replaced. In postwar England, the white youth expressed their resistance to the rapidly imposed social changes through oppositional values they saw in minority cultures, particularly black ones. To the war-shocked British young people, blacks appeared immaculate in their poverty — saints and exiles, free in their bondage. British social leaders and mores seemed flat and failed, by comparison. The Teddy Boys' disdain for bourgeoise patterns of work, manners, and narrow gender roles were soon exported to Germany, where Britain's armed forces had occupied the northern third of the country after the war. By 1960, the thriving bohemian/rock scene of Hamburg was ready to help launch the Beatles: five (at first) working-class natives of Liverpool, England, an Atlantic port city whose sailors had been bringing back American records since the war ended. The Beatles acknowledged African-American artists Little Richard and Chuck Berry as their artistic mentors.

Germany's "economic miracle" of the 1950s and its climb to solid NATO partnership in the following decades were accompanied by increasing "Americanization." American soldiers were the most popular in the countryside, especially blacks, who were warm and kind to German children. While controlling Germany between 1946 and 1949, the U.S. military government established 37 "America House" libraries and information centers throughout the country and redesigned the popular magazines *Stern* and *Der Spiegel* based on the American models *Time* and *Life*. Hollywood and Coca Cola took advantage of the country's dependence to plant the seeds of economic domination for their products. By the 1980s, U.S. films controlled 80 percent of the German box office and Coke, having tied its image to film stars, was everywhere and poised to gobble up the East German market once the Wall came down.

THE UNITED STATES OF EUROPE

In the late 1980s, a boom in the use of U.S. imagery occurred in European advertising. Levi-Strauss, the jeans maker, started the trend in 1986 when its London ad agency, a branch of the New York–based Bartle, Bogle & Hegarty, made the first of an award-winning series of ads picturing young Levis wearers in old Chevy trucks in U.S. southwestern desert landscapes. American settings, character types, and English language slogans were soon used by other European agencies to sell a variety of goods — Dutch radios, French TV, Italian jeans, razor blades, gasoline, candy bars, even European beers. In an obvious saturation, Europeans were using American themes and images to sell their own products to each other.

Advertising directors explained why: the impending integration of politics, education, and trade in 1993, to be known as the "European Community," had spurred them to find imagery acceptable across traditional cultural boundaries. "If you borrow an American atmosphere," said Mathieu Lorja, director of advertising for the Dutch electronics giant Philips, "it neutralizes the typical European cultural differences" (Tempest 1990: 9). He and other ad executives said that, although Europeans may prefer their own TV shows and movies, they prefer American ones over any other European country's. One study found that in the two most popular German magazines, *Stern* and *Spiegel*, the United States was the only country whose visual icons were being combined with ideological and emotional themes to sell things. Despite the approaching alliance of the European Community, the study found no images referring to "Europeanness" or continental unity. The "United States of Europe," an idea preached to the Europeans by the United States since the postwar Marshall Plan, seemed poised to make an entrance, but was still, as in dubbed movies, rehearsing with U.S. stand-ins (Englert 1990).[6]

GERMANY'S CRISES OF DIVERSITY

As Europe debated the limits of its closer integration, Germany began to debate its own liberal asylum law, which was saddling the country with two thirds of all who sought political asylum in nations of the European Community. To atone for the sins of the Nazi era, postwar Germany had written into its new constitution the most liberal law in Europe to accommodate those fleeing oppression. Germany's 79 million people are crowded into a land area the size of New England, New York, and New Jersey combined. There are only half as many Americans (39.4 million) occupying that equivalent area in the United States. Germany also has one of the most homogeneous populations among major nations, with only 7 percent of the population deriving from ethnic groups other than German and only about 3 percent nonwhite. The United States, by comparison, is more than 25 percent nonwhite, to say nothing of the variety of ethnic affiliations. In Germany, Turks are the biggest minority group by far, three times as large as the next in size, Croats and Serbs, and blacks represent less than 0.5 percent of the population (*Frankfurter Rundschau* 1991; *Hamburg State Pocket Book* 1992). Thus the appearance in their midst of growing numbers of Mediterranean, African, and Asian asylum-seekers was very noticeable to the average German.

In the late 1980s, many Germans called for limits to immigration. Far-right nationalists proposed returning all racial non-Germans to their presumed countries of origin, and hooligans attacked with fists and firebombs. The unification of East and West Germanies in 1989, after forty years of Cold War separation, multiplied these tensions. East Germans experienced the merging of the two states as colonization by the West (Borneman 1991). *Besserwessies*, a word play combining a slang term for know-it-all with the Westerners' oft-repeated opinion of their own side's superiority in all things, was the sarcastic "word of the year" among Easterners in 1991. With their cultural institutions and life plans abolished by the unification treaty and their economic status falling far short of their hopes, disillusioned and alienated lower class young men began scapegoating the non-Germans in their midst. The federal authorities, then based in Bonn in the West, inflamed tensions by dispersing groups of black and Muslim asylum-seekers throughout the rural Eastern countryside. Hooligans, usually identified as skinheads, began attacking foreigners. They were little restrained by the poorly equipped police, who were familiar with minimal outbursts from a docile populace under the thumb of a totalitarian regime and its army and secret police. Actually, there were more incidents in the former West, which is three times as large as the former East, but many of the most starkly brutal happened in the East. German debate intensified, with leftists holding immense candlelight processions and vigils in support of pluralism and rightists charging that the republic was being destroyed by aliens who wouldn't assimilate. After four years of heavy media coverage of this painful debate over national identity, the German parliament voted in 1994 to tighten the asylum restrictions.

ADVERTISING'S COMMODIFICATION OF DIFFERENCE

The mass media — particularly advertising — stood ready to exploit the circumstances sketched above. German advertising had been made over in the American style in the 1960s and 1970s. The top American agencies established subsidiaries in countries with consumer potential and staffed them with locals who could adapt U.S. techniques to the host cultures. American ad techniques proliferated. German ads formerly relied on a didactic expert in a white coat lecturing about a product, but American ad producers staged little dramas using music and appeals to envy and fear, all portrayed as "real life" (Masson & Thornburn 1975: 95–106).

These American-inspired advertising concepts hinge on the creation of "commodity-signs" — compositions combining a product with people in a social situation. These vignettes are designed to convey social meanings that we, the viewers, can easily grasp at a glance: McDonald's is really a haven for the family; jeans express your individuality in a safely conforming way; "lite" beer is an accessory of manly sports culture. Our glancing at hundreds of these ads, however fleeting or detached, is enough for us to recognize the accepted social meanings depicted. Glossing hundreds of condensed, formally-arranged advertising vignettes is an effective reinforcer of norms because the images and meanings slip right into the subconscious. Moreover, the scenes depicted are not what life is like in a literal sense, but what advertisers take to be normal. Advertisers don't want to shock us into critical thinking; their images deal in the views of life most familiar to the majority of the ad's intended audience. Associating a product with the scene gives viewers a way to attain the benefits of the social relationships depicted. As advertising scholar Robert Goldman and others have pointed out, this commodification of meanings is inherently an ideological process. Far from being innocuous, ads are a powerful political force that reinforce the cultural meanings that a majority would consider normal, such as the "acceptable kinds" of freedom, individuality, relationships, or gender roles (Goldman 1992).

So how would an ad campaign stand out in the crowd of conventionalized scenes? By using superior graphic design, to be sure, but an ad campaign might exploit public preoccupation with some current social issue by raising a new topic but limiting its power by hedging it in the context of old ones. Innovative material can thus be controlled by conventional counterpoint. Ads constructed in this way can become very popular because they have included new elements — such as racial pluralism in a society convulsed by intolerance. Even if close analysis of the ads reveals countervailing meanings that vitiate the ads' apparent boldness, by merely including minority images at all, the ads have offered a wider variety of people the freedom to make their own interpretations of formulaic stories and situations.

In the 1980s the experience of subordination became a leading theme in many mass media. Feeling subordinated, according to commentators like John Fiske and George Lipsitz, is a near-universal experience: minority groups are oppressed by majority groups and members of the dominant groups are oppressed by the system, whether bureaucracy or industrial workplace. The depiction of individuals struggling against injustice or overpowering odds can be read by people at many class levels as reflecting their own desires to resist inequality in social relationships. Ads that appear to depict people defying the normal constraints of a society, though in a "safe" way, can impress members of the majority that important issues are being addressed in a public way (Fiske 1989: 212).

One of the ways people can defy racial and class segregation is by forging bonds with someone from a less powerful, or more despised, group. African-American feminist critic bell hooks writes that mass culture is the current medium "that both publicly declares and perpetuates the idea that there is pleasure to be found in the acknowledgement and enjoyment of racial difference" (hooks 1992: 21). In the 1980s, interracial relationships first openly explored in the 1960s came back: black and white buddy movies (Eddie Murphy and Nick Nolte, Danny Glover and Mel Gibson) and interracial musical collaborations (Springsteen and Clemmons, Simon and Ladysmith Black Mambazo, Bonnie Raitt and John Lee Hooker). Ms. hooks points out that advertising's recent use of racial difference has been to portray racial difference as something that would seem to members of the dominant group as "a new delight, more intense, more satisfying than normal ways of doing and feeling" (hooks 1992: 21).

Just as Levis in 1986 started an era of U.S. imagery in European advertising, so Benetton, the Italian sportswear manufacturer, in 1985 inaugurated the current commodification of racial difference. For the Paris Summit in 1985 between Reagan and Gorbachev, Benetton rushed out a series of ads picturing a black boy and a white boy carrying U.S. and Russian flags. Of course, the ads got attention. Gorbachev said, as he was being driven along a Boulevard Champs-Elysée plastered with these ads, "Who *is* this Benetton, anyway?" (Picardie nd). Benetton became the international leader at showing how successful the commodification of otherness could be. Benetton had 5,500 stores in 80 countries. Their campaign, "The United Colors of Benetton," became famous for picturing people of different races together in provoking ways. Another Benetton shock technique included blurring the line between art, news reportage, and advertising by using in their ads pictures taken by photojournalists originally published as journalism. Even the trenchant advertising critic Leslie Savan admitted that this mix of boldness and ambiguity made her appreciate the new "non-ad" ad, which made her feel "quite the radical" (Savan 1992: 271). Seeing the sudden interplay between peoples of differing races in their ads in the late 1980s, progressive Germans must have felt the same.

COME TOGETHER: SO MUCH MORE TO BUY

In 1987, images of American eccentric types began symbolizing for Germans the polarization of social difference. In that year, the new German cigarette brand, West, launched an ad campaign featuring young lifestyle icons offering West to odd types. West's initial campaign had imitated Europe's number one brand, Marlboro, with pickup trucks in a western landscape, but the effort flopped. The new West campaign was shot entirely in Los Angeles by German fashion photographer Peter Lindbergh for the Hamburg agency Scholz & Friends. The West campaign seemed to "capture a zeitgeist," according to German media analyst Reinhold Misselbeck, when it appeared simultaneously with an unrelated, traveling exhibit of a series of Hollywood street portraits by German photographer Volker Corell, who had lived in Los Angeles since 1978 (Misselbeck 1992). The theme of this "spirit of the age" appeared to be compassion for eccentricity and an interest in social diversity. The exhibit was major art news in the big cities and drew heavy crowds.

A difference emerges when the texts of the two collections are compared: Corell's photos are head-on portraits, giving their subjects the dignity of sole focus and of making direct eye contact with viewers. Furthermore, Corell gives his portraits captions containing biographical sketches filled with pathos for his subjects, who range from porn stars and bar bouncers to cops and Salvation Army missionaries. In contrast, the West ads had, from the first, a burlesque edge to them. Their first grouping featured a fat "Old Elvis," a quite short and stocky "Al Pacino," and an obese "Old Lifeguard" (names attached by West). Then as the campaign evolved into its focus on pairs, the ads always subordinated the odd types to ideal types: the eccentrics are usually fat or older and always conventionally unattractive; they display social awkwardness through uncomprehending facial expressions and unbalanced body postures. Because it is invariably an ideal type (thinner, younger, prettier) who offers West to a subordinated type, the ads direct their audience's identification to the idealized "normal" figures who offer to help the others. Although the ads also exploit smoking's ability to keep smokers thin, they began to show ethnic types (such as an African "tribal king") among the "weirdos" who needed West's help to become acceptable. Although it is probably a step toward pluralism for German ads to even acknowledge the diversity West's ads do, the series' design retains a phobia for the different. Most of the others depicted   drawn from Los Angeles's agency rosters of "bizarre types" — have little to do with Germany. but the ads tapped into public anxiety over difference. With this campaign, West vaulted from dead last to the number three market spot among German brands, after Marlboro and HB.

One West ad shows a young American black man (with reversed baseball cap) offering West cigarettes to a fatter man dressed in African clothes and carrying a cane decorated with a skull: primitivism and death! The West campaign paired African types only with American black types, never with whites. The heavier "African" man wears a contorted, confused expression. Another West ad had a young black man, with baseball cap on backwards, raging directly into the camera with mouth wide open and eyes glaring. The text read, "Keinen Pfennig Mehr!" This translates as the idiom, "Not a penny more," using an image of black rage to refer to West's low price, the cheapest among German brands. Thus black protest at inequality — or a popular stereotype of a protesting person — became domesticated as a universal consumer beef. White smokers could feel radical and save some pennies, too.

Another German cigarette brand, Peter Stuyvesant, made intimate transgression of racial boundaries the explicit theme of their campaign: their ads showed people of different races talking intently at close range or enjoying touching each other. Stuyvesant added a layer of subversive authority to the general Benetton themes by adding John Lennon's song title "Come Together" to each ad vignette. The slogan evolved and added the line, "and learn to live as friends." This campaign emerged in 1989, at the time East Germany was throwing off its Stalinist leaders in the Autumn Revolution. In a true bonanza of "sponsored revolution," Stuyvesant workers in "Come Together" T-shirts handed out cigarettes in East Berlin's main square, Alexanderplatz, as Easterners, in their first free elections since Hitler took over in 1933, voted on uniting with West Germany. Stuyvesant rival West began using the slogan "Test the West" at the same time (Borneman 1991: 231).

Unlike the West campaign's sarcastic parody of social hierarchies, the Stuyvesant images, at first glance, portray the protagonists as formal equals. In 1979 the sociologist Erving Goffman's analysis showed how the formal arrangement of figures and their body language in ads represent women as more childlike, dependent, or "mentally drifting" than men. He called these persistent patterns "genderisms" (Goffman 1979: 34, 40–54, 57–83). Continuing to depict women as physically weaker, less authoritative, and emotionally dependent on men allowed advertisers to show an array of "women's libbers" without recognizing women's real gains in power during the years of the Women's Movement. In the 1980s, notes Robert Goldman, advertisers reacted to the growing economic power of nonwhite populations by adding people of color to their ads, but, as Goffman might have predicted, they show the races "in formal equity but on different footing." We might call these new uses of subordination cues by color, clothing, and body language "racialisms."

In one Stuyvesant ad, a young, male, white smoker gazes enthusiastically at a black saxophone player, a Sonny Rollins look-alike. The pairing suggests that the young white regards the jazz musician as a mentor or hero, but the white's image is positioned higher in the frame than the sax man, subtly subordinating the black man to his younger fan. In another Stuyvesant variation, a black woman, looking right at us with her mouth open wide as if singing or laughing, subordinates a less animated Asian man by covering one of his eyes. Mutual looking is a sign of equality; compromising someone's gaze, even playfully, is a subtle reminder of boundaries.

A third major tobacco company, HB, number two in the German market, beamed themselves into the "united colors" game with a campaign showing young black men and young white men at Star Trek–like control panels. Compared to the other two, the HB ads were ethereal and static, more like department store window displays than photojournalism, yet each ad had a black man in it, adding to the saturation of blackness in this very white country.

Near my house in Hamburg in 1992, I came upon an amazing concentration of billboards that showed how saturated German ad campaigns had become with black American images. A 100-foot-long string of three billboards facing a major street all featured pairs of American blacks. On the left billboard, Ray Charles and Marilyn Monroe types demonstrated, via an interplay of image and text, the range of programming offered by the federally funded cable TV service: "from plain chocolate" (Ray) "to sugar-sweet" (Marilyn). These food keys are not only color-based, of course, but for Germans also evoke World War II associations between American blacks and chocolate, and white sugar with "sweetness and light." (Filmmaker Klaus Goldinger told me a common story: when the first black he had ever seen, a GI at the Frankfurt train station in 1946, offered him some chocolate, little Klaus thought for years afterwards that blacks had invented it because of the color association. German bakeries and candy stores still carry a chocolate bonbon named "NegarKusse," or Negro Kisses.) In this billboard, dark glasses on the black man may evoke Ray Charles's blindness or the cool hiding of the eyes frequently seen among musicians and celebrities. Unbalancing the "seeing" is used for subordination as well. The blond Marilyn, gazing out at us and speaking, is clearly the higher-status person.

In the middle billboard of these three, a light-skinned woman with curly hair and a darker man are in close conversation over a Stuyvesant cigarette. The slogan, scrawled in English cursive writing across the bottom of the scene like a caption, now reads "Come Together — So Much More to Enjoy." This pairing reflects the social color hierarchy that makes lighter-skinned black women more desirable and also illustrates the genderism of placing the man in the controlling position behind the woman. The novelty of depicting two black people enjoying a private moment with each other — or even the progressive impulse of using nonwhites to sell products to whites — are held in check by this old graphic vocabulary of inequality.

On the right one of this trio of billboards, an ad for the cable company gives another example of the extremes you can expect when you get cable: "From art to cult." The underlying theme of difference as opposites is clear — the other pairings in this company's billboard series include from ice to fire, from bird (air) to snake (ground), and from turtle to racehorse. On this third billboard in Hamburg, in the German text, Art (*Kunst*) is personified by Beethoven, all leonine curls and intensely staring out at us. Cult is personified by the African-American blues legend, Jimi Hendrix. Hendrix's hair is wild, too, but he is depicted as slightly smaller than Beethoven's head in the frame. The opposing of Beethoven to Hendrix carries on, in addition to the obvious racial opposition, a century-old argument in Europe over the necessity of elevating high art over low art. The guardians of European cultural traditions have always attacked American popular culture as vulgar entertainment undermining "true culture," which is built on masterworks from established élite traditions. The German term *Kunst* embodies this sense of high art. In this billboard, as in the first one on the left, hierarchy is reinforced by denying the pair equal sight: Ludwig stares at us vigorously, defiantly, whereas Jimi's eyes are closed and his face is downcast in subordination.[7]

The very existence of multiracial ads can reverse the intended effect of their content. On the surface, the ads suggest that if different people just "came together" (with their advertised product's help) it would be a wonderful world (Satchmo's recording of "What a Wonderful World" was used in a 1992 Renault TV ad). On the other hand, the ads get attention — they "work" — because we know such sanitized togetherness is far from the everyday reality. As Jeffrey Peck has pointed out, the ads work to subvert their superficial union of difference in two ways. First, the ads remove all context — they depict only faces of different shapes floating on a neutral background. These people don't have the whole spectrum of cultural differences we deal with in the real world — language, custom, religion, etc. Second, by using sanitized American images, the ads provoke Germans and visitors alike "to ask why *their Auslander* [foreigners] can't be like these 'proper' foreigners [who are] well behaved, clean, and congenial" (Peck 1991). In all these ads, however, there are no Turks, Vietnamese, Tamils, Arabs, Yugoslavs, or Gypsies, who are precisely the immigrant groups attacked by skinheads at asylum centers and the very ones with whom Germans need to discuss coming together. Turks are nearly one-third of all foreigners in Germany, but in two years I found only one ad with people depicted as Turks in a German context, and never in the ad campaigns discussed in this paper.

MINSTRELS, SAMBOS, AND DEVILS

There is a final category of advertising image current in Germany during this period that makes explicit reference to the themes of blackness, primitivism, and blatant racism. These are concentrated in ads for jeans, many from Italian makers. An Italian jeanswear company named More and More had a logo, in 1991–92, composed of a quartet of black male singers with mouths so distortedly open in song that they evoked the minstrel blackface of Jolson fame. Cardboard cutouts of this minstrel quartet hung from ceilings and stood on counters in every jeanswear shop in Germany, which is a lot of stores. Another Italian jeanswear brand, Take Two, features a Jim Crow–era Sambo couple. They are caricatures of grinning simpletons. Several times I saw the Sambo poster paired in store windows with a conventionally beautiful "real" white couple (themselves a commodified version of desirable youth, of course). A young Turkish shop owner, seeing me photographing this pair of posters in his window, proudly presented the Sambo one to me as a gift. He brushed aside my questions about its archaic black stereotypes by saying, "Jeans, American; blacks, American; music, American. All together, all good!"

Jeans are a huge industry in Europe, even larger than the domestic American market, and Europeans have excorporated jeans (taken them from their American context). During this period, they were worn even by TV news anchors and guests in prime time. Ads for jeans in Europe in the early 1990s, embellishing Levis' decades-old "authentic Gold Rush" theme, have a strong nostalgia component. European graphic artists mix and match many icons from America's pastoral past, sometimes in comic, fractured references, to evoke a "Happy Days" era of fun and social peace. Hence these ads that would be considered inflammatory in the United States, Britain, or France are, in Germany, just another reference to a consumer's golden age (which is, come to think of it, historically an American scene).

The effort to control the political reaction to touchy subjects by casting them in figures from another culture can take advertisers into unfamiliar waters. In the middle of this West/Stuyvesant/Telekom/HB blitz of yuppie blackness, Benneton depicted a black boy beside a blond girl. She had blond curls, a puff-sleeved blue dress, and a full smile that evoked Shirley Temple; he had hair teased up into two horns, and gazed solemnly at us. When Benetton had to recall the "black devil" ad from the United States and Britain, creative director Oliviero Toscani complained that he was "only reflecting what already exists," not contributing to the demonization of blacks (Baker 1991: 17). Another Toscani ad for Benetton featured a white baby suckling at the breast of a black woman whose head was cut off by the frame. When this image was denounced in Britain, the United States, and other countries, Toscani and Benetton protested that they had never heard of the mammy wet-nurse tradition (Rodkin 1990: 52). Toscani and advertising artists like him believe they are using "the richest and most powerful form of communication in the world" to "unite the world" by making people "think and discuss" (Baker 1991: 17). They clearly see their ads as art.

Polling her seminar students after a semester of trying to evaluate these themes, African-American Studies professor bell hooks found them concluding that "something was happening" because these ads were causing the issues to come "out in the open." The students thought that the message of such ads was a breakthrough and a challenge to white supremacy and to all systems of domination (hooks 1992: 39). However, hooks states the following cautions: "Simply by expressing a desire for 'intimate' contact with black people, white people do not eradicate the politics of racial domination as they are made manifest in personal interaction. . . . [My] over-riding fear is that cultural, ethnic and racial differences will be continuously commodified and offered up as new dishes to enhance the white palate — that the Other will be eaten, consumed, and forgotten" (hooks 1992: 28, 39). hooks also finds in this genre of advertising a contributing factor in the rise of separatist attitudes among ethnic and racial minorities: "Concurrently, marginalized groups, deemed Other, who have been ignored or rendered invisible, can be seduced by the emphasis on Otherness, by its commodification, because it offers the promise of recognition and reconciliation. When the dominant culture demands that the Other be offered as a sign that progressive political change is taking place, . . . it invites a resurgence of essentialist cultural nationalism" (hooks 1992: 26). There is one true aspect of opposition here: the drawing of racial lines by people on either side of them is certainly opposite to what the "come together" type of ad seems to represent.

Assimilation has always been a painful, halting process. As Germany began to face its hardest work of assimilation, the unification of East and West and the accommodation of colonies of non-Germans and nonwhites throughout the country, advertisers rushed to be "First Over the Wall" with U.S. off-the-shelf images. This was a sponsored colonization of consciousness offered just at the time the country needed its clearest, most heartfelt thinking. Stuart and Elizabeth Ewen write, "The politics of consumption must be understood as something more than what to buy, or even what to boycott. Consumption is a social relationship, the dominant relationship in our society — one that makes it harder and harder for people to hold together, to create community" (Ewen & Ewen 1982). Though advertisers had gone beyond representing people of color as signs of the primitive and exotic, their new scenes of interactive hipness still dealt not in empathy and universality but in envy and fear. Some Germans may have come to share with some Americans that sense of betrayal that the democratic ideals of pluralism, tolerance, and equality could be weakened by one of the powerful media through which they are broadcast.

As the Test the West, Come Together, and From Art to Cult campaigns in Germany illustrate, the global hierarchy that leads other countries to use U.S. images to augment their own discussions of identity makes talking about actual life experience even trickier than it used to be.

NOTES

1. Savan, Leslie. *The Sponsored Life: Ads, TV, and American Culture.* Philadelphia, Pa.. Temple University Press, 1994, pp 1–3.

2. Erving Goffman. *Gender Advertisements.* New York: Harper & Row, 1979, pp. 1–9.

3. For full discussion of the primitive trope, see: Marianna Torgovnick, *Gone Primitive: Savage Intellects, Modern Lives.* Chicago, Ill.: University of Chicago Press, 1990; Henry Louis Gates, *"Race," Writing, and Difference.* Chicago, Ill.: University of Chicago Press, 1985; Sally Price, *Primitive Art in Civilized Places.* Chicago, Ill.: University of Chicago Press, 1989; Reinhold Grimm and Jost Hermand, eds., *Blacks and German Culture.* Madison: University of Wisconsin Press, 1986.

4. For the transfer of Teddy Boy values to Germany, see Kaspar Maase, "Halbstarke [hooligans] and Hegemony: Meanings of American Mass Culture in the Federal Republic of Germany During the 1950s." In R. Kroes, R. W. Rydell, and D.F.J. Bosscher, eds., *Cultural Transmissions and Receptions; American Mass Culture in Europe,* pp. 152–70. Amsterdam: FU Press, 1993.

5. Jack Kerouac, *On the Road*. New York: Penguin, 1972, p. 169.

6. The Marshall Plan was the first full-scale insertion of consumerism into Europe. See D. W. Ellwood, "The Marshall Plan and the Politics of Growth." In Peter M. R. Stirk and David Willis, eds., *Shaping Postwar Europe: European Unity and Disunity 1945–1957*. London: Pinter, 1991, pp. 15–26.

7. European elites have usually received U.S. popular culture with hostility. See C.W.E. Bigsby, *Superculture: American Popular Culture and Europe*. Bowling Green, Ohio: Bowling Green University Popular Press, 1975; *American Studies International* 28 (2), October 1990, special issue on U.S. mass culture abroad; R. Kroes, R. W. Rydell, and D.F.J. Bosscher, eds. *Transmissions and Receptions: American Mass Culture in Europe*. Amsterdam: VU Press, 1993.

REFERENCES

Baker, Lindsey. "Taking Advertising to its Limit." *The Guardian*, July 22, 1991, Style section p. 1.

Borneman, John. *After the Wall: East Meets West in the New Berlin*. New York: Basic Books, 1991.

Englert, Sylvia. "Can Freedom Help Sell Cameras?" Unpublished manuscript, University of Frankfurt, Center for the Study of North America, 1990.

Ewen, Stuart and Elizabeth Ewen. *Channels of Desire: Mass Images and the Shaping of American Consciousness*. New York: McGraw-Hill, 1982.

Fiske, John. *Reading the Popular*. New York: Unwin Hyman, 1989.

Frankfurter Rundschau (newspaper), April 4, 1991, p. A-4.

Gilman, Sander. *On Blackness Without Blacks*. Boston, Mass.: G. K. Hall, 1982.

Goffman, Erving. *Gender Advertisements*. New York: Harper & Row, 1979.

Goldman, Robert. *Reading Ads Socially*. London: Routledge, 1992.

Hamburg State Statistical Pocketbook. Hamburg: Staatsministeriumverlag, 1992, p. 44.

hooks, bell. *Black Looks: Race and Representation*. Boston, Mass.: South End Press, 1992.

Masson, Peter and Andrew Thorburn. "Advertising: The American Influence in Europe." In C.W.E. Bigsby, ed., *Superculture: American Popular Culture and Europe*. Bowling Green, Ohio: Bowling Green University Popular Press, 1975.

Misselbeck, Reinhold, ed. *People of Hollywood*. Exhibition catalogue. Frankfurt: Art Forum, 1992.

Peck, Jeffrey M. "Refugees as Foreigners: The Problem of Becoming German and Finding Home." Paper delivered at Trust and Refugee Conference, United Nations University, Helsinki, 1991.

Picardie, Ruth. "How to Get Ahead in Advertising." (British magazine, cover missing, no title, c. 1992).

Rodkin, Dennis. "How Colorful Can Ads Get?" *Mother Jones*, January 1990, p. 52.

Savan, Leslie. *The Sponsored Life: Ads, TV, and American Culture*. Philadelphia, Pa.: Temple University Press, 1994.

Tempest, Rone. "In Advertising World, Pan-European Often Means American." *International Herald Tribune*, December 28, 1990, p. A-9.

Italian jeans makers specialized in mining "nostalgic" images of past U.S. eras in their ads, like these Sambo figures from a poster in Hamburg in 1992. Courtesy of Steve Fox.

Three billboards juxtaposed in Hamburg, 1992, illustrate the saturation of "race of opposites" in early 1990s Germany. Courtesy of Steve Fox.

One of Oliviero Toscani's images for Benetton, Frankfurt, 1991. Many protested
that he was contributing to the demonization of Blacks with this "horned" image.
Toscani responded that he was exposing prejudice with this satirical juxtaposition.
Courtesy of Steve Fox.

7

Choosing Exile: Richard Wright, the Existentialists, and Cultural Exchange

Greg Robinson

Black American expatriates in France have long been active agents of cultural influence. Since as early as the mid-nineteenth century, when black Creoles, such as playwright Victor Sejour, left New Orleans and settled permanently on French soil, France has enjoyed a reputation as a haven for African Americans. For some, such as James Baldwin, France offered a refuge, free from the worst effects of American racism. For others, such as pioneer jazz musician Sidney Bechet, France offered opportunities to work. For countless painters, sculptors, and architects, France represented a gateway to high culture, where blacks could be educated and be granted entry into the milieu of the fine arts.

For much of this long history, the cultural influence was predominantly one-way: from France to America. France's impermeability to influence from its African-American guests reflected the confidence of the French in the superiority of their "civilization" and their traditional views of the United States as barren of culture, as well as popular condescension toward black Americans as children of nature wounded by American racism. Although a few figures — Josephine Baker, the most celebrated — did make a place for themselves within French culture, commentators persisted in analyzing their art through the vocabulary of the exotic and "'primitive."[1]

The most outstanding group of black Americans to move to France was the set of writers and intellectuals who came to Paris in the 1940s and

1950s, including such figures as Richard Wright, James Baldwin, Chester Himes, and William Gardner Smith. These intellectuals were the first black expatriates (and in some ways the first American emigrants generally) to interact with and influence their French hosts in any significant way. They were able to do this because of a peculiar mix of circumstances. The postwar world was a cultural flashpoint, a place of maximum flux and intermixture. Furthermore, at a time when American culture reached worldwide dominance, these intellectuals were the most influential representatives of American culture living in Paris (many of their works continue to be read and appreciated in the United States, especially in black circles). Similarly, the racial background of these intellectuals drew the special attention of the French, as France embarked on the difficult process of decolonization while the status of the expatriates as members of an oppressed minority group in their native country increased their visibility and influence. Although it sharpened their sense of themselves as Americans, it also attracted the sympathetic attention of many French who felt ambivalent or hostile toward the United States. Finally, the black expatriates were visible and involved in intellectual life because of their interaction with the two most important intellectual movements in France during the period: the French Existentialists and the Negritude movement among black African writers.

The central figure among the black American intellectuals in France was Richard Wright. Wright was the first black American novelist to achieve international fame, the first black American writer to settle in France during the postwar era, and the American who was most directly involved with the French. Wright's friendship and political collaboration with writers of the Existentialist movement, especially Jean-Paul Sartre, during the late 1940s is a notable example of the cultural and intellectual exchange between Americans and French in this period. Although their collaboration was brief, and their mutual understanding always limited, Wright influenced the French by his use of existential philosophy in deconstructing racial domination while they renewed his admiration for intellectual community and his sense of intellectual political commitment.

Many scholars have written about Wright's life in Paris, yet, as Paul Gilroy noted in *The Black Atlantic* (1993), the "critical consensus" about Wright's stay in Paris is overwhelmingly negative: "It is claimed that after moving to France Wright's work was corrupted by his dabbling in philosophical modes of thought entirely alien to his African American history and vernacular style."[2] Conversely, Wright's defenders have dismissed his embrace of existentialism as ephemeral, or have claimed that his interest in such ideas predated his move to France, with the result that he was largely unaffected by his new surroundings.[3]

It is obvious that Wright was not "seduced" out of his own modes of thought by an Existentialist siren song. Not only had Wright achieved intellectual maturity and established a fixed viewpoint and style by the time he got to France, but he also had achieved a thorough grounding in European philosophy. Ralph Ellison later recalled studying Dostoevski and Unamuno with Wright in the 1930s.[4] Wright appreciated French existentialism precisely because it offered a key to understanding the Russian and German authors he favored as well as a method of elaborating existing themes in his own work. He insisted repeatedly in interviews that his reading of Dostoevski made him an existentialist long before he met Sartre.[5] He did not feel intellectually inferior to his French hosts as James Baldwin charged. Wright empathized with the Existentialists' concentration on fear and dread, but felt he had a far clearer grasp of it as a result of his own background and experience. "When they lynch a black man in Mississippi, I am lynched. And that is not philosophy!"[6] In 1947, he wrote that their abstract description of existential angst as a barrier to human achievement was "a manifestation of a lack of effectiveness for political action among the intellectuals and the petty-bourgeoisie of the Western world."[7]

In any case, the debate over Wright's "seduction" misses the most important element in Wright's contact with the French, which involved his sense of a political mission. Before moving to France, Wright had been intimately involved in political and antiracist activism in the United States. As a member of the Communist Party during the 1930s, Wright attended conferences and wrote articles on literary and political topics for Party journals. For example, in his 1937 article "Blueprint for Negro Writing" in the short-lived magazine *New Challenge*, Wright attempted to set guidelines for the production of black fiction, which would make use of folk materials and black specificity without ignoring the larger connections between blacks and other proletarians.[8] Ultimately, however, Wright found it impossible to act as an intellectual within Party discipline. Although the Communists officially encouraged his fiction as "proletarian literature," Party members criticized Wright's attempts to show black life and the dehumanizing effects of prejudice realistically and his refusal to portray noble black and white workers. Wright was outraged at the Party's opportunistic stand on racial matters, and he began to feel that the Communists had welcomed and promoted him, not for his individual talent or ideas, but because his black skin made him a useful propaganda weapon. After a long period of silent dissent, in 1945 he publicly declared that he no longer considered the Party "a viable means for social change."[9]

Once Wright rejected Communism, he lost not only his vehicle for political change but also his reliance on the class-dominated Communist model of society, though he remained influenced by Marxian ideas.[10] He was forced to construct a new model of social analysis and a blueprint for political action. Wright rejected Black Nationalism as such — he was suspicious of the fascist tendencies within the black masses, and he bristled at the suggestion that he was intellectually dominated by his black identity — but his experience as a black American helped him to construct what he considered a profound sense of social forces.

Paul Gilroy correctly states that Wright's literary art was political beyond immediate protest over the specific predicament of African Americans.[11] Wright's fiction described black community life as unsparingly bleak and disordered.[12] However, as his nonfiction writings during the 1940s clearly demonstrate, Wright did not write in this fashion to scorn blacks or even to indict white racism; rather, he considered the unsettled behavior and condition of blacks an extreme example of the alienation faced by all Americans.[13] Accustomed to a life in stable, hierarchical, and relatively homogenous peasant societies, Americans lacked a cultural tradition to offset the dizzying changes and dehumanizing effects brought on by their rapid shift to an industrial society. Their hysterical attempts to impose such an order on their lives led them to extremes of violence and disorder. The entrenched pattern of oppression, poverty, and disenfranchisement to which blacks were subjected, as well as the extreme nature of the shift from agricultural society, increased black alienation, but the difference was in degree, not in kind.

In a famous phrase, Wright asserted that "the so-called Negro problem in America is not really a Negro problem at all, but a white problem, a phase of the general American problem."[14] Although he rejected what he called "the obvious, unnatural method of placing the moral blame of the Negro problem upon the Negro himself — as is all too often done,"[15] he also denied that racism was an isolated moral failing of American whites rather than a symptom of modernity. Lacking a mature standard to judge new developments, whites took refuge in familiar, if outdated, social patterns and stereotypes, and feared difference. They were thus unreceptive to rational or humanitarian appeals for equality. Conversely, black Americans were potential leaders in the struggle to overcome such alienation. As a colonized race that had industrialized alongside the colonists, they represented a bridge between the technological progress of the West and the cultural values of the Third World. As Wright explained in 1946,

"Negro life in the U.S.A. dramatically symbolizes the struggle of a people whose forefathers lived in a warm simple culture and who are now trying to live the new way of life that dominates our time: machine-civilization and all the consequences flowing from it."[16]

In late 1945, while seeking a way to give political expression to this developing view, Wright was officially invited to France by the French government. Even before his arrival, Wright's works enjoyed great popularity among French readers. During his tour, Wright found himself and his work celebrated, and he was ecstatic over his welcome.[17]

After spending several months in France, he and his family returned to New York, but they soon felt suffocated by the bigotry they encountered. (Wright experienced nearly universal social ostracism as part of an interracial couple, and he feared his young daughter would grow up stigmatized by American racism.) In 1947, he made the painful decision to emigrate permanently to France, and he made Paris his base until his death in 1960.[18]

Wright enjoyed life in Paris, despite the privations of postwar life and harassment by the United States government.[19] He felt genuinely relieved of the crushing burden of anxiety he felt as a black man in America.[20] "There is more freedom in one square block of France than in the entire United States," he claimed.[21] Wright attributed the relaxed attitude of the French toward racial minorities to the established heritage and worldwide prestige of French culture, which made Frenchmen less threatened by aspects of other cultures. As he explained to André Gide, the more secure men felt within their society, the less frightened they were of difference, and the less likely they were to be xenophobic, violent, and racist.[22] Despite his affection for France, Wright still considered himself an American. He retained his American citizenship and his passport throughout his stay in France and never learned to speak French with any facility. Wright claimed that he was living in "exile" from the racial situation in the United States. He remained attached to his native country, perhaps in spite of himself.

Once settled in his "city of refuge," Wright became close to various French intellectuals who were generally grouped under the Existentialist banner, including Jean-Paul Sartre and Albert Camus, whom he had met in New York. Of all his French acquaintances, Wright was actually the most friendly with Simone de Beauvoir. He hosted her on a tour of Harlem night life during her trip to America in the winter of 1947, and she mentioned him frequently in her travelogue L'Amerique au jour le jour (1948). Wright had long conversations with Sartre and with Beauvoir, who wrote in her memoirs that she considered him livelier and more interesting than French intellectuals. Wright's background made it possible for them to indulge their love of American culture without feeling compromised in their resentment of American society, and he fed the Existentialists' interest in American writers.

The Existentialists admired Wright's work, though for its dissection of American life more than its literary craftsmanship, and they publicized it heavily. Sartre published a translation of *Black Boy* (1945) in the Existentialist journal *Les Temps Modernes* during 1947, and featured Wright's 1945 lecture on black American literature as part of a special issue in mid-1948 devoted to the United States. Wright reciprocated by championing the work of the French in his writings and interviews. In 1948, he wrote an introduction to the published version of *The Respectful Prostitute*, the English translation of Sartre's play about racism in the American South.

Wright was impressed by the parallels between his and the Existentialists' theories of alienation. Just as Wright explained the predicament of blacks under Jim Crow as an extreme example of the alienation of modern humanity, the French saw their life under the German Occupation as an archetype for the modern experience. Because the least deviation from the "role" assigned them involved uncontrollable dangers of retaliation by the German occupiers, any form of resistance was an unpredictable and morally engaged act (Sartre later claimed that France had never been so free as under the Nazi occupation). Wright wrote in 1947 that Sartre was "the only Frenchman I've met who has voluntarily made this identification of the French experience [under the Nazi Occupation] with that of the rest of mankind. How rare a man is this Sartre! His ideas must be good for they lead him into the areas of life where man sees what is true."[23]

Although the ideas and intellectual concerns of Wright and the French — race, class, and American society — were strongly related during the postwar years, they differed greatly in their opinions and intellectual approaches. A full comparison of their ideas is outside the scope of this chapter, but both their areas of agreement and difference would play an important part in their alliance and eventual break, and a schematic view of their positions is therefore revealing.

Wright and the Existentialists agreed that the intellectual had a generalized mission to support humanist culture against the alienating effects of technology. The French associated the defense of freedom with support of the working class. This meant that, despite their opposition to totalitarianism (and the Communist Party's attacks on Existentialism), they felt a commitment to the Soviet Union as the ultimately liberating champion of the future proletarian society. They were, however, not party-line Stalinists, and they insisted on their liberty of thought and action.

Although their abstract view of (and ignorance of conditions in) the Soviet Union led them to support that nation, when they viewed the United States through the same kind of abstract lens, they opposed it as the symbol of soulless industrial capitalism. Like Wright, they stressed the alienating effect of technology on American life, but they considered it a product only of capitalist society.[24]

Wright, in contrast, remained wary of anti-Americanism. He wrote, "It is very easy to damn America by rejecting America and it is very hard to damn America while accepting America."[25]

In addition, although Wright agreed that industrialism was at the base of the threat to human freedom, he felt the Soviet Union represented an even greater threat than the West. In a 1948 article, he wrote, "As things stand now, the only difference [between East and West] is that Russia has taken our industrial methods and applied them with a ruthlessness which we cannot use because of our traditions of individual freedom."[26] Despite the influence of Marxism on his thinking, Wright contended that psychological, not economic, factors were at the root of oppression. In 1946, he asserted that "before anyone, Right or Left, can even take the attitude that something must be done, he must sense how the problem is reflected in the hearts of men."[27]

Ironically, the shared interest in issues of colonialism that probably drew them the closest was also the area in which they differed the most in their approaches. As postwar France began to face the difficult and contentious question of decolonization, the Existentialists not only supported movements for political independence in Africa and Asia but also grew interested in their cultural self-assertion as a way to throw off the structures of racial dominance. Wright, who considered the common experience of racial oppression a unifying force between American blacks and Africans, had long been involved in movements against colonialism. He championed African independence, and he agreed that cultural self-assertion was a way for Africans to liberate themselves mentally. Wright and Sartre were both original sponsors of the magazine of culture and ideas, *Presence Africaine*, which would become the chief organ of the Negritude movement.[28] However, the French wished to absorb themselves in the study of "natural" nonwestern culture in order to join the racial "other" and transcend their alienation from western capitalist society. (Sartre would later be attacked by the anthropologist Lévi-Strauss for his interest in the "primitive.") Wright, on the other hand, admired European culture and remained fundamentally Western in attitude. He enjoyed Western standards of living and comfort (Margaret Walker Alexander claims he made "a fetish" of cleanliness) and despite his hatred of colonialism was devoted to Western humanist and democratic ideals that the Existentialists considered bourgeois.[29]

Wright's collaboration with the Existentialists went beyond mutual intellectual interest and literary patronage. A large part of Wright's admiration for France stemmed from the prestige and power of intellectuals in French society. The Existentialists, in addition to their cultural dominance, played an especially important political role. Sartre and his associates wrote political pieces in popular journals (notably their own review, *Les Temps Modernes*) and organized demonstrations.

In ordinary circumstances, this joint interest in intellectual commitment would likely have remained largely literary and private; however, as the American presence in Paris increased during the late 1940s following the inauguration of the Marshall Plan, and talk of a military alliance grew widespread, the existentialists, fearing the imperialist tendencies of the Americans, grew alarmed.[30] Meanwhile, Wright became frightened that the increased American military presence (he remained critical of NATO throughout his life) and political involvement in France would lead to an increase in American-style racism and would kill off progressive anti-Stalinist forces. As the East-West conflict heated up, Wright and the French saw it as a prelude to war — the main threat to civilization. Wright began a political partnership with the Existentialists based on what his biographer, Michel Fabre, later described as their shared concern with the philosophical difficulty of bridging individual and political responsibility. Wright agreed with Sartre that it was "up to the individual to do what he can to uphold the concept of what it means to be human."[31]

Wright's most important joint venture with the Existentialists in this regard was the short-lived *Rassemblement Democratique et Revolutionnaire* (RDR), a movement started by Sartre and David Rousset that attempted to unite intellectuals of the non-Communist Left into a "third way" political force around the defense of European humanist culture, separate from both the totalitarianism of the Soviet Union and the essential evil of capitalism.[32]

Wright agreed that only through the actions of a group of like-minded partisans could such a "third road" be realized, although he had little hope that a political party of intellectuals could maintain its independence in the face of a massive political bipolarization. Wright was not a full-fledged member of the RDR. Simone de Beauvoir wrote in her memoirs that the organization was unwilling to invite any Americans to take part, although it would accept their collaboration.[33] Furthermore, according to Michel Fabre, "Wright would not allow himself to risk being deported by becoming involved in the affairs of a country that was protecting him." Instead, he was assigned, as a "militant intellectual," to help the RDR by criticizing American policy where appropriate.[34]

Wright's most striking contribution to the organization was a speech at a conference on "The Internationalism of the Mind" in Paris on December 14, 1948. Wright asserted that "The war against man is open!"[35] He explained that the twin dangers to cultural freedom were American opposition to intellectual life and Soviet dictatorship. "These two nations, Russia and America, believe they represent human freedom, and the human mind is sacrificed to these beliefs. . . . Writers and artists, listen to me: the leaders of the world are waging a war against you! They don't need you in the society they are contemplating . . . you will be reduced to complete powerlessness, to slavery."[36]

Wright seized on Garry Davis as an example of the alternatives to bipolarism. In October 1948, Davis, a former American bomber pilot, arrived in Paris. Claiming to represent "the little man," Davis renounced his American citizenship and led sit-ins at the United Nations (then meeting in Paris) demanding that the organization grant world citizenship as a weapon against nationalism and wars. Davis attracted huge crowds to his speeches and gained widespread attention by asking people to send him their names for a registry of world citizens, though some Americans and French denounced Davis's pacifist message as an attack on the Western will to resist Communism.

Wright enthusiastically backed him, and he joined a Council of Solidarity for Davis alongside French intellectuals such as Albert Camus, Andre Breton, and Emmanuel Mounier. *Le Monde* reported that Wright, Breton, and David Rousset sent messages of support to a meeting of the related movement "Citoyens du Monde" in Berlin.[37] Although the movement quickly fizzled, Wright defended his advocacy of world citizenship on the grounds that it would permit smaller nations to exercise their interest in voting against war. In an article on Davis in *Time* magazine, he said he considered Davis a great fighter for freedom. "Can the peoples [of the world] believe in the efforts of the U.S. for democracy and freedom when it is well known that the U.S. does not support her own democratic institutions?" he asked.[38]

As the year 1949 dawned, the contradictions within the RDR between pro-Americans and pro-Communists became more manifest. Sartre and Wright felt that Rousset, who was soliciting funds from the American Congress of Industrial Organizations, was too Rightist. In March, the Communist-inspired Peace Movement held an International Anti-War Day. The RDR responded by scheduling an International Day Against War and Fascism. Sartre, Maurice Merleau-Ponty, and Wright sent a joint message to the RDR meeting to be read after pro-Atlantic Pact statements by American delegates: "We condemn for the same reasons both the more or less undisguised annexations in Central and Eastern Europe by the USSR and the Atlantic Pact. It is by no means certain that this pact will slow up the coming of war. It may, on the contrary, hasten it. What is certain is that, a little sooner or a little later, it will contribute to make it inevitable."[39]

Wright stopped collaborating with the RDR after Sartre, who considered the organization too anti-Soviet, resigned in the summer of 1949. He was upset that his ideas had been ignored by the French, and that he had been used by the members of the RDR and allied groups as a tool to attack the United States.

Wright and the Existentialists returned to individual self-assertion against the unified terror of the Cold War, and they attempted to maintain a neutral position between the United States and the former Soviet Union. Wright refused to be drawn into attending pro-Communist events, but he kept his distance from American officials in Paris, and he continued to speak critically in interviews of American policy. Sartre supported his neutrality, despite his pro-Soviet inclinations. When the French Communist press launched a series of attacks on the two, they counterattacked by publishing a French translation of Wright's essay, "I Tried to be a Communist," a bitter account of the opportunism and intellectual sterility of the Communist Party, in *Les Temps Modernes*.[40]

However, Wright attempted one more time to collaborate with the Existentialists. In 1950, a group of black expatriates, fearing that the increased American presence in France would increase racial discrimination, organized a civil rights group. Wright, however, insisted that the threat was not simply to black rights but to intellectual freedom. As he wrote soon after, "To an extent that white Americans do not feel the capacity or the need, the U.S. Negroes have sought a solidarity with French attitudes as though for protective coloration, and they have caught, as if by contagion, the French apprehension of the loss of their freedom, of the fear of America and the dread of Russia."[41] At Wright's urging, the group was named the French-American Fellowship Club, and Sartre was the guest speaker at its first meeting. Once organized, the group sponsored demonstrations at institutions that had discriminatory racial policies, such as the American Hospital in Neuilly.[42] However, despite Wright's efforts, Sartre and his colleagues declined to become active in the Fellowship, which eventually folded for lack of funds.

After 1950, Wright gradually parted company with the Existentialists. Because he lived in Paris, he developed other relationships. He also evidently grew personally tired of Sartre, which affected his relations with Simone de Beauvoir and others. Also, after the outbreak of the Korean War, Sartre and the Existentialists moved completely into the Soviet camp (where they remained as fellow travelers for several years). Wright, despite his opposition to the war, was unable to tolerate the Soviet Union, and he characterized Sartre's decision to attend the Communist-backed Vienna Peace Conference as "a stupid move."[43] Conversely, the Existentialists were disturbed by Wright's anti-Communism. Although they had been willing to print "I Tried to be a Communist" in *Les Temps Modernes*, when Wright reprinted it in the famous anti-Communist anthology *The God That Failed* (1950) they feared it meant he had turned to the Right.

Furthermore, as Wright, in tandem with the intellectuals of the Negritude movement, became more fascinated with questions of colonialism and racial issues as dominant in human relations, he diverged from the group of *Les Temps Modernes*, whose political nexus retained its primary East-West focus. Wright was offended when he asked Sartre for help on an antiracist project, only to be reminded of the primary importance of the workers of Eastern Europe. On a few occasions, notably the anti-Gaullist demonstrations in 1958, Wright joined the Existentialists, but they had long since ceased to be intimates.

James Baldwin provided a clue to both the value and the limits of Wright's interchange with the French Existentialists when he wrote that he distrusted their association, not only because he felt there was little the French could give Wright, but that "ideas were always more real to them than people."[44] The Existentialists' concern with ideas over people meant presumably that they understood Wright in symbolic rather than personal terms. Beauvoir remarked that during the 1950s Wright lost interest in literature and turned into an "anti-Communist."[45] This comment (aside from revealing amazing ignorance of Wright's longstanding problems with the Communist Party) indicates that although the Existentialists were attracted by Wright they only absorbed ideas from him on a limited range of subjects.

At the same time, their tendency to abstraction and their habit of generalizing from their immediate circumstances, which were sometimes narrow, gave Wright great authority on these subjects in their eyes. Because they had little experience of writers of color, Wright's blackness and his championing of African literature automatically transformed him in their eyes into the representative of non-Western culture. Similarly, his working-class background gave him an existential authenticity as a stand-in for the proletariat. His ideas and examples in matters that touched on these areas were, thus, especially valid to them.

Wright's analysis of race relations influenced the French in various ways. Beauvoir credited Wright's discussion of racism with helping inspire her to analyze women's oppression.[46] *Black Boy*, which portrayed blacks faced with Jim Crow as paralyzed by fear and insecurity, was an important reference for Sartre's play about the Scottsboro Boys, *The Respectful Prostitute*, which described black people's obsessive urge, first to mask their hatred, and eventually to eliminate their personalities altogether. In his introduction to the play, Wright praised Sartre's "insight into the truth" of racial discrimination.[47]

Perhaps more importantly, the Existentialists' concentration on violence as a way for oppressed people to cast off imposed feelings of inferiority and powerlessness seems to bear the mark of Wright's idea, most memorably developed in his 1940 novel *Native Son*, that individual self-assertion, even through violence, was the only way to achieve a sense of self. In her landmark feminist work, *The Second Sex* (*Le Deuxieme Sexe*) (1949) (which cites *Native Son*), Beavoir comments that "Violence is the authentic proof of each one's loyalty to himself, to his passions, to his own will . . . anger or revolt that does not get into the muscles remains a figment of the imagination. In the United States it is quite impossible for a Negro, in the South, to use violence against the whites; this rule is the key to the mysterious "black soul": [the Negro's] whole way of feeling and acting are to be explained on the basis of the passivity to which he is condemned."[48] Although Sartre evidently never read *Native Son*, in September 1947 Wright wrote Dorothy Norman that Sartre had agreed that individual violence was the only way to combat racism and anti-Semitism. "Even the acts of terror of the Jews [in Palestine] which are futile are serving to keep alive somewhat the sense of what a man or a few men can do. From that point of view I find myself in deep sympathy with the desperate acts of the Jews when they strike out blindly at their enemies. I've felt the same sympathy when Negroes do the same. I don't want to feel this way, but what other way is there to feel?"[49] In his well-known introduction to Wright's disciple Frantz Fanon's 1960 book, *The Wretched of the Earth* (*Les Damnes de la Terre*), Sartre championed violence as a way of breaking the dependent relations between colonized and colonizer.[50]

What the French gave Wright, in terms of supporting his work and inspiring the Existential turn in his writings, which is particularly apparent in the novel *The Outsider* (1952),[51] is well documented. More subtly, they offered him what Michel Fabre called "an existentialist praxis."[52] Sartre had preached that intellectuals should necessarily engage themselves in political conflicts in support of humanist values. Obviously,

Richard Wright was not French, and for all the pretensions of the French Existentialists to universalism, they inevitably saw life in a particular fashion not easily shared by others. Still, Wright adapted the theory of "engagement" to advance his own philosophical ideas by political means. For example, when Wright formed the French-American Fellowship, he did so not as a black American, but as an exponent of philosophical freedom. He promoted the fellowship by using the methods of the French intellectuals. He wrote a group manifesto and organized press conferences and interviews to publicize it.

Richard Wright, during his first years in France, was able to interact directly and intimately with outstanding representatives of French culture, notably the Existentialists of *Les Temps Modernes*. Despite stark differences in their ideas and makeup, their common interest in overcoming human alienation, their mutual interest in issues of race and colonialism, and their interest in finding a humanist, spiritual path for humanity between the extremes symbolized by America and the former Soviet Union brought them into intellectual partnership and political collaboration for a time. If, in the end, their political and personal paths diverged, Wright still managed to school the French in his unique analysis of racial oppression, which shaped their views of "the other." In return, they renewed and expanded his political commitment as an intellectual.

NOTES

1. See, for example, Phyllis Rose. 1984. *Jazz Cleopatra*. New York.

2. Paul Gilroy. 1993. *The Black Atlantic: Modernity and Double Consciousness*, p. 156. Cambridge, Mass.: Harvard University Press.

3. For example, one critic writes, "It has been assumed commonly but erroneously that Richard Wright [first] imbibed the heady existentialist brew during his expatriate years in Paris." Nina Kresner Cobb. 1980. "Richard Wright: Exile and Existentialism." *Phylon* 40, p. 362.

4. Ishmael Reed, Quincy Troupe, and Steve Cannon. 1977. "The Essential Ellison," *Y'bird Magazine* 1 (August). Reprinted in Maryemma Graham and Amritjit Singh, eds. 1995, *Conversations with Ralph Ellsion*, pp. 345–46. Jackson: University of Mississippi Press.

5. Fabre, Michel. 1978. "Richard Wright and the French Existentialists," *MECUS* 2, pp. 39–52. Summarized in Kenneth Kinnamon, Comp. 1988. *A Richard Wright Bibiography: Fifty Years of Criticism and Commentary*. New York: Greenwood. This book is a truly invaluable resource for research on Wright.

6. Ibid.

7.   Constance Webb. 1968. *Richard Wright*, pp. 280–81. New York: G. P. Putnam.

8.   Richard Wright. 1937. "Blueprint for Negro Writing." *New Challenge* 2 (Fall): 53–64.

9.   For Wright's break with the Party, see, for example, Michel Fabre. 1993. *The Unfinished Quest of Richard Wright*, 2d ed., pp. 228–31. Urbana: University of Illinois Press; Annie Cohen-Salal. 1987. *Sartre: A Life*, p. 242. New York: Pantheon.

10.   Ralph Ellison recalled that when he visited Wright at the *Presence Africaine* offices in Paris in 1954, Wright told him that after he broke with the Communists he had nowhere else to go. Ralph Ellison. 1986. *Going to the Territory*, pp. 198–216. New York: Vintage.

11.   Gilroy, *The Black Atlantic*, p. 154.

12.   Wright's purpose has frequently been misunderstood. Margaret Walker and Allison Davis consider Wright's negative depiction of black communities a sign of self-hatred. See Allison Davis. 1983. *Leadership, Love, and Aggression*. San Diego, Calif.: Harcourt Brace Jovanovich; Margaret Walker. 1987. *Richard Wright: Daemonic Genius*. New York: Warner. In contrast, Ralph Ellison, in his polemic against protest writing, argued that Wright consciously exaggerated black pathology as a civil rights strategy. Ralph Ellison. 1964. *Shadow and Act*, p. 137. New York: Viking. Ellison's letters to Wright during the 1940s in the Richard Wright papers at Yale University's Beinecke Library show that he agreed that the black experience was key to understanding modern life.

13.   The most notable examples are Wright's "folk history" of black Americans in Richard Wright. 1941. *Twelve Million Black Voices*. New York: Viking; Richard Wright. 1945. "Introduction." In *Black Metropolis*, edited by St. Clair Drake and Horace Cayton, pp. xvii–xxxiv. New York: Harcourt Brace; the articles he published in Dorothy Norman's *Twice a Year* in 1947–1948.

14.   Richard Wright. 1948. "Introductory Note to *The Respectful Prostitute*." *Twice a Year* 18 (June–July): 14.

15.   Ibid.

16.   Reprinted as Richard Wright. 1946–1947. "A World View of the American Negro." *Twice a Year* 14–15 (Fall–Winter): 346–47. Wright's view of blacks' struggle against technology was not completely new; the seeds of his position can be found in Wright, "Introduction."

17.   Wright was disdainful, however, of the "forces of commerce" in France that had presented his work, and had "done a damn good job in painting the Negro as something exotic." Wright to Owen Dodson, June 9, 1946, reprinted in David Ray and Robert M. Farnsworth, Comps. 1973. *Richard Wright: Impressions and Perspectives*, p. 141. Ann Arbor: University of Michigan Press.

18.   To some critics, it appeared as if Wright had abandoned his former commitments. Nelson Algren and James Farrell, two left-wing novelists who had been Wright's friends from his Chicago days, scorned him for apparently running away from the racial and class struggle in America to take an extended holiday

in French cafés. Bettina Drew. 1987. *Nelson Algren: A Life on the Wild Side*, p. 301. New York: G. P. Putnam's Sons.

19. Despite his break with the Communist Party, Wright remained a strong critic of American racism, and was a target for the government during the anti-Communist hysteria that engulfed the country in the late 1940s and 1950s. See Addison Gayle. 1980. *Richard Wright: Ordeal of a Native Son*. Garden City, N.Y.: Doubleday.

20. James Baldwin. 1961. *Nobody Knows My Name*, p. 149. New York: Dell.

21. Richard Wright. 1950. "I Choose Exile." Unpublished essay. Richard Wright Papers, Beinecke Library, Yale University. Although James Baldwin, Wright's fellow expatriate, later criticized him for mistaking the freedom France offered talented black Americans for a true commitment to racial equality, Wright was aware that implicit in many denunciations of American racism was the desire of the French, unconscious of their own racism, to feel superior to a politically dominant power and to fight against American influence in France. Wright spoke sarcastically of the French who called the American embassy to denounce lynchings (see Dorothy Norman. 1987. *Encounters*, pp. 200–201. San Diego, Calif.: Harcourt, Brace, Jovanovich).

22. Fabre, *Unfinished Quest*, p. 304.

23. Fabre, *Unfinished Quest*, p. 322.

24. For a brilliant deconstruction of the existentialist distinction between the "contingent" evils of the Soviet Union and the "innate" evil of the capitalist West America represented, see Tony Judt. 1992. *Past Imperfect: French Intellectuals, 1944–1956*. Berkeley, Calif.: University of California Press.

25. Richard Wright to Gertrude Stein, April 12, 1946, quoted in Michel Fabre. 1973. "Wright's Exile." In *Richard Wright: Impressions and Perspectives*, Compiled by David Ray and Robert M. Farnsworth, pp. 123–24. Ann Arbor: University of Michigan Press.

26. Richard Wright, letter to Dorothy Norman, March 9, 1948, printed in *Twice a Year*, 10th Anniversary Issue, 1948, p. 72.

27. Richard Wright, letter to John Scanton, June 15, 1946. Quoted in Cobb. "Richard Wright: Exile and Existentialism," p. 363.

28. It was Jean-Paul Sartre. 1945. "L'Orphée Noir." *Presence Africaine* 1 (November–December): 220 (later reprinted in *Les Temps Modernes*), who coined the term "Negritude" to describe the common psychology and culture of people of color. See Lilyan Kesteloot. 1979. *Black Writers in French*, Ellen Conroy Kennedy, trans. Philadelphia, Pa.: Temple University Press.

29. Walker. *Richard Wright: Daemonic Genius*, p. 209.

30. Wright, unlike the Existentialists, favored the Marshall Plan in theory, and tried to organize a movement to have an additional "inner Marshall Plan" for American Negroes. See Fabre, *Unfinished Quest*, p. 601.

31. Fabre, *Unfinished Quest*, p. 322.

32. For a provocative analysis of the Existentialist position on Communism, see Judt, *Past Imperfect: French Intellectuals, 1944–1956*, p. 122 passim.

33. Simone de Beauvoir. 1962. *La Force des Choses*, p. 428. Paris: Gallimard.

34. Fabre, *Unfinished Quest*, p. 327.

35. Richard Wright. 1948. "L'Humanité est plus grande que l'Amerique ou la Russie." *Franc-Tireur*, December 16.

36. Wright, "L'Humanité est plus grande que l'Amerique ou la Russie."

37. *Le Monde*, 10 November 1948. Other notable French leftist intellectuals, including Vercours, André Gide, Albert Camus, (and Sartre, reluctantly) spoke in support of Davis. See Ronald Heymann. 1987. *Sartre*, p. 264. New York: Viking.

38. *Time*, March 9, 1949, p. 22.

39. Fabre, *Unfinished Quest*, p. 329.

40. Constance Webb. 1968. *Richard Wright*, p. 288. New York: G. P. Putnam.

41. Richard Wright. 1951. "American Negroes in France," *Crisis* 58 (June–July): 382.

42. Fabre, *Unfinished Quest*, pp. 357–60. Fabre notes that James Baldwin, who was active in the organization, later slammed it as an "English melodrama." Margaret Alexander Walker claims that Wright was in the habit of forming or joining social/professional groups, although basically a loner. See Walker, *Daemonic Genius*, p. 284.

43. Fabre, *Unfinished Quest*, p. 375.

44. Baldwin, *Nobody Knows My Name*, p. 148.

45. Simone de Beauvoir. *La Force Des Choses*, II, 260. Because Wright wrote several fictional works during the decade, one must interpret the statement to mean either that Beauvoir considered him essentially a novelist or that she did not like the content of his books. Ironically, the French Intellectuals wrote accounts of their journeys to other societies (Beauvoir's own work on China being a notable example), at the same time Wright was at work on his own travel books.

46. Deirdre Bair. 1990. *Simone de Beauvoir*, p. 267. New York: Summit Books. Paul Gilroy claims, rightly, that this comment deserves further analysis.

47. Jean-Paul Sartre. 1949. *The Respectful Prostitute*. New York: A. A. Knopf. Sartre in fact achieved his first general recognition in America as an analyst of prejudice. His influential essay, "Portrait of the Anti-Semite," was printed in translation in the *Partisan Review* in 1946, while his philosophical works were not translated for several years.

48. Simone de Beauvoir. 1974. *The Second Sex*, p. 330. New York: Vintage Books.

49. Richard Wright, letter to Dorothy Norman, September 1947. Reprinted in Dorothy Norman, *Encounters*, p. 205.

50.   Frantz Fanon. 1963. *The Wretched of the Earth*, Constance Farrington, trans. New York: Grove.
51.   Richard Wright. 1953. *The Outsider*. New York: Harper & Brothers.
52.   Fabre, *Unfinished Quest*, p. 560.

REFERENCES

Bair, Deirdre. 1990. *Simone de Beauvoir*. New York: Summit Books.

Baldwin, James. 1961. *Nobody Knows My Name*. New York: Dell.

Beauvoir, Simone de. 1973. *The Second Sex*. New York: Vintage.

Beauvoir, Simone de. 1962. *La Force des Choses*. Paris: Gallimard.

Beauvoir, Simone de. 1948. *L'Amerique au jour le jour*. Paris: P. Morihien.

Cobb, Nina Kresner. 1980. "Richard Wright: Exile and Existentialism." *Phylon* 40, pp. 362–83.

Cohen-Salal, Annie. 1987. *Sartre: A Life*. New York: Pantheon.

Davis, Allison. 1983. *Leadership, Love, and Aggression*. San Diego: Harcourt Brace Jovanovich.

Ellison, Ralph, correspondence. Richard Wright papers, Beinecke Library, Yale University.

Ellison, Ralph. 1986. *Going to the Territory*. New York: Vintage.

Ellison, Ralph. 1964. *Shadow and Act*. New York: Viking.

Fabre, Michel. 1993. *The Unfinished Quest of Richard Wright*, 2d ed. Urbana: University of Illinois Press.

Fabre, Michel. 1978. "Richard Wright and the French Existentialists." *MECUS* 2, pp. 39–52.

Fanon, Frantz. 1963. *The Wretched of the Earth*, Constance Farrington, trans. New York: Grove.

Gayle, Addison. 1980. *Richard Wright: Ordeal of a Native Son*. Garden City, N.Y.: Doubleday.

Gilroy, Paul. 1993. *The Black Atlantic: Modernity and Double Consciousness*. Cambridge, Mass.: Harvard University Press.

Heymann, Ronald. 1987. *Sartre*. New York: Viking.

Judt, Tony. 1992. *Past Imperfect: French Intellectuals, 1944–1956*. Berkeley: University of California Press.

Kesteloot, Lilyan. 1979. *Black Writers in French*, Ellen Conroy Kennedy, trans. Philadelphia, Pa.: Temple University Press.

Kinnamon, Kenneth, Comp. 1988. *A Richard Wright Bibliography: Fifty Years of Criticism and Commentary*. New York: Greenwood.

Norman, Dorothy. 1987. *Encounters*. San Diego, Calif.: Harcourt Brace Jovanovich.

Ray, David, and Robert M. Farnsworth, Comps. 1973. *Richard Wright: Impressions and Perspectives*. Ann Arbor: University of Michigan Press.

Reed, Ishmael, Quincy Troupe, and Steve Cannon. 1977. "The Essential Ellison." *Y'bird Magazine* 1 (August). Reprinted in Maryemma Graham and

Amritjit Singh, eds. 1995. *Conversations with Ralph Ellsion*. Jackson: University of Mississippi Press.

Rose, Phyllis. 1984. *Jazz Cleopatra*. New York: Vintage.

Sartre, Jean-Paul. 1947. "Black Boy." *Les Temps Modernes*.

Sartre, Jean-Paul. 1946. "Portrait of the Antisemite." *Partisan Review* 13(2) (Spring): 163–78.

Walker, Margaret. 1987. *Richard Wright: Daemonic Genius*. New York: Warner.

Webb, Constance. 1968. *Richard Wright*. New York: G. P. Putnam.

Wright, Richard. 1937. "Blueprint for Negro Writing." *New Challenge* 2 (Fall): 53–64.

Wright, Richard. 1941. *Twelve Million Black Voices*. New York: Viking.

Wright, Richard. 1945. *Black Boy*. New York: Harper's.

Wright, Richard. 1945. "Introduction." In *Black Metropolis*, edited by St. Clair Drake and Horace Cayton. New York: Harcourt Brace.

Wright, Richard. 1946–1947. "A World View of the American Negro." *Twice a Year* 14–15 (Fall–Winter): 346–47.

Wright, Richard. 1948. "Introductory Note to *The Respectful Prostitute*," *Twice a Year* 18 (June–July): 14.

Wright, Richard, letter to Dorothy Norman, March 9, 1948, printed in *Twice a Year*, 10th Anniversary Issue, (Spring): 72.

Wright, Richard. 1950. "I Choose Exile." Unpublished essay. Richard Wright Papers, Beinecke Library, Yale University.

Wright, Richard. 1951. "American Negroes in France." *Crisis* 58 (June–July): 382.

8

The Space between the Boundaries: Globalization and Americanization

Victor Roudometof and Roland Robertson

Formerly each society to which history gave rise within a framework of a particular mode of production, and which bore the stamp of that mode's inherent characteristics, shaped its own space. We have seen by what means this was done: by violence (wars and revolutions), by political and diplomatic cunning, and lastly, by labor. Today, our concern must be with space on a world scale (and indeed — beyond the surface of the earth — on the scale of interplanetary space), as well as with all the spaces subsidiary to it, at every possible level. No single place has disappeared completely; and all places without exception have undergone metamorphoses. What agency shapes space worldwide? None — no force, no power. For forces and powers contend with one another within space, strategically, in such a way that history, historicity, and the determinisms associated with these temporal notions lose their meaning. (Lefebvre 1991: 412)

The great obsession of the nineteenth century was, as we know, history: its themes of development and suspension; of crisis and cycle; and of the ever accumulating past, with its great preponderance of dead men and the menacing glaciation of the world. Perhaps the current epoch will be above all the epoch of space. We are in the epoch of simultaneity: we are in the epoch of juxtaposition, the epoch of the near and far, of the side-by-side, of the dispersed. We are at a moment, I believe, when our experience of the world is less that of a long life developing through time than that of a network that connects points and intersects with its own skein. One could perhaps say that certain ideological conflicts animating present-day polemics oppose the pious descendants of time and the determined inhabitants of space. (Foucault 1986: 22)

Vinny Vega: Do you know what the funniest thing about Europe is?

Jules: What?

Vinny Vega: It's the little differences. I mean they got the same shit there they got here but it's just there it's a little different.

Jules: Example?

Vinny Vega: Alright. Well, you can walk into a movie theater in Amsterdam and you can buy a beer. And I mean no paper cup, I mean a glass of beer. And in Paris you can buy a beer in McDonalds. Do you know what they call a quarter pound of cheese in Paris?

Jules: They do not call it a quarter pound of cheese?

Vinny Vega: No, man, they have the metric system, they wouldn't know what the fuck a quarter pound is.

Jules: What do they call it?

Vinny Vega: They call it Royal with cheese.

Jules: Royal with cheese?

Vinny Vega: That's right. (Tarantino 1994)

In the following discussion, we address this volume's research agenda from the perspective of globalization theory.[1] Our comments aim at connecting the research reports published in this volume with the general theoretical discourse on the themes of Americanization, cultural imperialism, and globalization. In particular, the argument developed in this chapter is an effort to theorize the process of globalization in connection with the problematic of time-space relations. We locate three different dimensions of time-space relations and we examine the manner in which these relations are being reconstructed. We argue that this reconstruction of sociotemporal relations constitutes a critical dimension of the process of globalization, and it clearly differentiates globalization from modernization. In the context of this examination we connect the arguments put forward in this volume with our general problematic of globalization.

TIME VERSUS SPACE: THE MYTHOLOGY
ABOUT GLOBALIZATION

If globalization is said to entail the "compression of the world and the intensification of consciousness of the world as whole" (Robertson 1992: 8), then the transformation of time and space lies very much at the heart of this process. Nevertheless, the theorization of the time-space problematic has been a theme traditionally underdeveloped in social theory; and only relatively recently has this theme achieved centrality for social theory and sociological research. One important aspect of the thematization of space and spatiality is that, in recent years, it has been a multidisciplinary project. The issues of territoriality and identity have been increasingly elaborated in a number of social sciences and other disciplines (Hall & Du Gay 1996; Shapiro & Alker 1996). It can be predicted confidently that interest in such matters will increase in the coming years — expanding the growth of concern with space and spatiality, at the expense, so to speak, of the long-standing concern with time and temporality. This development is leading to the reconstruction of canonical ways of thinking about the world as a whole.

Lefebvre's monumental work *The Production of Space* (1991) can be considered one of the pioneer contributions in the rethinking of sociotemporal relations. Following Lefebvre, Soja (1989; 1996: 65–75) identifies the following dialectically linked triad of sociospatial configurations. First, there is the perceived space, that is, the empirical space of human interactions, a concept very similar to what Giddens (1984) has termed "locales." Second, there are representations of space (conceived space), the space within which agents think and work and where ideological, political, and cultural conflicts take place. Lastly, there are spaces of representation (lived space), that is, the space inhabited and used by cultural producers, the space where innovation and imagination can provide the terrain for changing power relations within the other two spaces.

The process of globalization encompasses transformations in all three respects. In particular, globalization involves the reconstruction of the time-space axis of the human condition, thereby reorganizing both the actual "objective" conditions of social life as well as the perceived "subjective" understanding of the agents. The reorganization of perceived space provides the terrain where some of the most visible examples of this process can be readily observed. In fact, numerous commentators have illustrated the reconstruction of perceived space using the proliferation of mass media as a key research site: CNN, McDonalds, Coca Cola, and so on. Prominently, a vast number of "places" around the world make even nonspecialist tourists aware of their migration across space. Electronic communication, with its simultaneity, destabilizes the sense of "place" as a terrain where "interaction" entails co-presence. These examples could be multiplied; but the effects of globalization cannot be constrained only within the perceived space. They are extended into both conceived and lived space. Indeed, globalization in the sociological and anthropological sense itself involves the continuing construction of space (as well as time and history).

Let us address first the transformations observed with the domain of conceived space. Within this field, globalization is a problematic concept, a terrain for ideological contestation. As globalization involves the reorganization of human experience, it can only be theorized by taking into account both time and space. Nevertheless, a pervasive characteristic of much of globalization discourse has been the juxtaposition of the proponents of time, narrative, and historicism against the proponents of space and simultaneity, a contrast aptly captured by Foucault in the beginning of this chapter. We can recognize the proponents of time and historicism in the attempts to periodicize globalization as a recent twentieth-century phenomenon (Reich 1992; Lash & Urry 1987; cf. Hirst & Thompson 1996; Cox 1997). This strategy largely follows preexisting conceptual categories. It mechanically extends nineteenth-century conceptual schemes to capture transformations that tend to exhaust the limits of these older paradigms. Not surprisingly, critics have pointed out that the novelty of the so-called information revolution has been overestimated (Harvey 1995: 9; see also Arrighi 1998). The novel character of other inventions from the past — such as the telegraph, automobile, radio, and telephone — impressed people to an equal extent in their day.

We can also recognize similar tendencies in attempts to identify globalization as an ideological construct of late twentieth-century capitalism and to classify it as responsible for the cultural "underdevelopment" or the "confused" identity of the global periphery (Friedman 1995: 69–90; Dhaouadi 1990: 193–208; Ferguson 1992: 69–93). The common thread of such analyses lies in their persistent advocacy of time-based historicism, in their determination to construct narratives that aim to update nineteenth-century Marxist historicism, and in their uncritical endorsement of peripheral "authenticity" (cf. Soja 1989). The conceptualization of a time-based process of globalization disregards the problematic of space and spatial-social connections.

Perhaps the best representative of this trend is Giddens's (1990) analysis of "globalisation" as a consequence of modernity.[2] Giddens (1991: 22) recognizes that "globalisation has to be understood as a dialectical phenomenon, in which events at one pole of a distanciated relation often produce divergent or even contrary occurrences at another." In his own discussion on "globalisation," however, he identifies modernity as involving time-space distancing as well as the disembedding of social relations, that is, the "lifting out" of social relations from local contexts and their restructuring across time and space (Giddens 1990: 10–21). The end result is that modernity and globality become closely interwoven in a manner that allows Giddens to postulate "globalisation" as the "consequence" of modernity (cf. Robertson 1992: 138–45).

Giddens's interpretation disregards Foucault's (1986: 22) highly relevant observation — cited at the beginning of this chapter — about the importance of history for European modernity. As Foucault reminds us, nineteenth-century European modernity entailed a particular historicism (as expressed in Comte, Spencer, and others) that located European "civilization" in an evolutionary chain of ever increasing complexity (for a general overview of these theories, see Ritzer 1992: 99–143). This historicism provided a time-based narrative in which "civilization" slowly moved from its original heartlands of Near East and Ancient Greece toward its eventual home in northern and western Europe. The spatial shift was treated as unproblematic, while emphasis was placed on the evolutionary components of the process. The twentieth-century sociological enterprise of "modernization theory" involved similar assumptions in its insistence that societies were changing or would change along similar or converging paths.

The importance of the spatial dimension is particularly well revealed when one considers Giddens's (1985) view of nationalism as an essentially marginal and transient phenomenon without deep roots in the individuals' "life-world." This highly selective perspective allows Giddens to be blind to what Billig (1995) calls "banal" nationalism — more specifically, to the pervasive nature and everyday rituals of nationalism in the societies of late modernity. Indeed, the project of nationalism entails the reorganization of social space as a means of ensuring the national homogenization (in ethnic or "racial" terms) of a particular territory (McNeill 1985). It leads to the standardization of space in a particular format governed by boundaries, passports, and the effective control of movement between spatial boundaries.

This manipulation of space allows the symbolic establishment of relations between a people and a particular space. In this manner — and with the help of cultural representation as much as the power of the state — "identity" is territorialized in relation to a "soil" (Malkki 1992). This territorialization is established in a twofold manner: first, via the standardization of the "space" occupied by a group and, second, by constructing a time-based narrative that disregards historical ruptures and discontinuities in order to construct a genealogy for a particular population. It is, indeed, the lack of a direct engagement with these issues that leads Giddens to a confusion between European modernity, which entailed a particular reconfiguration of social-spatial relations in the form of the nation-state, and globalization, which involves the reconstruction of social-spatial relations.

Through such processes, however, people develop a sense of belonging associated with a specific national homeland (Malkki 1992). This standardization of space in the form of the modern nation-state helps to develop the identity as a conceptual category. In turn, identity is a prime tool through which national ideologies construct a facade of national homogenization. Indeed, identity has only recently been conceptualized as entailing collective forms of social solidarity within a particular group (Handler 1994: 27–40; Gupta & Ferguson 1992: 6–23). In this new reconceptualization, greatly enhanced by the popularization and globalization of the concept of identity in the course of the twentieth century, historical memory provides for the constant recreation of identity among a population. Historical or social scientific writings constitute the means through which such associations are created and reproduced (Lowenthal 1994: 41–60). The use of the historical record is political, because national history provides a population with heroes, monuments, and other evidence regarding the existence of their identity over time (Horne 1984). Perhaps the most important facet of this process is the tendency to forget the biases inscribed in national narratives and the prejudices that are being reproduced in everyday life through them. Contemporary nations are frequently heavily dependent on narratives of historical deconstruction. Such narratives aim to provide revisionist accounts of the past as a means of justifying one's actions in the present. Commenting on this embrace of history with politics, Bhabha's questions are not as rhetorical as they may seem: "Do we best cope with the reality of 'being contemporary,' its conflicts and crises, its losses and lacerations, by endowing history with a long memory that we then interrupt, or startle, with our own amnesia? How did we allow ourselves to forget . . . that the nationalist violence between Hindus and Muslims lies just under the skin of India's secular modernity? Should we not have 'remembered' that the old Balkan tribes would form again?" (1996: 59). Of course, issues of bias and selective memory are not (nor can they be) confined to the aforementioned so-called faraway places. The case of Martin Bernal's *Black Athena* (1987), hailed as a deconstruction of a historical interpretation that concealed the place of black Africa in world history, reveals that the employment of the historical record in the field of identity politics is a theme of not only global periphery but also postmodern American core society.

"GLOCALIZATION" AND THE MAKING
OF EUROPEAN DIFFERENCE

The intellectual debate on "Americanization" consists in large part of a debate between proponents of time and proponents of space. Proponents of time view the process of globalization as involving a growing homogenization of local cultures, a trend closely related to the spread of capitalism in a global scale, and the concomitant subordination and erosion of local difference (for example, Ritzer 1993; see Tomlinson 1991 for a critical assessment). Their argument is largely derivative of earlier discussions regarding global convergence of different societies toward a common pattern of development. In response to this line of argument, the proponents of space point out that such a cultural homogenization has failed to materialize. This observation leads to the thesis that globalization involves the interpenetration of particularism and universalism rather than the supposed triumph of Western universalism over local particularisms (Robertson 1992: 97–105; 1995b).

From our viewpoint, globalization is akin to, and perhaps should be referred to more accurately as, "glocalization": the simultaneous adaptation of cultural items in different locales via the appropriation and production of local practices and traditions. According to the *Oxford Dictionary of New Words* (1991: 134), the term "glocalization" derives from the Japanese notion of *dochakuka*, originally the agricultural principle of adapting farming techniques to local conditions. According to the dictionary, the term became "one of the main marketing buzzwords of the beginning of the nineties." Glocalization in its business sense represents a direct acknowledgment by corporate actors of the necessity to cater to — and, indeed, invent — local conditions, producing and transforming commercial items so they become marketable in different regions and cultures (Swyngedouw 1997; see Gannon 1994 for an example of the manner in which diversity is incorporated into international management). Instead of monolithic standardization, then, local heterogeneity becomes the normative standard. Cultural, as well as institutional, homogeneity and heterogeneity are, therefore, pivotal features of the globalizing process. Although cultural diffusion can transform a locale, the recurrent "invention of traditions" makes it possible to preserve, create, or recreate cultural heterogeneity at the local level. The concept of glocalization thus eliminates much of the fashionable "pre-global" discourse concerning particularism versus universalism (Robertson 1992; Buell 1994; Walzer 1994; Spybey 1996: 154–55) because it entails the recognition that local and national cultures are constructed via reference to global discursive formations (see Robertson 1995a: 24–44).

Some of the chapters featured in this volume make specific reference to or allude to the cultural syncretism implicit within the concept of glocalization. As such, their arguments have a direct bearing as not only concerete examples of glocalization but also illustrations of the complexity of the issues involved in the intellectual debate on Americanization. In particular, Bergmann's discussion (Chapter 3, this volume) of the spectrum of Americanization in German politics between 1840 and 1990 illustrates the manner in which Americanization has provided a reference point for German political discourse. The perception of America as the "other" was a construct put forward by different groups with competing political agendas. Just like nineteenth- and twentieth-century Russians, Germans were divided into proponents and opponents of Americanization. The concept itself was heavily influenced by the competing political agendas of the various groups involved in these debates. Among them, perhaps the portrayal of Americanization as a foe by the Nazi regime illustrates the manner in which cultural difference can be invoked to justify political intolerance.

As Bergmann's and Robinson's chapters in this volume illustrate, however, actual cross-cultural contacts between the United States' intellectuals and French and German intellectuals have been widespread and pervasive. The postulate of Americanization, therefore, owes much to the desire to preserve myths of national uniqueness — and concomitantly, the privileged position of particular status groups closely associated with such myths. This process of "inventing traditions" (Hobsbawm & Ranger 1983) requires an outside target. The rise of the United States to a position of great global power in the course of the twentieth century — particularly since 1917 when the United States entered World War I — has provided such a seemingly legitimate target.[3] In this sense, the United States has replaced England, which, in the nineteenth century, provided both a reference point and an external foe for nation-building on the Continent.

Of course, this does not negate the actual reality of cultural diffusion of American cultural items in Europe. In direct reference to the problem of cross-cultural transmission, the Americanization thesis is worth considering in relation to Castoriadis's (1987) argument that American capitalism involves a colonization of the "imaginary," that is, a particular ordering of the ways in which actors think about the world and themselves. In its most broad interpretation, the argument indeed seems to be a plausible one; nevertheless, this thesis assumes that the meaning of cultural objects is universally fixed or centered and, therefore, the presence or employment of cultural objects throughout can be used as an indication of the domination of the social imaginary by the ideological infrastructure of postmodern capitalism. This assumption, however, brushes over serious issues of cultural diffusion and agency. As Simmel (1950) observed almost a century ago, the form of a cultural object is separate from its content, or its particular meaning for the local actors. If the two qualities of cultural objects cannot be treated as identical, then the question of whether the presence of American-based cultural objects reflects a growing process of Americanization can be dealt with as an empirical, and not a philosophical, question.[4] In fact, Fox's contribution (Chapter 6, this volume) shows this process at work in his discussion of the quite distinct way in which African-American images are used in German advertising.

In their discussion of modern Greek youth culture, Epitropoulos and Roudometof (Chapter 5, this volume) show that, in fact, even those manifestations of youth consumer culture that are most closely related to what is generally perceived as American culture (clubs, music), are filtered through the context of local cultures. What takes place at the level of consumer culture illustrates the manner in which agents manipulate the repertoire of the available options according to local meaning-contexts. In the case of modern Greek youth culture (similar in many respects to those of other Southern European countries), the magnet of modernity is expressed through the eyes of America. The social transformation of local societies, their transition from their own tradition to their own particular modernity, becomes a matter of experiencing and acting out in an American way. In this transformation — aptly captured in the Italian film *Cinema Paradiso* — modernity is identified with the consumption of American cultural items, but the role these items play in the local culture is a matter of the local dynamics. In other words, local agents appropriate and recontextualize consumer items according to their own frame of reference. In this process, cultural heterogeneity is reconstructed via a cultural syncretism of imported commercial items and local practices.

The dialogue from Quentin Tarantino's *Pulp Fiction* near the beginning of this chapter is exemplary of this construction of difference. As stated in the dialogue, it is the "little differences" that separate Europe from the United States, and it is not accidental that — in an ironic inversion of Ritzer's (1993) thesis — it is multinational McDonalds that provide a site where these differences can be clearly observed. Transnational business has recognized the necessity for preserving and accommodating — even promoting — local difference. This process of adapting commercial objects to local needs has given rise to the concept of glocalization — a term that indicates at a linguistic level the interpenetration of the local with the global (Robertson 1995a). Such processes indicate that discussions of Americanization need to take into account the particular manner in which this ideological construct is utilized within particular societies.

In his discussion of the former Soviet Union's political and legal system, David Lempert (Chapter 4, this volume) points out the problematic nature of Westernization for that country. Simply put, Westernization has provided a means through which internal control has been historically exercised in the diverse Russian Empire of the nineteenth century. In the late 1980s, Lempert argues, members of the former Soviet managerial élite as well as lawyers utilized American models in order to reconstruct the emerging post-Soviet legal and political system in a manner that allowed formal and informal appropriation of wealth and power on their behalf.

This process was uneven, because American models have been selectively imported to facilitate not the genuine democratization of Soviet life but the enhancement of the power of these élites. In this context, federalism, the use of government force, the separation of powers, and other American organizational models were divorced from their general context and applied selectively. Mass media promoted this trend by suggesting that — because Soviets and Europeans were the same — it would be possible to find the "magic formula" that would lead the Soviets to achieve American living standards.

LIVING IN THE SPACE BETWEEN THE BOUNDARIES

To conclude this discussion, we will address the transformation of Soja's (1996) third dimension of the lived space. Our comments here are intended as preliminary, and by no means as a final word on this issue. As already suggested in the course of this discussion, Western modernity entailed the standardization of specific time-space configurations such as the Western European nation-state and the intellectual, material, and political infrastructure it required. Subsequently, Western interpretations of globalization often advocate the peaceful coexistence with the "other" on the basis of Western moral, political, and cultural codes. This Eurocentric (or indeed American-centered) claim to universality does not do justice to the actual problematic of globalization. The proliferation of difference is, as we have already argued, central to the process of glocalization.

Although the process of consolidating the European nation-state was under way, other cultures and civilizations have had the opportunity to observe and critically adapt aspects of the Western European experience to their own projects of modernization. This cross-cultural emulation of organizational models has opened up the space for different regions of the globe to construct their own specific routes into and forms of modernity (Robertson 1990, 1995b; Therbon 1995). Such cross-cultural emulation lies very much at the heart of the conceptualization of globalization as a long-term process, one that involves systematic contact among different cultures and civilizations. The critical difference, however, between contacts that have occurred during earlier pre-modern periods and contacts that have been taking place during the modern post-1800 period, is the radically accelerated speed of social change.

Although the Western European process of nation-building entailed the reorganization of the world into distinct nation-states and colonial empires, the proliferation of Western cultural presence entailed increased contacts with the non-Western "other." If, for the majority of the people inhabiting the pre-modern world, lived space was located at the level of the village, then, for citizens of the modern world, lived space has been structured both at the level of the nation-state and, increasingly, at the international or global level. For the post-1960 period, these processes have become increasingly visible within the industrial and post-industrial societies of Western Europe and the United States. With the end of European colonial empires after 1950, however, and the concomitant movement of non-Western states into the global arena, Western modernity has no longer the monopoly as the key agent of glocalization. Baudrillard's (1983) proclamation of the "end of the social" may well be understood as involving the end of this carefully constructed myth of homogeneity and Western supremacy. After all, "society" has been a nineteenth-century Western European creation that owed much to the process of incorporating the peasantry and the working class into the national unit.

Increasingly, the lived space of individuals and collectivities extends beyond the boundaries of the nation-state. Tourism, immigration, and other forms of population movement are among the key ingredients in this process; and they provide visible manifestations of the relativization of the nation-state as the central unit of social organization. Global economic restructuring entails the reorganization of the division of labor within large corporations — with extensive headquarters located in advanced capitalist societies while the actual plans are relocated in the global periphery (Sassen 1996: 6–30; Lash & Urry 1994). This reorganization of economic activity leads to the need for transnational legal regimes to foster a common set of global rules as a means of ensuring the standardization of legal codes on a global basis (Held 1996). The entire process does not entail the decline of the state's territoriality and sovereignty, but it significantly restructures their meaning; some of the state's earlier functions are transferred to new international institutions (the World Trade Organization and the post-1992 European Union provide examples of this trend).[5] The circulation of goods is accompanied by the circulation of people; with about 120 million immigrants world wide, the spatial boundaries erected in the course of the nineteenth century by the attempt to construct nationally and culturally integrated territories are being reconfigured. The challenge posed by the new immigrant communities is closely related to the post-1945 shift toward global accountability on behalf of the state (Sassen 1996: 59–100; Esman 1992: 3–42). Indeed, the process of reconstructing Europe under the aegis of the European Union entails the development of strategies to deal with the immigration wave into Europe. Debates on the prospective inclusion of various countries into the European Union are a means of discussing not only these countries' possible entrance into the Union, but also to delineate the boundaries of the New Europe (Schopflin & Wood 1989).

During the post–World War II period, the nation-state has been gradually reconceptualized as an agent responsible for the human rights of every person within its territory (Jacobson 1996), and this provides a terrain for minority and immigrant groups to participate within the state's political body. Such participation is possible even when the immigrant groups do not, in fact, have formal membership in the state's citizenship body (Mitchell & Russell 1996; Soysal 1994). Protection of minorities becomes an issue of global importance, because a significant percentage of conflicts involves issues of minority rights (Gurr 1993; Preece 1997: 345–64).

We are experiencing, then, a situation in which more and more people and groups are going to exist in a time-space configuration that will include elements of diverse cultures. In Soja's (1996) work, Los Angeles provides a prominent example of such a time-space configuration, but it is not unique. Indeed, mass communication offers the possibility of living in the space between state and cultural boundaries that were hitherto considered immovable. Immigrant communities characteristically experience this, but they are not the only ones anymore, now that simultaneous communication allows contact without physical co-presence.[6]

Increased cross-cultural contact leads to attitudes of endorsement of forms of cultural syncretism or to advocacy of cultural purity (Dahlen 1997). These two types of orientation are described by Hannerz (1990) as "cosmopolitan" and "local." Cosmopolitanism "is an aesthetic stance of openness toward divergent cultural experiences, a search for contrasts rather than uniformity" (Hannerz 1990: 239). Inevitably, it is also a feature of those classes and occupational groups who can afford it or have to experience it as part of their work environment. Cultural fragmentation among these lines provides political leaders globe-wide with the ability to seize this cultural repertoire for their own purposes. It is in this context that "culture" becomes the conceptual battleground of political conflicts (Wallerstein 1990) and where cultural differences become politicized as differences between "civilizations," each of which stands for incommensurate cultural values (Huntington 1996).[7] At the same time, the professionalization of "intellectual communication" is contributing greatly to the accentuation of cultural and civilizational uniqueness. The "interculturalists" have a vested interest in such, even though they ostensibly claim to make intellectual communication easier (Robertson 1992: 172; Dahlen 1997).

CONCLUSION

In this brief presentation, we have attempted only to locate the preceding chapters in a broad analytic context, with special reference to spatiality as a salient aspect of contemporary globalization, or what Albrow (1997) calls the Global Age. We have not, it should be emphasized, sought to consider, or reconsider, in detail the rich and complex issue of Americanization in either analytic or comparative-empirical terms. Also, we have not, in broader terms, discussed fully the equally complex contemporary issue of cultural imperialism, this being the primary framework in which the matter of Americanization is currently raised and pursued.

We have, nonetheless, argued briefly that the discourse of American cultural imperialism has in recent years greatly neglected spatial considerations. We, in contrast, have insisted upon these, with particular reference to the concept of glocalization. Glocalization is essentially a refinement of the older concept of globalization (which has become increasingly problematic as it has become more and more identified with economically driven globe-wide homogenization). Glocalization refers directly to the ways in which globalization necessarily involves the adaptation of global processes to local circumstances. To this extent, we maintain that globalization, when refined by the concept of glocalization, is a self-limiting process.

Although he does not consider the themes of globalization and cultural imperialism in precisely these terms, Tomlinson's (1991) important argument is, we believe, consistent with ours. In his book on cultural imperialism, Tomlinson discusses a number of discourses of globalization (for example, media imperialism, cultural imperialism and nationality, the culture of capitalism, and modernity and development) and concludes that each is deficient and should be transcended by the concept of globalization. In the course of his discussion, Tomlinson frequently rejects the global homogenization thesis by invoking the resilience — "constructed" or otherwise — of other cultures.

None of this is to deny all the elements of the very widespread Americanization thesis, but this thesis has become so firmly entrenched — not least within the United States itself — that we strongly propose that skepticism about the Americanization of the world is a most fruitful strategy. This is not only for the reasons already indicated, with particular reference to glocalization, but also because the "strong" version of the Americanization thesis neglects at least two crucial factors. On the one hand, it fails to consider the proposition that the United States is only weakly integrated into world culture in a variety of respects, ranging from its increasing use of capital punishment to everyday aspects of social life — perhaps most notably attitudes toward sexuality and the erotic. On the other hand, it neglects the degree of penetration of American society by a similar kind of "foreign" phenomena, such as cuisines of various kinds (notably Chinese and Italian), architecture (such as the various classical styles, as well as Japanese and other styles), and so on. It is, in fact, these kinds of "cultural flow" that make globalization (or glocalization) a much more sociologically attractive orientation than the discourse of cultural imperialism or Americanization.

In this sense, it is necessary to separate issues of perception and reality within the Americanization debate. If some of the chapters in this volume suggest that cultural syncretism rather than wholesale cultural homogenization is the result of cross-cultural contacts, we should juxtapose this reality of syncretism with the very popular perception of Americanization. Americanization then, constitutes a field for cultural wars within specific countries; and as such, it provides a useful research site for understanding the manner in which local cultural politics are shaped by and also contribute to the overall process of globalization.

NOTES

1. For general statements on globalization, see Robertson (1992), the special issue of *Theory, Culture, and Society* (Featherstone 1990), Roudometof (1994), Friedman (1994), Spybey (1996), Albrow (1997), Appadurai (1996), and the useful introduction to the literature by Waters (1995). For earlier formulations of some of the arguments put forward in this discussion, see Robertson (1995a).

2. Giddens's inadequate treatment of the spatial dimension has been the subject of widespread criticism. See Soja (1989, 1996), Pred (1990), and the essays in Gregory and Urry (1985).

3. See Greenfeld (1991) for an excellent discussion of continental class resentment toward the English in the course of the nineteenth century. See also Mathy (1993) for a good discussion of the French intellectuals' attitude toward the United States particularly during the twentieth century.

4. Certainly, as McLuhan (1964) argues, the emergence of different forms can give rise to new kinds of content. This does not, however, imply that the content-form relationship is not subject to cross-cultural variation — nor does it suggest that selective appropriation is a theoretical impossibility. For further discussion, see Roudometof (1994).

5. This process has fueled an entire debate on the "crisis" of the nation-state. For some characteristic statements, see Hobsbawm (1990), Bereciatru (1994), Luke (1995), Smith (1991), and Sassen (1996).

6. Iyer's (1989) descriptions of Asia could certainly be read as exemplary of the manner in which these processes are by no means limited within the context of the societies of late modernity. The proliferation of diasporas in the second half of the twentieth century represents another important facet of globalization. In sharp contrast to the original meaning of the term "diaspora community," used to indicate the Jews exiled from their homeland, contemporary interpretations include the Armenian, Maghrebi, Turkish, Palestinian, Cuban, Greek, and, perhaps, Chinese diasporas (Safran 1991: 83–84). The list is certainly not an exhaustive one, but it illustrates, in a concrete manner, the ability of local expatriate groups to preserve their ties with their homeland.

7. Modern day cultural wars still focus on people's claims to have an exclusive relationship to their soil. Such conflicts, however, have been globalized because transnational national communities can be located in not only contested regions but also wherever local communities have settled. The cultural conflicts among Macedonian and Greek immigrants in Australia in the 1980s and 1990s illustrate the manner in which an identity that rests on an exclusive relationship to a particular soil can become a heated issue. In this conflict, each side claims to be the only one to have the exclusive right of symbolic ownership to Macedonia (Danforth 1995; see also Roudometof 1996). It is critical to note that the Australian contenders bear a purely symbolic relationship to the very soil they so fiercely defend. Such examples of long-distance nationalism (Anderson 1993) will, no doubt, become more of a regular occurrence in the next century.

REFERENCES

Albrow, Martin. 1997. *The Global Age*. Stanford, Calif.: Stanford University Press.

Anderson, Benedict. 1993. "The New World Disorder." *New Left Review* 193 (May–June): 3–14.

Appadurai, Arjun. 1996. *Modernity at Large: Cultural Dimensions of Globalization*. Minneapolis: University of Minnesota Press.

Arrighi, Giovanni. 1998. "Globalization and the Rise of East Asia." *International Sociology* 13(1): 59–77.

Baudrillard, Jean. 1983. *In the Shadow of the Silent Majorities or The End of the Social and Other Essays*. New York: Semiotext(e).

Bereciatru, Guruta Jáuregui. 1994. *Decline of the Nation-State*. Reno: University of Nevada Press.

Bernal, Martin. 1987. *Black Athena: The Afroasiatic Roots of Classical Civilization*. London: Free Association.

Bhabha, Homi K. 1996. "Culture's In-Between." In *Questions of Cultural Identity*, edited by Stuart Hall and Paul Du Gay, pp. 53–60. London: Sage.

Billig, Michael. 1995. *Banal Nationalism*. London: Sage.

Buell, Frederick. 1994. *National Culture and the New Global System*. Baltimore, Md.: Johns Hopkins University Press.

Castoriadis, Cornelios. 1987. *The Imaginary Constitution of Society*. London: Polity.

Dahlen, Tommy. 1997. *Among the Interdisciplinarists. An Emergent Profession and the Packaging of Knowledge*. Stockholm: Stockholm University, Department of Anthropology.

Danforth, Loring. 1995. *The Macedonian Conflict: Ethnic Conflict in a Transnational World*. Princeton, N.J.: Princeton University Press.

Dhaouadi, Mahmoud. 1990. "An Operational Analysis of the Phenomenon of the Other Underdevelopment in the Arab World and in the Third World." In *Globalization, Knowledge, and Society*, edited by Martin Albrow and Elizabeth King, pp. 193–208. London: Sage.

Esman, Milton J. 1992. "The Political Fallout of International Migration." *Diaspora* 2(1): 3–42.

Featherstone, Mike. 1990. *Global Culture: Nationalism, Globalization, and Modernity*. London: Sage.

Ferguson, Marjorie. 1992. "The Mythology About Globalization." *European Journal of Communication* 7: 69–93.

Friedman, Jonathan. 1994. *Cultural Identity and Global Process*. London: Sage.

Friedman, Jonathan. 1995. "Global System, Globalization, and the Parameters of Modernity." In *Global Modernities*, edited by Mike Featherstone, Scott Lash, and Roland Robertson, pp. 69–90. London: Sage.

Foucault, Michel. 1986. "Of Other Spaces." *Diacritics* 16: 22–27.

Gannon, Martin J. and Associates. 1994. *Understanding Global Cultures*. London: Sage.

Giddens, Anthony. 1984. *The Constitution of Society*. Berkeley: University of California Press.

Giddens, Anthony. 1985. *The Nation-State and Violence*. Berkeley: University of California Press.

Giddens, Anthony. 1990. *The Consequences of Modernity*. Stanford, Calif.: Stanford University Press.

Giddens, Anthony. 1991. *Modernity and Self-Identity*. Oxford: Polity.

Greenfeld, Liah. 1991. *Nationalism: Five Roads to Modernity*. Cambridge, Mass.: Harvard University Press.

Gregory, Derek and John Urry (eds.). 1985. *Social Relations and Spatial Structures*. New York: St. Martin's Press.

Gupta, Akhil and James Ferguson. 1992. "Beyond 'Culture': Space, Identity, and the Politics of Difference." *Cultural Anthropology* 7(10): 6–23.

Gurr, Ted Robert. 1993. *Minorities at Risk: A Global View of Ethnopolitical Conflict*. Washington, D.C.: United States Institute of Peace Press.

Hall, Stuart and Paul Du Gay (eds.). 1996. *Questions of Cultural Identity*. London: Sage.

Handler, Richard. 1994. "Is 'Identity' a Useful Cross-Cultural Concept?" In *Commemorations: The Politics of National Identity*, edited by John R. Gills, pp. 27–40. Princeton, N.J.: Princeton University Press.

Hannerz, Ulf. 1990. "Cosmopolitans and Locals in World Culture." *Theory, Culture, and Society* (7): 237–51.

Harvey, David. 1995. "Globalization in Question." *Rethinking Marxism* 8(4): 1–17.

Held, David. 1996. *Democracy and the Global Order: From the Modern State to Cosmopolitan Governance*. Stanford, Calif.: Stanford University Press.

Hirst, Paul and Grahame Thompson. 1996. *Globalization in Question: The International Economy and the Possibilities of Governance*. Cambridge: Polity.

Hobsbawm, Eric. 1990. *Nations and Nationalism Since 1780*. Cambridge: Cambridge University Press.

Hobsbawm, Eric and Terence Ranger (eds.). 1983. *The Invention of Tradition*. Cambridge: Cambridge University Press.

Horne, Donald. 1984. *The Great Museum: The Re-presentation of History*. London: Pluto.

Huntington, Samuel P. 1996. *The Clash of Civilizations and the Remaking of World Order*. New York: Simon and Schuster.

Iyer, Pico. 1989. *Video Nights in Kathmandu and Other Reports from the Not-So-Far-East*. New York: Vintage.

Jacobson, David. 1996. *Rights Across Borders: Immigration and the Decline of Citizenship*. Baltimore, Md.: Johns Hopkins University Press.

Lash, Scott, and John Urry. 1987. *The End of Organized Capitalism*. London: Sage.

Lash, Scott, and John Urry. 1994. *Economies of Signs and Space*. London: Sage.

Lefebvre, Henri. 1991. *The Production of Space*, translated by Donald Nicholson-Smith. Cambridge: Basil Blackwell.

Lowenthal, David. 1994. "Identity, Heritage, and History." In *Commemorations: The Politics of National Identity*, edited by John R. Gills, pp. 41–60.

Princeton, N.J.: Princeton University Press.

Luke, Timothy W. 1995. "New World Order or Neo-world Orders: Power, Politics, and Ideology in Informalizing Glocalities." In *Global Modernities*, edited by Mike Featherstone, Scott Lash, and Roland Robertson, pp. 91–107. London: Sage.

Malkki, Liisa. 1992. "National Geographies: The Rooting of Peoples and the Territorialization of National Identity Among Scholars and Refugees." *Cultural Anthropology* 7(1): 24–44.

Mathy, Jean-Philippe. 1993. *Extreme Occident*. Chicago, Ill.: University of Chicago Press.

McLuhan, Marshall. 1964. *Understanding Media. The Extensions of Man*. Cambridge, Mass.: MIT Press.

McNeill, William. 1985. *Polyethnicity and National Unity in World History*. Toronto: University of Toronto Press.

Mitchell, Mark and Dave Russell. 1996. "Immigration, Citizenship, and the Nation-State in the New Europe." In *Nation and Identity in Contemporary Europe*, edited by Brian Jenkins and Spyros A. Sofos, pp. 54–80. London: Routledge.

Pred, Allan. 1990. *Making Histories and Constructing Human Geographies: The Local Transformation of Practice, Power Relations, and Consciousness*. Boulder, Colo.: Westview.

Preece, Jennifer Jackson. 1997. "National Minority Rights vs. State Sovereignty in Europe: Changing Norms in International Relations?" *Nations and Nationalism* 3(3): 345–64.

Reich, Robert B. 1992. *The Work of Nations: Preparing Ourselves for the Twenty-First Century Capitalism*. New York: Vintage.

Ritzer, George. 1992. *Classical Sociological Theory*. New York: McGraw-Hill.

Ritzer, George. 1993. *The McDonaldization of Society: An Investigation into the Changing Character of Contemporary Social Life*. Newbury Park, Calif.: Pine Forge Press.

Robertson, Roland. 1990. "Japan and the USA: The Interpenetration of National Identities and the Debate about Orientalism." In *Dominant Ideologies*, edited by Nikolas Abercombie, S. Hill, and Brian S. Turner, pp. 182–98. London: Urwin Hymon.

Robertson, Roland. 1992. *Globalization: Social Theory and Global Culture*. London: Sage.

Robertson, Roland. 1995a. "Glocalization: Time-Space and Homogeneity-Heterogeneity." In *Global Modernities*, edited by Mike Featherstone, Scott Lash, and Roland Robertson, pp. 25–44. London: Sage.

Robertson, Roland. 1995b. "Theory, Specificity, Change: Emulation, Selective Incorporation, and Modernization." In *Social Change and Modernization: Lessons from Eastern Europe*, edited by B. Grancelli, pp. 213–32. New York: Walter de Gruyter.

Robertson, Roland. 1996. "The Theory and the Discourses of Globalization."

Kyoto Journal of Sociology 4 (December): 233–50.

Roudometof, Victor. 1994 "Globalization or Modernity?" *Comparative Civiliza-tions Review* 31 (Fall): 18–45.

Roudometof, Victor. 1996. "Nationalism and Identity Politics in the Balkans: Greece and the Macedonian Question." *Journal of Modern Greek Studies* 14 (Fall): 253–301.

Sassen, Saskia. 1996. *Losing Control? Sovereignty in An Age of Globalization*. New York: Columbia University Press.

Schopflin, George and Nancy Wood (eds.). 1989. *In Search of Central Europe*. Cambridge: Polity.

Shapiro, Michael J. and Hayward R. Alker (eds.). 1996. *Challenging Boundaries*. Minneapolis: University of Minnesota Press.

Shirley, Rodney W. 1987. *The Mapping of the World: Early Printed World Maps*. London: Holland Press.

Simmel, Georg. 1950. *The Sociology of Georg Simmel*, translated and with an introduction by Kurt H. Wolff. New York: Free Press.

Smith, Anthony D. 1991. *National Identity*. Reno: University of Nevada Press.

Soja, Edward W. 1989. *Postmodern Geographies: The Reassertion of Space in Critical Social Theory*. London: Verso.

Soja, Edward W. 1996. *Third Space: Journeys to Los Angeles and Other Real-and-Imagined Places*. Cambridge: Basil Blackwell.

Soysal, Yasemih N. 1994. *Limits of Citizenship: Migrants and Post-National Membership in Europe*. Chicago, Ill.: University of Chicago Press.

Spybey, Tony. 1996. *Globalization and World Society*. Cambridge: Polity.

Swyngedouw, Erik. 1997. "Neither Global nor Local: 'Glocalization' and the Politics of Scale." In *Spaces of Globalization: Reasserting the Power of the Local*, edited by Kevin R. Cox, pp. 137–66. New York: Guilford Press.

Tarantino, Quentin. 1994. *Pulp Fiction*. Los Angeles: Miramax. Movie.

The Oxford Dictionary of New Words. 1991. Compiled by S. Tulloch. Oxford: Oxford University Press.

Therbon, Goran. 1995. "Routes to/through Modernity." In *Global Modernities*, edited by Mike Featherstone, Scott Lash, and Roland Robertson, pp. 108–23. London: Sage.

Tomlinson, John. 1991. *Cultural Imperialism*. Baltimore, Md.: Johns Hopkins University Press.

Tornatore, Guiseppe. 1988. *Cinema Paradiso*. Rome: Christaldifilm. Movie

Wallerstein, Immanuel. 1990. "Culture as the Ideological Battleground of the Modern World-System." *Theory, Culture, and Society* 7: 31–56.

Walzer, Michael. 1994. *Thick and Thin*. Cambridge, Mass.: Harvard University Press.

Waters, Malcolm. 1995. *Globalization*. London: Routledge.

Index

About the Contributors

Peter Bergmann is associate professor of history at the University of Connecticut. He is the author of *Nietzsche, "The Last Antipolitical German"* (1987) and coeditor of *East Europe Reads Nietzsche* (1998).

Ruben Berrios currently works as a researcher at the University of Pittsburgh.

Mike-Frank G. Epitropoulos is a doctoral student and teaching fellow in sociology at the University of Pittsburgh and holds adjunct appointments at Duquesne University and Point Park College. His principal research interests and publications have been in development, tourism, and political economy.

Steve Fox is program administrator for the New Mexico Endowment for the Humanities in Albuquerque. He writes about aspects of popular culture in the West in the Cold War years.

Jun Kanamitsu is a doctoral candidate in sociology at the University of Pittsburgh.

Samuel A. Kugel is professor at the Institute of History of Science and Technology at the Russian Academy of Science in St. Petersburg where he leads the Center for Sociology of Science and Technology.

David Lempert, adjunct associate professor at George Washington University, attorney, international consultant, and president of Unseen American Projects, Inc., is the first U.S. anthropologist to have conducted field work in urban Russia. He is author of *Daily Life in a Crumbling Empire: The Absorption of Russia into the World Economy* (1996), *Escape from the Ivory Tower: Student Adventures in Democratic Experiential Education, A Model Development Plan: New Strategies and Perspectives* (Praeger 1995), and *A Return to Democracy: The Modern Democracy Amendments.*

James F. Luther is a graduate student in sociology at the University of Pittsburgh.

Roland Robertson is professor of sociology and religious studies at the University of Pittsburgh. He has published widely. His most recent works include *Talcott Parsons: Theorist of Modernity* (1991); *Religion and Global Order* (1991); *Globalization: Social Theory and Global Culture* (1992); and *Global Modernities* (1995).

Greg Robinson is a doctoral candidate in American history at New York University. He has contributed to *Prospects: An Annual of American Culture Studies* and *Presidential Studies Quarterly.*

Keri L. Rodriguez is a graduate student in sociology at the University of Pittsburgh.

Victor Roudometof is assistant professor of political sociology at the American College of Thessaloniki. His most recent contributions include the *Journal of Modern Greek Studies* and the *East European Quarterly.* He is currently editing a volume about Macedonia.

Thomas Schott is associate professor of sociology and West European studies at the University of Pittsburgh. His teaching, consulting, and publications focus on the global institutionalization of science and technology and the globe-spanning networks in scientific and technological research.

ISBN 0-275-95051-4

90000>

EAN

9 780275 950514

HARDCOVER BAR CODE